Victura

JAMES W.
GRAHAM

Victura

THE *K*ENNEDYS,
A SAILBOAT,
AND THE SEA

FORE
EDGE

ForeEdge

An imprint of University Press of New England

First paperback edition 2015

Manufactured in the United States of America

Designed by Eric M. Brooks

Typeset in Centaur by Passumpsic Publishing

For permission to reproduce any of the material in this book, contact

Brandeis University Press, 415 South Street, Waltham, MA 02453,

or visit brandeisuniversitypress.com

Paperback ISBN: 978-1-61168-865-8

Ebook ISBN: 978-1-61168-599-2

The Library of Congress has cataloged the hardcover edition as follows:

Graham, James W.
Victura : the Kennedys, a sailboat, and the sea / James W. Graham.
    pages   cm.
Includes bibliographical references and index.
ISBN 978-1-61168-411-7 (cloth : alk. paper)
1. Kennedy family. 2. Kennedy, John F. (John Fitzgerald), 1917–1963.
3. Victura (Boat). 4. Sailing. I. Title.
GV810.92.K46G73   2014
973.9220922—dc23   2013036504

Page 266 constitutes a continuation of the copyright page.

To Linda,
with love

Ulysses ALFRED, LORD TENNYSON

It little profits that an idle king,
By this still hearth, among these barren crags,
Match'd with an aged wife, I mete and dole
Unequal laws unto a savage race,
That hoard, and sleep, and feed, and know not me.

I cannot rest from travel: I will drink
Life to the lees: All times I have enjoy'd
Greatly, have suffer'd greatly, both with those
That loved me, and alone, on shore, and when
Thro' scudding drifts the rainy Hyades
Vext the dim sea: I am become a name;
For always roaming with a hungry heart
Much have I seen and known; cities of men
And manners, climates, councils, governments,
Myself not least, but honour'd of them all;
And drunk delight of battle with my peers,
Far on the ringing plains of windy Troy.

I am a part of all that I have met;
Yet all experience is an arch wherethro'
Gleams that untravell'd world whose margin fades
For ever and forever when I move.
How dull it is to pause, to make an end,
To rust unburnish'd, not to shine in use!
As tho' to breathe were life! Life piled on life
Were all too little, and of one to me
Little remains: but every hour is saved
From that eternal silence, something more,
A bringer of new things; and vile it were
For some three suns to store and hoard myself,
And this gray spirit yearning in desire
To follow knowledge like a sinking star,
Beyond the utmost bound of human thought.

This is my son, mine own Telemachus,
To whom I leave the sceptre and the isle,—
Well-loved of me, discerning to fulfil
This labour, by slow prudence to make mild
A rugged people, and thro' soft degrees
Subdue them to the useful and the good.
Most blameless is he, centred in the sphere
Of common duties, decent not to fail
In offices of tenderness, and pay
Meet adoration to my household gods,
When I am gone. He works his work, I mine.

There lies the port; the vessel puffs her sail:
There gloom the dark broad seas. My mariners,
Souls that have toil'd, and wrought, and thought with me—
That ever with a frolic welcome took
The thunder and the sunshine, and opposed
Free hearts, free foreheads—you and I are old;
Old age hath yet his honour and his toil;
Death closes all: but something ere the end,
Some work of noble note, may yet be done,
Not unbecoming men that strove with Gods.
The lights begin to twinkle from the rocks:
The long day wanes: the slow moon climbs: the deep
Moans round with many voices. Come, my friends,
'Tis not too late to seek a newer world.
Push off, and sitting well in order smite
The sounding furrows; for my purpose holds
To sail beyond the sunset, and the baths
Of all the western stars, until I die.
It may be that the gulfs will wash us down:
It may be we shall touch the Happy Isles,
And see the great Achilles, whom we knew.
Tho' much is taken, much abides; and tho'
We are not now that strength which in old days
Moved earth and heaven; that which we are, we are;
One equal temper of heroic hearts,
Made weak by time and fate, but strong in will
To strive, to seek, to find, and not to yield.

CONTENTS

Illustrations appear after page 118

BOOK I)

Christenings

CHAPTER I

Metaphor for Life

The day before he died President John F. Kennedy and his wife, Jacqueline, arrived at the Rice Hotel in Houston, Texas, taking a room freshly remodeled for their short stay. They had three and a half hours to rest and dine together before heading out for two evening appearances and the day's end. Jack, sitting in a rocking chair, wearing just his shorts, worked on a speech and doodled on a sheet of hotel notepaper.[1]

Later, their public obligations satisfied, they retired to another hotel closer to the next day's events. Jacqueline saw Jack, in his pajamas, kneel by his bed to say a prayer. She told a friend a few weeks later, "It was just like a little childish mannerism, I suppose, like brushing your teeth or something. But I thought that was so sweet. It used to amuse me so, standing there." She compared his religious rituals to "superstition." She wasn't sure he was a true believer, "but if it was that way, he wanted to have that on his side."[2]

The next morning, with the president and first lady in Dallas for their motorcade's nightmarish turn past the book depository, the Rice Hotel housecleaning staff found the doodle the president had left in his room. It was a simple pencil drawing of a little sailboat, beating through the waves.

Jack Kennedy often drew such sailboats during White House meetings or while on the phone. Sometimes, he put a gaff rig on the mast, like the one on the *Victura*. Somewhere in their minds, throughout their lives, Jack and his brothers and sisters were always at sea. Sailing influenced how they thought, how they competed, the content of public speeches, how as a family they celebrated happy events or managed grief, how they grew close to one another.

Of the nine children of Joseph and Rose Kennedy, the ones most influenced by and enamored with sailing were Jack; his older brother, Joe; and their younger siblings, Ted, Eunice, and Robert. When they were young, sailing was a topic of ongoing earnest discussion, sometimes led by their father.

They would constantly ask one another, What made us lose a race? What gear needed replacing? At what cost? What sailing instructors should we hire? What kind of sails? How do we launch the spinnaker faster? Who can we get to crew? How fast the wind and how high the waves?

As they grew older and moved into independent lives, they always came back to sailing, coordinating return trips to their seaside Cape Cod home, sometimes arranging their lives around regattas, making time for a sail every day. Their children and grandchildren were still doing the same eighty years after they first went for a sail on *Victura*.

When Robert's young wife, Ethel, joined the family, she perfectly blended in, not least because she brought her own love of sailing. Jacqueline, enamored less with the races and more with sailing's beauty, wrote poetry about and drew pictures of sailboats years before she met Jack. Whatever the lofty position a Kennedy held, helicopters, airplanes, and motorcades all eventually pointed back to Hyannis Port in time for sailing races.

Once together at sea the Kennedys riveted their attention on the race or, if just cruising, spent hours in conversation while watching sunsets; worrying over storm clouds; taking drenching waves over the gunwale; shivering, almost hypothermic; holding soggy sandwiches pulled from the cooler.

Older Kennedys taught younger ones. They grounded their boat on sandbars, at least once crashing into a buoy. They thought nothing of jumping into the water if necessary to lighten the load and speed the boat. They yelled when mistakes were made, punched one another even, laughed about it afterward. The stronger the Cape winds, the whiter the whitecaps, the better. They took friends out who became lifelong pals after passing tests of seaworthiness or camaraderie.

Once they became parents they used sailing to connect with their children, including nephews and nieces whose fathers were lost. They learned seamanship and survival skills, which they swear saved Jack's life in World War II. Sailing, they said, gave their lives perspective and helped them explore how to cope with the complexity that comes with being a Kennedy—the privileges, the attention, and the "buzz saws of life."[3] They sailed at night too, quietly taking in the infinite stars, distance, space, and horizon and said it gave them insights into life's mysteries. "Sailing, for me, has always been a metaphor for life," wrote Ted in his memoir, *True Compass*, written eighty years after the family first summered in Hyannis Port.[4]

The family had many sailboats, but the favorite was *Victura*. They kept it the longest and sailed it most, over almost fifty years. It was wooden and modest in size, twenty-five feet in length, spare of accommodation, and gaff rigged, a sail configuration thought quaint today even though folks still say the shorter mast height prevents a knockdown in a gale. About two hundred one-design Wianno Seniors identical to *Victura* have been built for families like the Kennedys who summer or live on Cape Cod's South Shore. Thus they fairly compete on boats of equal specifications in races around Nantucket Sound.

That *Victura* survived so long, a small boat in such big seas, is surprising itself. Acquired in 1932, struck by lightening in 1936, dragged onto the beach by war-injured Jack during a hurricane in 1944, and nearly lost in a 2003 harbor fire that took twenty other sailboats like it, *Victura* once sprung a leak and started sinking beneath Ted's aging and none-too-small size, as the senator resignedly watched boats in the race pass him by until he could get a tow. After they gave *Victura* to a museum, they bought a new Wianno Senior, called it *Victura* too and sail it to this day.

Now, when a Kennedy dies and his or her loved ones stand to speak words of consolation, they often turn to the imagery of sailing and to their stories of *Victura*. At Ted's death in 2009, four eulogists told stories of being with him on *Victura*. Less than two years later, when Ted's daughter, Kara, died of cancer at age fifty-one, her brother Patrick said, "Dad now has his first mate, his crew with him, as they set sail," and quoted Eugene O'Neill, "I dissolved in the sea, became white sails and flying spray, became beauty and rhythm, became moonlight and the ship and the high dim-starred sky!"

Jack did not know his stay at the Rice Hotel was his last day on earth, but his thoughts went back to the Cape and the sea that night because that is where Kennedy minds always drift. All through his life Jack was sick with one illness or another, but sailing freed him, filled his lungs, tanned his skin when it was ashen or yellow, separated him from worries ashore, and gave him seclusion with family and friends.

Robert, a less accomplished sailor who married young and had less time for racing, still loved taking his children out on the water. Before he died at forty-two, after fathering eleven children, he bought a "sister boat" to *Victura* and called it *Resolute*. For years following Robert's death, when the weather was warm enough, and even when it was not, his surviving family sailed *Resolute* almost every day. Brothers, sisters, and nephews of Jack bought Wianno Seniors, so *Victura* and *Resolute* begat *Headstart*, another *Victura*, and *Ptarmigan*. These begat *Santa Maria* and *Dingle*.

Ted, perhaps the most dedicated—some might say obsessive—sailor, lived a long life of ups and downs, the opposite of the short lives of Jack and Robert. They rose together on a steady and uninterrupted path to the White House, but Ted lived almost as long as the other two combined, beaten down by tragedies, some fated, some self-inflicted. Sailing reminded Ted to keep plowing onward, no matter the wind or current or competition. The younger Kennedys picked up on that.

The daughters of Joe and Rose Kennedy had less family pressure to achieve political success, for theirs was an era of male primogeniture, but Eunice grew up to be as forceful and effective a leader of social change in America as her brothers. Perhaps not so coincidentally she was also among the most accomplished sailors.

Over the years the images of the Kennedys at sea defined the family brand and gave birth to the Kennedy myth. Kennedys under sail were the picture of adventurousness, wholesomeness, vigor, and family. They commanded the elements and the political world. Jack Kennedy's navy experience in World War II became an epic tale of seafaring heroism, retold throughout his political career. A 1953 *Life* cover photo of Jack and Jacqueline on the bow of *Victura*, along with their larger storyline, presented them as beautiful, privileged, sophisticated, glamorous, and destined for something great. Media forms like television were fast evolving and multiplying, their effects just being understood, and Jack and Jackie were well cast for the new era.

As Robert and Ted grew older and entered the picture as politicians themselves, they had children who took to the sea as had their parents. The image of the Kennedys at sea became affixed in public consciousness for the rest of the twentieth century and into the next.

The story of *Victura*, more than the tale of a small sailboat, is a story of a steeled family and uncommon upbringing in a particular time and place, under specific circumstances, some created with deliberateness by parents who had the means, some shaped by world events and accidents of fate. All of these combined to deeply influence the lives of a few extraordinary people who, more than most, helped define America in the second half of the twentieth century. From these circumstances grew the Kennedys and all they became. Always integral to it all was a simple, small sailboat. *Victura.*

~ In 1925 the Kennedys of Boston first summered at Hyannis Port, renting Malcolm Cottage and buying it two years later.[5] It was many-gabled with white clapboard and green shutters, roomy, to be sure, but less ostentatious than some along the shore. The more prevalent exterior of homes on Cape Cod is weathered gray cedar shake shingles framed in trim so brightly white you squint from the sun's reflection. Brick or stone construction was and is a rarity on the Cape. Walking the neighborhoods today, you are never out of sight of wind speed and direction indicators in the form of weathervanes on roof peaks and American flags flapping from front porches or high on poles. Between the sea and the white Kennedy house was one of the tallest of flagpoles around, visible from far offshore.

The other primary luxuries of the house were the invigorating sea breezes, a broad two-acre lawn facing the water, a long stretch of beach, and the beautiful Nantucket Sound seascape of sea sage and grasses, shore birds and sailboats, sky and ocean. Joe Sr. early on hired an architect to enlarge the house and, like an architect himself, sought to methodically enlarge his children's potential for exceptional achievement. His and Rose's plans for them included excellent boarding schools, competitive sports, and the Ivy League. On the agenda were constant outdoor adventures; exposure to diverse experiences, places, and people; and always lively, mind-engaging dinner table conversation and debate. Joe treated his children like intelligent adults, teaching them responsibility and helping them see themselves as fully engaged citizens of the world with important future roles to play.

~ Decades after their arrival in Hyannis Port, Rose in her old age made it a habit of dining one-on-one with each of her twenty-nine grandchildren. With them she looked back to those early Cape years and their extraordinary family history. She told them of the "help wanted" signs in the Boston store windows she remembered as a child, where the initials "N.I.N.A." were all that was necessary to convey that, "no Irish need apply," as though code made the discrimination tasteful.[6] Rose's father became mayor of Boston, and the man she married achieved even more. But even when Joe's fortune, celebrity, and political influence were well established, social acceptance remained beyond their grasp.

The Catholic grandson of an Irish immigrant, son of a Boston barkeep turned successful businessman, by 1926 Joe was already worth $2 million. He could build a fortune but never divest himself of his Irish, non-Protestant, new-money identity, three strikes against true acceptance by Boston Brahmins. Precocious about business—the press said he was at age twenty-five the youngest bank president in the country—Joe was perhaps naive about social acceptance.

Three years before that first summer in Hyannis Port, the family had tried a summer in Cohasset, seeking and expecting membership in that community's golf club. As Joe's friends lobbied for the club election committee's approval, one eventually wrote to another that accepting Joe's family "wouldn't be as easy sailing as I imagined."[7] Club elders spent the entire summer deliberating, humiliatingly stringing them along, before rejecting the Kennedys.

This sort of occurrence wasn't lost on the children. Much later, after Jack's presidency, Robert Kennedy recalled his father's 1927 decision to leave their home in Boston. Robert made the family sound not just discriminated against, but underprivileged. Reminded that his family then was hardly poor, leaving town as they did in a private rail car, Robert said, "Yes, but—it was symbolic. The business establishment, the clubs, the golf course—at least that was what I was told at a very young age."[8]

"That's exactly why I left Boston," Joe Sr. told a reporter years later, speaking of his decision not to raise his Irish Catholic children there, moving them instead to a new family household in New York, while keeping their summer place at the Cape. "I didn't want them to go through what I had to go through when I was growing up there. They wouldn't have asked my daughters to join their deb clubs, not that our girls would have joined anyway—they never gave two cents for that society stuff. But the point is they wouldn't have been asked in Boston."[9]

Jacqueline said of the Kennedys, "They always seem to have a sort of persecution thing about them, don't they? I notice the way Mrs. [Rose] Kennedy speaks even now . . . 'is someone a Catholic?' or 'are they Irish?' As if it's—you know, I guess they've had such persecution."[10]

Some among the Kennedy's old-money immediate neighbors referred to their summer residence as the "Irish House," teeming as it was with loud, over-active children whose great-grandparents came from Ireland. It would take a few decades, some electoral successes, and the acquisition of neighboring properties before it became known as the "Kennedy Compound."

Rejected in Cohasset, they tried summering in Hyannis Port, and in some ways the outcome was not much more promising. The Kennedys sought membership in the local golf club and were rejected yet again. One of Rose's biographers claims she encouraged her husband to invest in a local yacht club that had closed for financial reasons. They calculated, so the story goes, that a yacht club would not be able to deny membership to a founding member.[11]

The story is probably untrue, but the family did fully embrace sailing from the earliest times, along with the social scene surrounding races. They wanted acceptance, and aside from the fun of the sport it was also a point of entry to higher society. Thus, quickly and firmly anchored was the Kennedy family association with Cape Cod sailing.

The Kennedy family was tight-knit for many reasons; a shared sense of persecution being just one. The boys viciously competed, brother against brother, until an outsider presented a threat of any kind and transformed sibling rivals into unbeatable allies. A playmate later recalled, "No matter what anyone else had done, the Kennedy children always praised each other's accomplishments to the skies. While it was amusing and touching for a time, it got to be rather tiresome after a while."[12]

The children were loud at play, aggressive and tireless on the family lawn and in sailboat races, a culture clash with the seen-not-heard children of the neighbors. Other parents were disapproving. So Joe and Rose kept to themselves as a family, perhaps not entirely by their own choice, despite Rose's later alternate history: "Years ago we decided that our kids were going to be our best friends and that we could never see too much of them. Since we couldn't do both, it was better to bring up our family than to go out to dinners. My husband's business often took him away from home and when all of us had time to be together we didn't want to share it with outsiders."[13]

Thus, in that summer of 1925, the Kennedy children first dug their toes in the sandy beach at Hyannis Port and became with their parents a self-dependent family, focused for the most part on one another. They did not exclude outsiders—there were many playmates—but they made their family relationships the most important they had. Joe's eldest son, Joe Jr., turned nine. Jack was seven. They had four sisters—Rosemary, six; Kathleen, five; Eunice, three; and Patricia, one—and a little brother, Robert, less than a year old. Another sister, Jean, and the youngest of the family, Ted, followed in 1928 and 1932.

Much has been written of the noisy, rowdy Kennedy household, the win-at-all-cost touch football, the swimming and sailing, where anything short of first place demanded explanation. Less often noted is the sheer beauty of their surroundings. It was a joyous escape from the urban life of Boston and New York and the stifling New England boarding schools.

The world the Kennedys could gaze at from their vast front porch at Nantucket Sound boasted always-changing canvases of sea etched by winds, colored by clouds and reflected sparkling sun, animated by gliding gulls and graceful schooners. There were walks on the beach and ventures to the roaring Outer Cape, the gentle rolls of beach grass-covered dunes all along the way. From the big house Joe's second-floor bedroom had a balcony where he could sit and watch it all, most importantly his children, never walking but always running across the lawn; the sea dotted with their boats; and the horizon they would all cross in their epic ways.

CHAPTER 2)

Bred to Win

Around 1961, when the daughter of President and Mrs. John F. Kennedy was about three, her mother asked her to memorize two short poems. Caroline surprised her father by reciting both from memory. "I remember his delight, and my own," said Caroline decades later.[1] They were by Edna St. Vincent Millay:

FIRST FIG
My candle burns at both ends;
        It will not last the night;
But ah, my foes, and oh, my friends—
        It gives a lovely light!

SECOND FIG
Safe upon the solid rock the ugly houses stand:
Come and see my shining palace built upon the sand![2]

In the same summer of 1925 that the Kennedys arrived on the Cape's South Shore, another palace on the sand was established on Cape Cod. This one had no association with the Kennedys and was actually so small it could barely be called a house. A thirty-six-year-old veteran of the Great War bought land and the following year hired a carpenter to build a tiny cottage, perching it precariously on a dune just twenty feet above the high water mark. About twenty miles to the northeast, around the bend of the Cape's elbow, fronting east and unprotected on the Atlantic oceanfront, it sat alone, exposed ship-like to the sea. Its owner called his cottage "fo'castle."

The following year the owner planned a two-week September visit to his new cottage, but his rapture for the setting made him extend the visit to November. He returned frequently in the seasons immediately following, alone, and took to writing about all he saw of nature's rhythms, the sea, the effect of wind on dunes, and the sense-numbing pounding of waves.

"I simply wanted a place to come to in the summer," he wrote, "one cozy enough to be visited in winter could I manage to get down." Consisting of two rooms that together measured just twenty-by-sixteen feet, the house he designed "showed, perhaps, a somewhat amateur enthusiasm for windows. I had ten."[3]

He was Henry Beston, and his writings of nature were something altogether new. He was later compared to Thoreau, another nature chronicler who had written of Cape Cod seventy years earlier. Beston's poetic observations of nature and its rhythms more directly anticipated post-1960s environmentalists. His sensitivity to humankind's relationship to nature, influenced by a previous time spent with Navajo Indians in New Mexico, showed a mystical sense of nature's great interconnectedness. On Cape Cod affluent summertime invaders like the Kennedys must have been an affront to Beston. Some say Beston bridged a twentieth-century gap between the Teddy Roosevelt conservationist era and the environmentalism of people such as Rachel Carson, who later cited Beston as one of her only true literary inspirations.

Beston's masterwork, "The Outermost House," was well reviewed when published in 1928, and its reputation grew within the lifetime of Joe Kennedy's children. Whether Beston and the Kennedys ever encountered one another in those years is not known, but in that setting and that time were two men sowing seeds: Beston creating a new way of thinking about nature, and Joseph P. Kennedy Sr. consciously, sometimes audaciously, nurturing in his children a culture of political aristocracy and ambition.

In summer, in those same early months that the Kennedys were first exploring the Cape, Beston wrote of the beauty found there in the tiniest details: "The duneland air burns with the smell of sand, ocean and sun. On the tops of hills, the grass stands at its tallest and greenest, its new straw-green seed plumes rising through a dead crop of last year's withered spears. On some leaves there is already a tiny spot of orange wither at the very tip, and thin lines of wither descending on either edge. Grasses in the salt meadows are fruiting; there are brownish and greenish-yellow patches on the levels of summer green."[4]

Thoreau wrote of Cape Cod three quarters of a century before the Kennedys and others affluent families arrived, but he saw them coming:

> The time must come when this coast will be a place of resort for those New-Englanders who really wish to visit the seaside. At present it is wholly unknown to the fashionable world, and probably it will never be agreeable to them. If it is merely a ten-pin alley, or a circular railway, or an ocean of mint-julep, that the visitor is in search of,—if he thinks more of the wine than the brine, as I suspect some do at Newport,— I trust that for a long time he will be disappointed here.

After renting it for two summers, Joe Kennedy bought Malcolm Cottage and hired its original architect, doubling its size, and adding a sipping room and wine cellar that resembled a ship's hull. Joe planned wine *and* brine.

~ Even before they acquired the house, in 1927 the family had its first small sailboat.[5] Joe Jr. and Jack christened it the *Rose Elizabeth*, after their mother, and won their first race that year. They took to sailing quickly and naturally. Joe Sr. recalled that the older boys "were out in sailboats alone here in Hyannis Port when they were so small you couldn't see their heads. It looked from shore as if the boats were empty."[6]

Leo Damore, a Cape Cod resident who interviewed innumerable locals in the 1960s, said that although Joe Sr. was "not a knowledgeable sailor himself, he nonetheless followed the boats his children raced, taking note of anyone who carelessly fouled a mark or appeared to be giving less than his whole effort to winning. Afterward the culprit would be certain to receive a blistering tongue-lashing in front of the other children and be sent from the dinner table in disgrace to eat in the kitchen. But all would be forgiven once the recalcitrant confessed his mistake and promised to try harder the next time."[7]

By all accounts Joe Sr. was a demanding but demonstrably affectionate father. Moreover, he was deeply *interested* in his children. They deeply loved him in return, though a JFK biographer said their love had an "element of fear" to it, "not so much dread of his tongue lashings, although these were colorful and memorable, but rather fear of failing to measure up to his expectations."[8]

A decades-long family friend of Jack and the entire family, "Lem" Billings, recalled first meeting Joe Sr. when Jack brought him along to Palm Springs:

> Mr. Kennedy shook my hand and looked at me with a pair of eyes which I will never forget. I can only describe them as the strongest I have ever seen. When he looked at you, you felt he saw you as you had never been seen before. He had the terrifying ability to look at you as you look at yourself. Mr. Kennedy is the only man I ever met who could do this. As I came to know those eyes over the years, I learned that they could help you search through your own being for the answers to the very questions you had come to him to ask. That ability is certainly one of the keys to the greatness of the family he created.[9]

Whether or not Joe was calculating enough to believe he strengthened the children's bonds by giving them in common a constant fear of paternal disapproval, they all loved him and consciously embraced sailing as an activity that tightened the weave of family fabric. The children called one of the earliest boats, a sixteen-foot Wianno Junior, *The Eight-of-Us*. After Bobby and Jean were born, it changed to *Tenovus*.[10] When Ted arrived unexpectedly, a second Wianno Junior was christened, *One More*.[11] Joe Jr. later named yet another new boat for his littlest brother, the *Teddy*.[12]

If winning a race in their first summer of sailing wasn't enough to fill their heads with aspirations, a brief moment of "fame" as young sea rescuers administered another strong dose of self-confidence. Sitting on the porch with their father, Joe Jr. and Jack spotted an overturned boat in the harbor. They rushed to *Rose Elizabeth*, sailed out, and found a man exhausted, clinging to the boat. The twelve- and ten-year-old boys pulled him into their little boat, a feat the older Kennedys made known to the *Boston Post*, which reported the "daring rescue."[13]

Sailors learn more from mistakes and close calls than from successes. One such learning experience was Jack's at age thirteen. Nantucket Sound waters are normally predictable enough, but as the season grows late predictability diminishes. After a summer spent in familiar conditions, weather changes are particularly surprising. Before Jack was to start his first term at Canterbury School in Connecticut, he and his younger sister

Kathleen, or "Kick," set out under sail for nearby Osterville. A day that started out calm took a bad turn on their return leg. A squall blew up, then a dense fog rolled in. Back home, brother Joe and their father, having watched the weather change, strained their eyes to find them in the haze, growing more anxious as minutes ticked away. Jack had sailed the route many times in clear weather, so experience helped him find his way, fighting the squall and feeling his way home. Safely at dock, Jack was "nonchalant" about it.[14]

They stayed close to shore in those early years, but how tempting it must have been to venture a little farther out each time! Rose kept an eye on them, and whenever any of her children took a friend out sailing, she made sure the parents knew. There was a big flagpole on the lawn between the house and shoreline, which Rose used to signal her children when they were offshore. She or a gardener would lower the flag if she wanted them to come in.

The enormity of the greater challenges offered by the vast sea beyond would have been immediately evident on family outings a few short miles down the road to the Outer Cape's Atlantic coastline, with its huge dunes overlooking endless wild ocean. The often-peaceful sounds of the more protected Mid Cape shoreline are a sharp contrast to the outer shore's roar and the pounding of waves that shake the ground below your feet. Visits there must have made the Kennedys Mid Cape home seem like a shelter from the chaotic world beyond, from nature's unpredictable, sometimes violent course. When you saw storms on Nantucket Sound, you thought how much more awful it must be out at sea, off the Outer Cape.

Thoreau described the "roaring of the breakers, and the ceaseless flux and reflux of the waves, . . . they did not for a moment cease to dash and roar, with such a tumult that, if you had been there, you could scarcely have heard my voice the while . . . I doubt if Homer's Mediterranean Sea ever sounded so loud as this." After returning to Boston, Thoreau said, "I seemed to hear the sea roar, as if I lived in a shell, for a week afterward."[15]

Beston devoted a whole chapter to his observations of Outer Cape waves. "From across the moors, the great levels of the marsh, and the bulwark of the dunes resounds the long wintry roaring of the sea. Listen to it a while, and it will seem but one remote and formidable sound; listen still longer and you will discern in it a symphony of breaker thunderings, an endless, distant, elemental cannonade. There is beauty in it, and ancient terror. I heard it last night . . . there was no wind, the leafless trees were still, all the village was abed, and the whole somber world was awesome with the sound."[16]

Those visits would give the Kennedy children a visceral sense of the hazards and challenges the wider distant world offered, the oceans and continents they would soon explore as young men and women. During those first years at Hyannis Port, elsewhere on that eastern seaboard, in New York City and in Washington and out across the Atlantic, they were on the eve of the stock market crash and the Great Depression. Soon President Roosevelt would appoint Joe Sr. as the first chair of the Securities and Exchange Commission, created to fix a broken stock market after the 1929 crash, and then ambassador to the Court of Saint James, placing the family in London, where they would witness the coming war.

In nonsummer months there would be boarding schools for Joe Jr., Jack, and the other children as they grew older. Thoughts of their return to the Cape were ever-present, and their father believed in giving Joe and Jack decision-making authority concerning sailboats to teach them responsibility and build self-confidence. So during the school year, their thoughts and correspondence were filled with the coming season's boating decisions. To what seems an extraordinary degree, choices concerning acquisitions, repairs, and outfitting were made with close consultation of the eldest sons, sometimes delegated entirely to them, often with no small financial consequence. Joe Jr.'s and Jack's letters discussed the merits of one vessel over another, prospective hired boat hands, relative costs, and other factors. Joe Sr. held veto authority but showed his sons he respected their opinions.

After a couple of summers at Hyannis Port, as Joe Jr. and Jack grew more skilled at sailing the small Wianno Juniors, they dreamed, as sailors do, of bigger boats. In January 1930, as fourteen-year-old Joe Jr. finished a letter to his father, he added an additional note:

Dad, I just had this letter already sealed when I got a letter from J. Alden Yacht Broker. I had asked him to send me some of the particulars of some of his boats. I am sending you details of one which I think is an excellent buy. I know you won't have hardly any time to look at it, but when you consider Crosby's 25 foot boats 2nd hand for $1,200 and they have a rotten cabin and no motor. I have had the Junior designes [*sic*] for three years and I am sure I will be able to sail this.[17]

He must have been referring to a Wianno Senior Class sloop, 25 feet in length, 17.5 feet at the waterline, 8 feet wide, each carrying enough lead ballast to achieve a weight of at least 4,100 pounds. They were and still are built by the Crosby Yacht Yard of Osterville, Massachusetts, founded in 1850 and situated six miles west of Hyannis Port. It would be two years before they acquired a Wianno Senior, but in the intervening months the discussion of other boating options was continual.

In May 1930 Edward Moore, personal secretary to Joe Sr., sent Joe Jr. more information about boats for sale. "Some of these look pretty good to me but how the price will strike Daddy, of course, I don't know. It will be a good thing to have a bunch of possibilities ready for him when he gets back."

Joe Jr. replied, "These boats look very good to me. The Friendship sloop is kind of old so I don't know how she is. The other, by the picture, looks just the kind I would like. Maybe we could get it cheaper." Twelve days later Joe Jr. had second thoughts after learning of a cruising opportunity. "I was wondering whether to wait another year before getting a boat. . . . If I [take the cruise] I will know more about sailing."[18]

The following spring Joe Jr. wrote to his father with grand plans:

I went to Boston last weekend to look at some boats. I talked it over with George Connelly and his partner, and I think this is the best idea. There are no sloops around Boston [of] the kind I want. I looked at some, but I didn't like them. We thought it would be best to get a small schooner or yawl about 35–40 feet. That is about 5 feet larger than the sloop. Then to have a man on it for the first month and go cruising, in that way I would learn how to navigate, and also to learn how to sail it. George Connelly thinks we could get a good young man for around $80.00 a month. Another advantage to either a yawl or small schooner is that if caught in a blow, you could let down one of the sails and keep on sailing, while in a sloop, you would have to take down the mainsail, and reef it.[19]

A year later, in 1932, Jack was fifteen and weighing in on many things nautical. His father invited him to advise on the hiring of a family "skipper" to help maintain boats and teach sailing. Wrote Jack, "the skipper—Everett Tallman—that you named in the telegram seems to me to be a good man. He is a nice fellow and while he may not [know] too much about the fine pts. of sailing yet is, I think, a worker, and knows quite a little. Thus, I think that he would be the best man."[20]

By the winter and spring of 1932 the family made its most momentous boating decision. They decided on a Wianno Senior. Decades later that purchase was often described as a gift from Joe Sr. to his son Jack. Yet letters show Joe Jr. was actively involved in every boat acquisition, including this one, and in the years immediately following, Joe appears to have sailed it as often as Jack. Newspaper accounts of races from the 1930s identify the sailboat as belonging to Joe Jr. More likely it was acquired for the family as a whole. It might have been Jack's favorite over the years, but others in the family regularly sailed it too.

Wilton Crosby of the Crosby Yacht Building and Storage Company, in Osterville, sent Joe Sr. detailed specifications of the Wianno Senior, adding, "You probably know these boats very well and know how they sail, so it will be useless for us to try to tell you how well this class has performed in the Wianno Yacht Club. We are building four of these boats this winter and would like very much to build one for you."[21]

The order was placed, and Joe Jr. and Jack followed the work's progress. It was actually one of two boats ordered by the family that year; the other was the Wianno Junior that Joe named the *Teddy*. In March Joe Jr. wrote to another of his father's assistants, C. J. Scollard, with instructions concerning both boats' specifications and delivery, indicating that the second boat's name was Jack's to bestow. After discussing *Teddy*, Joe wrote, "Jack gave you the list of the colors on the other boat. Bottom-gold, side-white, deck-buff color. Jack is in the infirmary so I cannot find the name of the boat, but I will tell him to let you know as soon as possible."[22]

From boarding school in late spring Jack addressed a letter to his mother: "Dear Mother, Did you talk over the name of the boat with Joe. What did he think?" He concluded the letter with, "It was too bad about the Lindbergh baby. Please give my love to all. Lots of Love, Jack."[23] On May 23 Scollard wrote to Crosby, "Regarding the Senior Wianno One Design Boat which you [are] building for Mr. Joseph P. Kennedy, the following has been selected: *VICTURA.* Please have this name placed on the boat."[24]

Others have written that Jack said the name had "something to do with winning." In a 1960 interview shortly before his election to the presidency, Jack told a writer for *Sports Illustrated* that *Victura* was Latin for "about to conquer."[25] It was true. Ariane Schwartz, a Dartmouth College authority on Latin language and literature, said that "victura," is the feminine form of "victurus." "The form comes from the perfect passive participle of both the verb to live (vivo) and . . . to win/conquer (vinco)," she explains. "'Victurus' is the future active participle, so 'victura' means 'about to live' or 'about to conquer.' It's feminine, I imagine, because the Latin word for ship is feminine. So you can interpret the name as a blend of the two— the ship will last a long time—it will fare well and outshine others."[26]

Jack, 15, middling student of Latin, found a name both pleasing to the ear and perfect for a boat he would race.

After a few seasons the boat's color above the waterline was changed to navy blue. Colors can vary, but everything else about one-design sailboats must stay the same if it is to be raced. Every Wianno Senior has been built to precisely the same hull design and rigging specifications and the same sail area for main, jib, and spinnaker. The addition of ballast prevents any weight advantage. "Each tapered edge of a wooden centerboard or wooden rudder must be bound by a 1/2 inch half-round or half-oval metal rod," says one of a long list of association design rules. "All spars must be of solid Sitka spruce, and may be made from a single piece or from two or more pieces laminated together. The dimensions of existing spars may not be altered and all new spars shall have the dimensions shown [in an accompanying diagram], provided that the gaff and boom may be shortened."[27]

The first boats had planks of old-growth cypress over white oak framing. It had a cramped cuddy in which two might sleep in a pinch, but it was really a day sailor. An admiring 1989 profile in *Wooden Boat* magazine noted, "Bent to Sitka-spruce spars was a breathtaking cloud of canvas: some 72 square feet of jib and a whacking 294 square feet of mainsail on a waterline length of 17 feet!"[28] A modern boat designer would never employ a gaff-rigged, four-sided mainsail, but surviving boats today have Cape Cod yesteryear charm. The boat's wide beam, ballast, short mast, and the weight of its racing crew of four reliably kept it from knock-downs in a gale. Crosby was so confident in his design that it is said he offered a $1,000 prize to anyone who could capsize a Wianno.[29]

The concept of one-design sailboat racing was only about fifty years old when the Kennedy children were introduced to it. The idea is that when each boat is identical, winning depends on the skills of skipper and crew rather than boat design. Earlier, to race fairly, dissimilar boats were assigned handicaps or were grouped by classes of similar size, shape, and sail area. The result was costly for the boat owner, because design improvements meant constantly investing in newer boats to stay competitive. In 1887 members of the Royal Cork Yacht Club, in County Cork on Ireland's southern coast, decided to build several identical racing dinghies called the "Water Wag." The one-design idea spread quickly and led to the design of numerous other fleets of alternate design and size. Today, Hobie Cats, Sunfish, and J/24s are popular one-design racers.

In 1913 H. Manley Crosby, son of the Osterville boatyard founder, was approached by a member of the nearby Wianno Yacht Club. Would he create a boat designed for, as one later boat enthusiast asked, "safe day sailing and racing . . . a fast, handy, handsome, seaworthy, rugged, shoal-draft knockabout, appropriate for the notoriously shallow and choppy waters of Nantucket Sound"? Crosby would. Fourteen club members agreed to place orders, and in that single winter of 1913–14 the Crosbys somehow produced fourteen new boats, a production output never again exceeded in a single year. They came close in 1930, despite the Depression, when he lowered his price and completed orders for eleven more boats.[30]

Manley Crosby had fours sons helping him in the early years: Malcolm, Carroll, Wilton, and Horace. Grandsons Bradford, Wilton Jr., Theodore, and Malcolm Jr. continued the boat building as decades passed and improved their techniques as they did so. In earlier years they would cut tree branches that had grown in the angled or curved shapes they needed. They replaced that with wood steaming and bending techniques. "The hulls were framed and planked right side up, but the process was facilitated by careening the hull over on its ear, first one side and then the other." They reused molds to replicate the boat hull, but "because they were set up by eye, there are slight variations between the boats built" in the earlier decades.[31]

Boats built up until about the time of *Victura* were held together with galvanized boat nails or screws, and the boat's distinctive round cabin trunk—the vertical part wrapping around the upper cabin with oval porthole windows—was made of a single piece of oak, steamed and bent. To counterbalance the massive sails, the bottom had an iron keel of six hundred pounds and an equal weight of lead ballast stowed below.[32] Over the century that followed about 200 were built and 120 survive, 4 of them in museums. Since 2001, with the market for new wooden boats all but vanishing, Wianno Seniors have been made of fiberglass, weighed down to give new owners no advantage.

"You go up the coast here all the way up through Maine, there are different types of boats that have similar characteristics," said Ted Kennedy Sr. "But this boat was obviously made for just this kind of wind, this kind of sea and these kinds of currents. And these are outstanding performers."[33]

The idea of one-design racing might have had special appeal to the patriarch of the Kennedy clan. It was painfully clear to him that no matter his lofty status in business, nothing could change the New England social status of an Irish Catholic. It must have been especially pleasing to see his children and the Brahmins brought to a level playing field offshore. Perhaps that helps explain Joe Sr.'s emotional response to the wins and losses of his children and the intensity of his scorn for half effort.

~ The Wianno Senior outlived other boats that arose in the early days of one-design sailing. The result today is a small group of boat owners committed to meticulously maintaining the specifications and characteristics of a boat that long ago was far surpassed by boat design engineering technology. Owners' arguments in defense of the gaff rig sound like a defense of the pope's worldview in the time of Galileo. But their faith in the superiority of the boat is absolute and so too is their commitment to being the best competitor on the water. Max Kennedy, Robert's son and the owner of the Wianno Senior *Ptarmigan*, the last of the Seniors made of wood, observed that one local sailor who is a four-time J/24 world champion, involving tens of thousands of competitors, sometimes wins when racing in a Wianno Senior but more often loses to one of the obsessive regulars on that boat.[34]

According to a local newspaper profile of the fleet's devotees, "While all the boats have names, owners tend to refer to Seniors by hull number. It's a lineage thing. For example, Burnes's father, Bunny (No. 14), married Ruth Carney (No. 82) and begat Richard (No. 148), father of Gordon (No. 185)."[35]

"It's almost as if the Senior is the common ground, like a golf course, that binds people and generations together," said Steven Morris, a former owner now living in Maine. Few people would get married on the afternoon of a race, he said, because guests would not show up. "How obsessive can skippers get?" Morris asked. "I remember waking up and looking out the window at the treetops before I even said good morning to my wife. The direction and strength of the wind determined how I tuned the boat and selected my crew."[36]

The Kennedys have bigger boats and the means to own them, but in 2012 Eunice Kennedy Shriver's son Mark bought #203, the green-hulled *Dingle*, from a local owner of Irish descent. "I really like the Seniors most because they're big enough to put five, ten people on it, but everybody's got a job," said Mark. A bigger boat is too removed from the water and the elements:

> For me, the water's splashing over the front of the boat, or the boat's tipping and you have to sit on the side and hike out in order to flatten it. The kids, if they want more action, they can go to the front of the boat. They can sit on the boom; they can drag. . . . But when we tack somebody needs to make sure the mainsheet's ok; somebody's got to make sure the jib's released and the other jib sheet's brought in; somebody's got to grab the mooring. You don't have a big crew, you're doing the work and you're close to the water. If a big wave hits the side of a Senior it comes right over the edge there. If it's cold, everybody

screams; if it's sunny and beautiful out, everybody goes "ahh," and you have the salt water hit you in the face. That's life. That's beautiful. And you're not twenty feet in the air, on top of a boat looking down— you're right on the water. I love that.[37]

One does not merely buy a Senior. Ownership is bestowed. For some, the transfer feels sacramental. The current chair of the Wianno Senior Class Association, Tim Fulham, became owner of #143, *Pertelote*, when he and his wife bought it together as a wedding present to each other.

Richard Ulian wrote a book-length encomium to the Wianno Senior, disguised as *Sailing, An Informal Primer*.[38] He spends as much of the book on romantic affection for his #7, *Tirza*, and for Nantucket Sound as he does on sailing fundamentals. Ulian maintains that the boat picks the owner, not the other way around, and he remembered first spotting *Tirza*, recently restored, at Crosby's Boat Yard. He took it for a trial sail and fell in love but did not have enough money to buy it. *Tirza* would not leave his mind, and Ulian wanted that Senior and no other. Two years later he tracked down the man who bought the boat from Crosby's and wrote him a note asking that he be contacted if ever the owner wanted to sell his Senior. Ulian almost immediately received a phone call.

"How did you know I wanted to sell the boat?"

"I didn't."

The owner named a price that was lower than he had paid. After a moment he offered an even lower price.

"I want someone to have it who'll care for her," he told Ulian.

A week later Ulian showed up to close the transaction. "The boat lay dockside," wrote Ulian, "gleaming white, freshly painted, impeccably varnished." Ulian wrote the check and handed it over. The owner hesitated.

"Are you sure you want to do this?" Ulian asked.

"No. But my wife does. I caught my foot in the mainsheet during a jibe last fall—pulled me almost out of the boat, the way she saw it. She made me promise to sell."

"I don't want to take it from you like that," said Ulian. "Won't you talk to your wife again?"

Ulian thought he saw moisture in his eyes. "No, I have to sell."[39]

~ The Kennedy children of Joe and Rose were famously active in many sports. The personal fitness trainer hired in the early years had the children out on the lawn at seven in the morning for calisthenics and "could be heard on a quiet morning from Nantucket Sound to Cape Cod Bay." There were swimming competitions, touch football on the lawn, and, when weather wasn't cooperating, board games and charades indoors. But sailing was the favorite pastime and to win in the regattas, many in the household had a role, including hired help and local workers.

In what is one of the earliest photograph of *Victura*, published in the *Boston Globe* on July 15, 1934, seventeen-year-old Jack is on the bow, twisting his head to better hear something Bobby, eight, is saying. Bobby's buzz-cut head is barely up to Jack's belt. The photo caption reads, "Bob advises his brother John how to bend the jib of the *Victura*." Perhaps only in 1930s New England would a newspaper expect its readers to know without explanation that "bend the jib" means tying a line to the foresail's peak so it can be raised.[40]

Before one afternoon race Jack sailed a practice run on *Victura* and afterward left the sails improperly secured against gusty winds. One was torn. With time before the race running short, the damaged sail was rushed to a local seamstress, whose normal work for the family involved the girls' skirts. "It was a big job," said the seamstress. "The sail was virtually in ribbons—they really needed a new one—but because of the race I dropped everything to get the job done on time."[41]

The Kennedys are said to have been notoriously bad about paying bills, so when a Kennedy chauffeur came to collect the repaired sail and rush it back for the race, the seamstress demanded seven dollars. "No money, no sails," she insisted. The chauffeur angrily described the urgent need to get *Victura* to the starting line, but the seamstress was unmoved. After returning to Hyannis Port to get the seven dollars, the chauffeur delivered the sail in time for Jack to win, but at a loss to the seamstress: "It was the last sail that was ever brought to me again."[42]

Major races in those years were more than boating events; they were social ceremony. "Those watching the race arrived at the long Wianno Club pier at the end of Wianno Avenue . . . dressed for the occasion. The women wore long skirts, large-brimmed hats, and white gloves; the men, impeccable blue blazers, white flannels, and commodore caps."[43]

Among the more colorful characters in those years were the Parlett sisters. Both Mary and Edna owned their own Wianno Seniors, and, according to one account, "each had a man, politely called 'the professional,' who was responsible for the day-to-day care and sailing of the boat. At race time, the professional sailed the sisters' boats to the starting line and prepared for the race, after which a shore launch brought the sisters out. Mary and Edna, dressed in their finery, graciously stepped down from the launch onto the decks of their respective Wianno Seniors to begin the race. The professional's role was like that of the royal groom who saddled and held the horse for the well-attended Queen of England."[44]

Damore writes, "The Kennedys customarily crewed their own boats during the time when as many as 35 boats of the Wianno, Osterville and Hyannis Port fleets hired professional crews. A crewman frequently earned up to $75 for two races a week. During the mid-1930s it was not unusual to see the 'skippers' of such boats hit the decks wearing afternoon wash-silk frocks; they would sit on canvas camp chairs, white gloves on the tillers, 'sailing' to victory, for the rules allowed professionals to do everything but touch the tiller."[45]

Joe Jr. and Jack needed no royal groom and would wear no white gloves, for they thoroughly enjoyed the details and chores of making their boats race ready. They personally crewed their boats; otherwise, what was the point? But they did have plenty of professional help ashore. The "skippers" the family hired oversaw the children's sailing activities and maintained the boats, for maintenance is something boat owners love and hate, but mostly hate. The first such skipper was James A. "Jimmie" MacClean, who despite having coast guard and merchant marine experience, spent much time ashore taking the children to town for ice cream and elsewhere. As Joe and Jack grew older, a saltier skipper came aboard: John "Eric" Ericson, tall, loud, course, and fond of drink. He claimed that beer mixed into undercoat paint added buoyancy. He shouted orders at the boys with a Norwegian accent. Joe Sr. thought the boys needed to learn from a kind of man they would not likely encounter in the prep school and the Ivy League in years to come.[46]

In the same summer of 1932 that *Victura* was delivered, George Connelly, a yacht broker who regularly gave the family nautical advice, recommended one Rodney Tibbetts in a letter suggesting the qualities Joe Sr. might have looked for in a "skipper" for the boys. Joe was seventeen, Jack fifteen. "Tibbetts is a big strong rugged fellow weighing over 200 pounds, well groomed, and very congenial. . . . I imagine you want a man to teach the boys navigation, how to handle the boat so they will have some confidence, and above all to know that they are in good hands and safe from any unnecessary risks. . . . He is clean cut, a clean liver, and his language is as clean as you would want it." Joe Sr. could not have been impressed when Connelly then added, "On the sailing end of it I believe he knows as much as the next man. I don't believe there is any mystery in sailing a boat; a lot depends on judgment, luck and the boat itself." Mr. Tibbetts apparently was not hired.[47]

Though boys had hired help and instruction, they also knew work. For boat bottom maintenance, Joe scraped barnacles and applied paint. Jack cared so much about the condition of his sails he kept them in his bedroom, despite his mother's wishes.[48] When Joe and Jack later also sailed Star-class boats, they "loved to putter around their boats," to do all the detail work necessary to be competitive.[49]

The Kennedy family relationship with personal hard work and the working classes was somewhat reflective of the times. Kennedys were privileged and ambitious, imbued with both a sense of entitlement and a strong work ethic. Their father often sent the boys on errands of the sort other families used hired help to perform. Though only three generations removed from their working-class Irish immigrant forbearers and gaining perhaps some consciousness of class distinctions that still worked against Irish Catholics of any income, the Kennedy children nonetheless could take the hired help for granted. They were known to be awful tippers. "Stepping off a boat onto the Hyannis Port pier, the children would shed articles of clothing as they marched along," expecting someone else to pick up after them. Housekeepers at Hyannis Port "complained about Jack's room: the wet towels in a heap on the floor, the tangle of ties in one corner, the bureau drawers turned over and emptied in the middle of the bed in a hurried search for some wanted item."[50] Jack was known to run down the dock toward a boat, tossing articles of clothing aside, expecting the help to collect them. Jack's boarding school, Choate, reported to his parents that he "has little sense of the material values and can seldom locate his possessions."[51]

The year 1937 was Luella Hennessey's first as a nurse brought into the family then and for decades afterward whenever a Kennedy was ailing or a child was born. That summer all the brothers and sisters "wanted to sail and it was quite difficult to get somebody to crew. I recall one afternoon that I raced as crew for Jack. He was getting along pretty well and as we were coming down towards the goal line he threatened to make me jump overboard, so that it would lessen the weight and he would be sure to win, but he didn't quite make me do it."[52]

Where their upbringing was concerned, their father, so intentional as a parent about so much, gave careful thought to how they experienced privilege. He sought to free them of concern about material possessions but still make them deeply driven to work harder than any peer or competitor. They were to take for granted their high position in society, yet never leave their position unguarded and unearned. They were to be supremely self-confident yet vigorously competitive and fearful of anything less than winning. "Kennedy wanted his children to start life on the heights to which he had lifted them. . . . He hoped to instill in them that natural confidence possible only to people who never had cause to doubt their social position," writes Doris Kearns Goodwin. "The sense of privilege he inculcated in his children did not allow for laziness or lack of effort. If they were to move into the ranks of the most successful, they had to become a tiny aristocracy of talent."[53]

As early as the late 1940s Joe Sr. spoke of his preference that his children pursue public service rather than business. "The country's got plenty of businessmen," he said. "We chance to be in a position in which [our sons] can be spared the necessity of supporting themselves. Spared that, why shouldn't they better try to qualify to serve their country in some needed capacity?"[54]

So while Joe and Rose did not expect their children to work to pay their own way—to do chores such as paint a boathouse, mow the lawn, or clean house—they did insist they work at being competitive with the highest intensity and sense of purpose. They demanded disciplined effort focused above all on winning. Whether in sport or in school, they were to come in first or do their absolute utmost to achieve first. There are many accounts of friends and family who watched with amazement at the extent to which Joe Sr. demanded success and at the way the children fought on one another's behalf for their success, at least when they were not viciously competing with one another.

Paul Chase, a friend of Jack's and frequent guest at the Cape said, "Mr. K. really did preach that winning was everything. Several times Jack asked me to crew for him when he could not find anyone else. Once we lost badly, and caught a half-hour lecture from the 'old man' on our return to shore. He said he had watched the race and that he was disgusted with both of us. There was no sense, he claimed, in going into a race unless you did your damnedest to win, an endeavor at which we failed miserably. He was really angry with us."[55]

Joe Sr. was a font of platitudes about competing and doing one's best. Trite at times, what his exhortations lacked in depth, they gained by being forcefully said and emphatically reinforced with displays of joy at victories and clear disappointment at less than an all-out effort. He closely supervised other sports too—swimming, tennis, football, golf. When they went off to boarding schools, he wrote letters to all his children, filling them with praise and critique on everything from penmanship to behavior to grades. The children seem to have accepted it not as paternal domination but an expression of love. It's said they worshipped their father, or at least idolized him. It was a relationship driven both by fear of disappointment and delight at his pride. What truly motivated probably depended on the child.

Joe Sr.'s message to his children was lost on no member of the family:

Rose: "Even in school games and races, we always took an interest. We went, and watched, and then talked about it afterwards. If they didn't win, we tried to find out why."[56] She said her husband's mantra was "We don't want any losers around here. In this family we want winners. . . . Don't come in second or third—that doesn't count—but win."[57]

Bobby: "There was no such thing as half-trying. . . . Whether it was running a race or catching a football, competing in school—we were to try. And we were to try harder than anyone else. We might not be the best, and none of us were, but we were to make the effort to be best."[58]

Ted: "If we were racing a sailboat, [Joe Sr.] was there in his cruiser. One time we did badly. He felt it was because we were not paying attention. There was absolute silence at dinner that evening."[59]

Eunice, the best of the female sailors in the family: "If we won, he got terribly enthusiastic. . . . The thing he always kept telling us was that coming in second was just no good. The important thing was to win, don't come in second or third, that doesn't count—but win, win, win."[60] "I was 24 before I knew I didn't have to win something every day."[61]

Jewel Reed, wife of Jack's World War II buddy James: "The [dinner] table was dynamic and Mr. Kennedy was checking up on everybody about whether they had come in first or second or third in tennis or yachting or whatever. And he wanted them to be number one. That stuck with me a long time. I remembered how intensely he had focused on their winning."[62]

A waitress that served the Kennedys: "They would run from Stone and Gable across the street and onto the lawn and you never got a sense that it was for the joy of running. You got a sense that it was for the joy of seeing who could win. . . . I never once found it an offensive competitiveness, by the way."[63]

On one occasion Jack said his father was "always rather harsh" but added, "I don't think his health was good, he was always living at a nervous pitch, he was speculating and all the rest. So he was always somewhat peremptory. . . . He was always emphasizing racing, that we always do well. . . . I make this point, that he set rather a stand for action."[64] On another occasion Jack said of Kennedy family competitiveness, "That's overrated. We played together and we played against each other in sports and there's always the desire of the younger brother or sister to show up an older one on something, but it was never more than that. Drive, yes; competition, no. Although I will say he'd ride our asses pretty hard if we lost in the sailing races."[65]

Conventional wisdom has it that Joe Sr.'s emphasis on winning was his way of grooming future leaders. He may have had survival skills in mind as well. His grandson Christopher maintains that families of that generation anticipated the likelihood that sons might have to fight a war and that the navy was going to play a big role in any future conflict. Seamanship and swimming skills could save lives. Even a child's teeth-brushing habits were important because they might one day need healthy teeth to grip a crewmate's strap to swim them to safety. Christopher believes his grandfather considered sailing a "martial art."

Joe Sr. demanded they know starboard from port; less discussed was knowing right from wrong. Some have said the high standards Joe Sr. set for his children did not extend to the realm of moral choices. The Kennedys would later speak of their family as having a culture of public service to others, a trait more attributable to Rose's influence and her Catholicism. Joe alluded to public service from time to time, but it seemed more aligned with political ambition than moral purpose. "Joe Kennedy stressed winning, excellence and competition, but he taught little about ethics and morals," wrote the JFK biographer, Michael O'Brien, an impression others shared.[66] Much has also been written about the amoral example Joe Sr. set for his children with respect to marital fidelity. Joe's admonitions in letters and reminiscences, oft-cited as they are, were all about winning and doing one's best, not so much about doing the right thing. When Jack was in trouble at boarding school for his participation in a misbehaving secret group of boys called the "Muckers Club," his father was called to meet the headmaster to discuss his son's possible expulsion. Joe feigned concern until the headmaster was out of earshot, then whispered to Jack that had *he* organized the group he would not have spelled it with an "M." Perhaps Joe was like many fathers who left the children's moral education to the mother and to the professionals, in this case the Catholic Church. Joe had a way of compartmentalizing daily life and religion.

As the children of Joe and Rose matured, moral purpose arose as a motivating factor. Robert in particular displayed it, but it was in the others too. That must have been Rose's influence. She was Catholic to the core, and the religious life she preached and lived was fully implanted for life in the minds of her children. Rose attended church daily and quizzed the children on catechism. She later said, "I wanted them to form a habit of making God and religion a part of their daily lives, not something to be reserved for Sunday."[67]

Childhood catechism took hold in their later lives. "By 1938, Joe Jr. had been the head of the Catholic Club at Harvard, thirteen-year-old Bobby was an altar boy and Eunice was displaying missionary zeal about converting their Protestant friends," according to Kathleen Kennedy's biographer.[68] Jack attended Sunday Mass all though Harvard, though his occasional irreverent remarks about the church were often a worry to his parents.

The children were not taught that coming in first ranked with getting to heaven. But the family's win-at-all-cost behavior struck some as unsportsmanlike. When Joe Jr. lost a race and went through the inevitable postrace debrief with his father, he blamed it on his aged and misshapen sail. Eric, the family skipper, was instructed to order a new one. Powered by new cloth, Joe started winning again until competitors took a closer look at the new sail. It appeared the gaff was riding higher on the mast than would be possible if the sail were regulation size. Was Joe cheating with extra sail area? That was no small accusation in Nantucket waters, where honor mattered. Eventually the family attributed the mistake to Eric, a boating professional they believed could be trusted with such matters. The alibi worked, but suspicion lingered.[69]

When Jack was nineteen he took an old boarding school friend out in a motorboat to watch a sailboat race that included Joe Jr. in one boat and another old classmate, Herb Merrick, in another. Jack's friend recalled, "When Herb started to pass Joe, Jack gunned our boat in front of Herb to slow him down."[70] The incident was probably more playfulness than cheating.

Sometimes religion and competition were conflated, as when Eunice announced at a sail race's start, "'All right, now: everyone say a Hail Mary.'"[71]

CHAPTER 3

At Once Rivalrous and Loyal

≋≋≋ Off-season the Kennedy children lived apart at boarding schools or alternated as a family between Boston and New York City. When apart, their collective longing to return to the sea came through in letters. Three from May 1934 were of a common theme. Joe Jr., studying in London, wrote to eight-year-old Robert, "I'll be glad to get back to the Cape for the racing. You'll probably be big enough to act as crew during the races. . . . Work hard in school, Bob, and eat lots of spinach so you'll be able to hold onto the ropes this summer." Kick wrote her mother at the Cape, "I hope you have a nice time watching the fleet," and Joe Sr. wrote Joe Jr. that President Roosevelt's son and daughter-in-law were to summer across nearby Buzzards Bay and had acquired a Wianno Senior they hoped to race, "so maybe you will have a crew for August."[1]

No doubt they enjoyed cities and their boarding school classmates, but stepping out of the car at Hyannis Port, feeling the Cape breeze, breathing air of salt and sea grass, was a liberating moment, a time for losing shirts and hours. They could spend a whole day in bathing suits and worry about few things more complicated than yacht club dances, fitness for a swim race, or the readiness of *Victura* or *Tenovus*. Walking alongshore they could watch the piping plovers—a bird still abundant in those years—establishing their bowl-shaped nests of sand on the beaches, having completed their migratory return in April. Sometimes they would see black skimmers flying inches above the water, lower beak longer than upper, scooping up food near the surface. In boarding school they were a slave to the clocks on the wall. Here the clock-like rhythm of nature was all around with comforting, unconfining constancy, ebb current slowly swinging to ebb tide, the winds quickening almost as sure as sunrise to a twenty-five-knot-or-more sou'wester starting every afternoon around one o'clock, the house's towering flagpole a sundial casting an hour's hand shadow around the big play place of their great lawn.

The return to the family routines of Hyannis Port was a coming home to an adventurous normal. It's a measure of how much they loved it that they and the following generation of Kennedys spent their lives returning, buying adjacent properties, trying new boats. The house was full of and surrounded by the incessant noise of brothers and sisters, brisk air, constant nursing of bumps and bruises, and boisterous conversation at dinner, led with calculation by their father to instill understanding of and curiosity about world affairs and politics. There were many sports played, but much time was devoted to sailing, to tinkering with boats to improve performance, to practicing maneuvers, to frequent races. They cruised and raced offshore, at first always within eyeshot of their front porch.

Brothers and sisters grew better at sailing every year. By summer's end of 1934 Kathleen, fourteen, and Eunice, thirteen, had won trophies, as did Joe Jr. The following year, wrote a chronicler of the lives of the girls, "the young Kennedys led by Eunice, Kathleen and Pat . . . plus Rosemary, Jack and Joe Jr., came away with 14 first prizes, 13 seconds and 13 thirds in 76 starts." Every year July and August calendars were full of racing. Over seven of those prewar years, collectively putting all they had into the races, "the Kennedys took away more prizes than anyone else, carrying away a bounty of loving cups, silver trays, bound books, clocks and desk sets as they left the port at the end of summer."[2]

There was also the science of calculated risk to learn; weather could not be reliably predicted in those days, and the wind could be wild. During the Hyannis Port Yacht Club Labor Day races of 1936, Joe Jr. skippered *Victura* and Eunice *Tenovus*, "in a strong southwest breeze and rough sea which caused the withdrawal of five of the small yachts."[3] In July 1937, a newspaper reported, "It was a day to dowse topsails at Edgartown Yacht Club regatta today, but the skippers didn't believe in dowsing anything and held on or dragged canvas during the wild-puffs of wind that reached half-gale force out of the southwest. . . . The fleet of nearly 200 boats sailed a series of races in unusually fast time, while leaving a string of crippled boats in their wake, a string that kept the Coast Guard busy rescuing the crews and towing in the wreckage." Sailing *Victura*, Joe took second in his division, a minute behind the winner, who covered the 6.4-mile course in seventy-five minutes.[4]

Joe and Eunice showed equal measures of determination under sail: "Eunice needed no example: she was as aggressive at the tiller as he. The goal was victory, the style wild: split-second timing at the start, recklessness at the windward buoy, disregard for the risk of a tiny misjudgment. Joe carried full canvas when others reefed; he had a gut sense of the touch of the breeze in light winds and a special feel on the tiller; he was last to head up for safety in a squall and first to ease off again."[5]

It is likely Jack crewed for his brother in those races in *Victura*, but surviving sailing records do not reveal as much about Jack. He must have gained plenty of helmsman's experience though, because he enjoyed such competitive success when he entered college.

~ In their years together on *Victura*, Joe and Jack found trouble as well as triumph. In a race good sailors intensely focus on the details of sail trim and tactics, little tolerant of idle chat, famously prone to heated language. This was certainly true of those who sailed *Victura* and the other Wiannos. "If the crew didn't get physically struck it was an amazing thing. I mean there is almost no Wianno racer there who didn't witness crew being thrown off or hit," recalled Robert's son Chris, describing later Cape experiences that resembled those of his father and uncles.[6]

One Senior sailor, Jean Kiley Wells, recalled an incident in the 1930s: "The Edgartown regattas were, needless to say, the highlights of the sailing seasons. I was always well-chaperoned by one or both parents, but even so it was a fun time. One Saturday afternoon, our Senior, the *El Cid*, and the *Victura*, captained by Jack Kennedy, collided. The Race Committee threw out both protests as the stories differed totally. It made no difference as we were both quite unsuccessful that day."[7]

The reward for all that tension on water is a tradition as inviolable as a skipper's authority: after-race drinks. There, tensions are lubricated away, friction forgotten, sailing adventures retold, mishaps inducing laughter instead of anger. After racing in the 1935 Edgartown Regatta in the summer before Jack went away to Harvard, the two Kennedy boys instigated a wilder-than-usual party at a local hotel, so boisterous that police were summoned. Joe and Jack were arrested. The role of alcohol in that incident is unrecorded, and Joe Sr. was known to disapprove of overconsumption, not wanting to validate the Irish stereotype. Upon learning of his sons' incarceration, Joe Sr. thought a night in jail would do them good. The *El Cid*'s Wells said, "The Wianno sailors at that time had a bad reputation in Edgartown and as I recall, some were on a blacklist in the hotels and lodging."[8]

It would not be the last time an Edgartown Regatta ended badly for a son of Joe Kennedy.

~ Joe Sr. made clear his high aspirations for all this children, but it was obvious that his firstborn and namesake was the anointed. The parents spoke of the importance of the younger children learning from the good example of their older brothers and sisters, so they expected model behavior from Joe and, though he sometimes fell short, he liked the role. At a young age, Joe Jr. assumed airs of authority over his siblings. He was beheld with some awe by the younger ones, particularly Ted, seventeen years younger, making his and Joe's relationship more paternal than fraternal.

Joe Jr. was smart, studious, athletic, handsome, witty, and poised. His teasing was vicious with a large dose of sarcasm, a means of asserting authority that did not necessarily enlarge his popularity. Jack's later description echoed that of others and was as good as anyone's:

> I have always felt that Joe achieved his greatest success as the oldest brother. Very early in life he acquired a sense of responsibility towards his brothers and sisters, and I do not think that he ever forgot it. Towards me who was nearly his own age, this responsibility consisted in setting a standard that was uniformly high. . . . I suppose I knew Joe as well as anyone and yet, I sometimes wonder whether I ever really knew him. He had always a slight detachment from things around him—a wall of reserve which few people ever succeeded in penetrating. I do not mean by this that Joe was ponderous and heavy in his attitude. Far from it—I do not know anyone with whom I would rather have spent an evening or played golf or, in fact, done anything. He had a keen wit and saw the humorous side of people and situations quicker than anyone I have ever known.

This was written in 1945 by a veteran back from war. Jack continued, "He would spend long hours throwing a football with Bobby, swimming with Teddy, and teaching the younger girls how to sail. He was always close to Kick and was particularly close to her during some difficult times. I think that if the Kennedy children now or ever amount to anything, it will be due more to Joe's behavior and his constant example than to any other factor."[9] One wonders now: even more than their father and mother?

Joe Jr. and Jack grew closer over time, but in those younger years Jack found second fiddle a position not to his liking. They were intensely competitive with each other, prone to squabbles. Jack, small of build, was not one to be cowed even if he rarely won a fight. Robert later told an interviewer that "he and [sisters] Pat and Jean would gape from the stairway, or hide, as the two struggled on the living-room floor; the style of the family was to let Jack fight it out on his own."[10]

That was something, given Jack's frailty then. The origins of his frequent illnesses were a mystery to his parents and doctors. Medical science at the time disallowed a good diagnosis, and his father sought much advice about it. Jack required so much medical attention in 1933 and 1934 that his father said Jack's physician would be presenting an article on Jack to the American Medical Association, "because it is only one of the few recoveries of a condition bordering on leukemia, and it was the general impression of the doctors that his chances were about five out of one hundred that he ever could have lived."[11] Not until after the war was he diagnosed with Addison's disease.

Even in college, friends still saw the two as competitors. Harvard classmate Thomas Bilodeau recalled, "The touch football was not a matter of strategy with the Kennedy family. It was a matter of blood and thunder. . . . Both the boys could never be on the same team. Whichever one Joe was on, Jack would always take the opposite team. There was great competitive spirit between the two boys."[12]

Joe Jr. had a temper too, and sailing brought that out. Jack, Eunice, and the other siblings often crewed for Joe in *Victura*. Eunice recalled, "he was very good, but he had quite a strong temper and would be cross as a billy goat and would blame somebody else when he didn't win."[13] When Teddy was a young boy he pleaded with Joe Jr. to take him along for his first race.

Teddy managed to acquire a lifelong love of sailing despite that day's experience with Joe. When Teddy was twelve or thirteen, after Joe was lost in the war, he was asked by Jack to record in writing that first race:

> I recall the day the year before he [Joe] went to England. It was in the summer, and I asked Joe if I could race with him. He agreed to this so we started down to the pier, about five minutes before the race. We had our sails up just as the gun went for the start. This was the first race I had ever been in. We were going along very nicely when he suddenly told me to pull in the jib. I had no idea what he was talking about. He repeated the command again in a little louder tone. Meanwhile, we were slowly getting further and further away from the other boats. Joe suddenly leaped up and grabbed the jib. I was a little scared, but suddenly he seized me by the pants and threw me into the cold water.
>
> I was scared to death practically. I then heard a splash, and I felt his hand grip my shirt, and then he lifted me into the boat. We continued the race and came in second. On the way home from the pier he told me to be quiet about what happened that afternoon. One fault Joe had was he just was easily mad in a race, as you have witnessed. But he always meant well and was a very good sailor and swimmer.[14]

Joe's long shadow was both a burden and a place to hide. Jack was less disciplined and more carefree, and he lacked his older brother's paternalistic nature. He showed less sense of purpose, more sense of humor. Joe was always destined for politics, but Jack envisioned an academic career, perhaps as a writer. Joe was organized and diligent about his assignments, whether he liked them or not. Not so Jack, writes Doris Kearns Goodwin. "Jack was unpardonably sloppy at home and lazy at school, interested only in the things that pleased him."[15]

Bilodeau recalled,

> There were certain differences between the two boys. Joe was quick. He would not put up in any way with intellectual stupidity; he could not stand people who could not understand problems quickly. He couldn't put up with mediocrity in any way. On the other hand, although Jack may have had the same feelings, he was a much more flexible person.

He seemed to be somewhat more understanding of mediocrity. And it seems to me that he was able with his personality to have won a great many people whom he couldn't have won if he had been at all quick to flare up at stupidity.[16]

As summers passed by and the personalities of the younger boys emerged, another biographer saw a developing dynamic:

Joe [Jr.] would often serve as a surrogate parent, filling in as enforcer and role model during the frequent absences of Joe Sr. and Rose. Jack would act as the family's detached observer, commenting and dissecting the proceedings as much as participating in them. Bobby was the fierce-willed altar boy, fighting for every scrap of ground he could get with a kind of messianic zeal, and Ted was the roll-with-the-punches guy. In short, Joe Jr. was the family's star, Jack its wit, Bobby its soul, and Ted its laugh. . . . Joe Sr. genuinely expected all four sons to be president. He gloated when they were children that he would outdo the Adams family, which only had two presidents.[17]

It would be many years before the contributions of the females of that generation would be fully appreciated.

~ Nonfamily members appeared on the scene through friendships with the children, some becoming lifelong friends, others not blending in or keeping up with the quick pace. Joe Jr. started a habit of bringing friends from boarding school for extended visits, and the others followed Joe's example by bringing their own friends. The parents approved since it kept their own children closer at hand. Joe Sr. generally ignored the friends of the other children. At the always-lively dinnertime conversations, any friends who tried to chime in discovered their participation unwelcome. Joe Sr. pretended not to hear them.

A common theme of friends' reminiscences was the trials at sea. Bilodeau, Joe's heavyset classmate, found that Joe and Jack sometimes competed for him as crew. "When the wind was heavy, both Joe and Jack vied for my affections. . . . I recall we were coming down to the finish line, and the winds let up and we were on a run. The boat was slowing down with my weight, and Jack turned to me and said, 'Over the side, boy. We've got to relieve ourselves of some weight.' So right out there in open water, I proceeded to just go over the side, and he ran on to win the race."[18]

~ Physical size was useful in high wind, but competitive sailing on a boat like *Victura* generally did not require size or brute strength, which was good for Jack. It was more strategic and technical. Skill at team building helped, Bilodeau's experience being a poor example. Sailors needed to know the engineering of the boat and master the infinite influences on its per-formance—wind speed, gusting and direction, water current, and wave. They needed an instinct for the subtle touch of the tiller in light wind and to be an interpreter of small variances in the sail's luff. That suited Jack.

Robert Kennedy's son Christopher, born in 1963, sails the family's new *Victura*, which itself is now among the older of the wooden Wianno Se-niors. Chris speaks of the almost infinite number of factors to consider, not to mention mastery of sailing terminology:

You can rake the mast forward by pulling out some of the wedges around where the mast goes through the deck and tightening down the forestay and loosening the side stays. . . . You can raise the entire rig, the gaff itself. You can pull the downhaul down. You can pull the peak up. You can lower the peak. You can pull the outhaul out. You can pull the outhaul out on the peak. You can set the luff lines. The leach. It's just endless, endless. That's just on the main [sail]. You've got the jib. . . . You can set that in a particular location on the forestay, tighten the downhaul. That's even before you get into just pulling the main in and out.

There are a million ways to continue to make things better and then to react and change. You know, just always improving, improving and keeping at it. And then there are enormous wind shifts out there. So a race can look lost and then the wind will back around the course, and it'll all of the sudden be favoring the boats that went their own route, favored their own course, didn't follow the leader.[19]

~ A quick student, Jack had day-after-day outings to learn the nuances of the *Victura*. Perhaps his most memorable race as a young man began with his decision to outfit *Victura* with a new mahogany tiller. In his late teens he was old enough to saw and plane a piece of wood into a perfect handle to steer the boat, and he was eager to try it out. After all that work and anticipation, he wasn't going to let weather stop him. The best record of that day is J. Julius Fanta's 1968 account, one that may have a few factual improvisations but which was at least written close enough in time to make available to Fanta some reasonably reliable secondhand accounts.[20]

The summer weeks leading up to the day of the race had been one hot windless day after another, a prison of a season for a sailor, and out of Nantucket Sound's character. With early fall came winds so high they might have warranted a small-craft advisory had the harbor at Hyannis Port been equipped to issue one. Jack's teen rivals showed up for the scheduled race to find a sign on the harbor bulletin board: "No Race Today." That also meant no race committee supervision for anyone venturing out. With white caps and rig-straining wind all around, brother Joe Jr. and the other young skippers were of no mind to question authority. They started back down the dock to shore.

"What are you going to do when it blows?" Jack said. "C'mon, let's have a race of our own."

Although alpha maleness was now factored in, given the age and temperament of those involved, Joe nonetheless replied, "Are you nuts?"

"We've been out in worse weather. What are we, a bunch of sissies?"

This pack of wolves would not so easily cede alpha. Six boats were readied for racing. Jack unbolted his old tiller and replaced it with the new one of fresh-lacquered mahogany. The other was tossed into the cuddy. For each competitor, the first consideration was whether to reef sails, which reduced sail area by lowering the mainsail a few inches and securing it with a line of ties parallel to the sail boom. When winds exceed, say twenty-five knots, depending on the vessel, an over-canvassed boat could tip or "heel" far enough to lose speed and give a good scare. A really good gust risks a knockdown. Wianno Seniors may be hard to capsize, but they make for a wet crew in any good breeze. With waves so big, this was going to be a soaking, a long struggle of pulling in sheets and a wracking of nerves as gusts sent the boat heeling beyond forty-five degrees. It was bold to put out under full sail, but many did. Jack was smart enough to reef.

If a horse race started the way a sailboat race begins, horses would gallop back and forth before the starting line, dodging and weaving until the starting bell, at which point all would push, shove, and crowd across the line at whatever position luck and timing afforded. For Jack, getting an advantaged position at the line meant tacking, or zigzagging, back and forth, easing and pulling the mainsheet to speed or slow the boat so the timing was just right. "Jibing" means turning with the wind behind, causing a sudden big swing of the boom and requiring a quick duck to miss a head knocking. Unplanned jibes could be painful, and the chaos of a race's start meant a lot was unplanned.

"A hidden danger, though rare, is a jibe by a boat close beside you," according to Richard Ulian, writing about Wianno Seniors, a boat with a long boom. "His boom sweeps very low across your cockpit. His crew is ready for a jibe. You and your crew may not be; in fact, you may have your backs turned to the danger. I have known people to be knocked out of their boats unconscious this way, with long-term injury resulting."[21]

With boats moving at top speed, crowding around the starting line, zigging and zagging in front and aside, the other big worry was collision. Avoiding one meant split-second knowledge of right-of-way. Sometimes a boat suddenly flashed in front of you, blocked from view by your jib sail.

Meanwhile, Jack was trying to settle into a muscle-memory comfort zone of intuitive response to gust and wave. When he could he glanced to check proper sail shape for the wind and double-checked lines so they were secure and untangled. His boat skipped unintentionally across the starting line before the start, so he called "hard-a-lee" to his crewmates and brought it back.

A quick turn, a gust, a wave and CRACK! Suddenly Jack was holding his new tiller handle, snapped off from the rudder head. He had no control. Rudderless boats turn naturally into the wind and stop. *Victura*'s momentum vanished, sail luffing wildly, boom jerking back and forth, as competitors streamed across the start and left Jack behind. "Thought you wanted to race!" said one passerby. Another noted the irony of Jack's bravado on the dock. As boat motion made the nub of the rudder head jerk clockwise, then counterclockwise, Jack unbolted what was left of his precious worthless tiller and tried to reinstall the old one. If only the rudder head would stop turning back and forth just long enough so he could reattach it! The loud popping flap-rattle of a luffing sail freshened his anger, but he stayed in control. Few sailors carry spare tillers, but at least he had that bit of luck. Agonizing moments passed until he tightened the bolt.

The rudder responded, and he trimmed his sails to cross the starting line. The luffing stopped, and he heard the satisfying silence of smooth sail trim and a steady beat forward. The other boats were all beating in parallel, half a leg of the course ahead. Pushing through, over and under white-capped swells, Jack struggled with the weather helm, where fighting a sailboat's tendency to turn into the wind causes the rudder to rob the boat of forward momentum. It was something between a roller coaster and bull ride. The crew stretched as far over the starboard gunwale as possible, straining their abdomens and leaning their weight to windward, upper bodies hanging out over the waves, to keep the hull as flat on the water as possible, because flatter is faster. Jack was carving as straight a line as he could, trying to keep the telltales on his sails horizontal, and he was gaining. The vibration of wind and shroud made the boat's hull emit a baritone hum like a great bass instrument.

He had not caught up with the other trailing boat until after rounding the first buoy. He was making progress though. Knocking past his first opponent, Jack took fifth position. Even in the best wind, sailboats like Wianno Seniors may not move with much more speed than a human can run, but when the weather is extreme, beads of water stinging, wind scraping skin with salt, waves exploding over the bow, sails dripping water, you feel like a race car driver. As you slowly edge past your opponent, both of you pummeled by weather, you're close enough to see helplessness in their eyes. That satisfied Jack.

Jack passed one, then another, muscles tiring from the pull of the tiller against the current. He pulled even with the boat behind the leader. The leader was, of course, his brother Joe, the best sailor in the group. The weather was worsening. As his bow inched up into second place, a sudden gust, the hardest one yet, hit both second-place boats. Jack heard yelling and in the corner of his eye saw crew from the other boat falling into the water, the boat's hull nearly on its side. At the same instant, another CRACK! Jack's tiller was still firm on the rudder. The noise was from overhead. His mind flashed: how's my mast? He leaned back and studied the rigging above. The gaff, which held the top of the mainsail aloft, was in two pieces. The sharp splinters of the now-loose pole dangled by the top of his mainsail, the shackle on the gaff's end broken too. The sail was folded down on itself. The four-sided mainsail was now held fast by only the three remaining corners, creating a smaller sail area. Those lines and sailcloth that still functioned were straining where they weren't designed to strain.

The other boat's crew was rescued by a race committee boat whose crew had decided to stick around just in case. Good thing. Jack had to choose between the risk of further damaging *Victura*'s mainsail or dropping out of the race. The wind was blowing stronger still. So much could go wrong. As Jack weighed options, he saw he was keeping up with Joe and maybe even gaining. The now intense wind might actually give Jack an advantage. With smaller sail area exposed, he might heel less and thus gain boat speed. Joe was fighting his own boat to keep its hull at less than forty-five degrees, water rushing along his gunwale and into his cockpit. *Victura* was just behind, the finish line just far enough away to give Jack time to close the gap.

Jack was not going to miss this opportunity. His snapped gaff rigging dangling inelegantly above, his hull flatter on the water than Joe's, he slowly made his way forward. There were moments when Jack gained on Joe, then Joe gained the lead back. They tried different tactics. At the finish line, ahead by just half a length, was Jack. Even a competitor like Joe took pride in his brother.[22]

CHAPTER 4

Chemistry

≋≋≋ Joe and Jack, the oldest of the boys, entered the 1930s aged fifteen and thirteen. Ted, the youngest, was born in 1932. So those prewar summers at the Cape were crucial formative ones for a Kennedy generation that would in the 1940s meet many fates and then, in the case of the survivors, move on to lives of such extraordinary distinction they helped define the later half of the American Century. Of the nine Kennedy children, one became president, one became U.S. attorney general and a U.S. senator, and another was the fourth-longest serving U.S. senator in history. Three, including two daughters, received the Presidential Medal of Freedom, the nation's highest civilian honor. One daughter helped redefine how people around the world treat and think about people who have disabilities. Another daughter was U.S. ambassador to Ireland, instrumental in bringing a peace settlement to northern Ireland. The oldest daughter after Rosemary married the heir apparent to a British duke. Patricia married a Hollywood leading man. The oldest son was posthumously awarded the Navy Cross, the navy's highest decoration.

There are times and places in history where circumstances converge and human chemistry is just right to create something extraordinary. Hyannis Port in the 1930s was not Gertrude Stein's apartment in 1920s Paris, nor was it Liverpool in the late 1950s when the Beatles formed a band. The Kennedys were just children summering by a seashore. But given what grew out of that time and the turns of fate to come in the years right afterward, something was at work then to influence what they thought about, what their aspirations would be, what motivated them. They would later say it was parental influence, and perhaps so. It must also have been sibling influence. As a place, Hyannis Port, its windswept waters, and its sailboats have remained a Kennedy touchstone ever since. Year after year, as pages turned on extraordinary family chapters, heroic and tragic, they always returned, rejoined, and reaffirmed family at Hyannis Port and offshore at sail, especially on *Victura*.

After Joe and Jack, Rosemary was next oldest, first daughter in the Kennedy family, born seventeen months after Jack. As she grew older, she showed increasing signs of struggle with learning. Walking came late. Reading was much harder. Eventually symptoms revealed problems beyond those of work habit or proneness to distraction. She had an intellectual disability—retardation as it was known then, though they never applied the word to her. How she would have been diagnosed by today's standards is a subject of some disagreement. Like cancer, mental disability was unspoken of in those days, and Rosemary's siblings protected her. They acted in public as though nothing was wrong and because of their numbers could always ensure someone was with her. She was by no means hidden from public view as were similarly afflicted children of other families. She is in all the family photographs of the early years and routinely joined brothers and sisters at youth social events, with brothers asking her to dance and Eunice always playing with her and keeping her company. Less was recorded of her childhood in Hyannis Port, no doubt because the youthful accomplishments, accolades, and sporting achievements of the others were for her so few and modest.

During Rosemary's adolescence in the 1930s, she began showing increasing signs of emotional volatility and mood swings. Brain science being in such infancy, doctors recommended a prefrontal lobotomy, shockingly extreme in hindsight but state of the art at the time. She underwent the procedure in 1941 when she was twenty-three, and the consequent brain damage required she be institutionalized for the rest of her life. Members of the family long afterward were haunted by the episode and the treatment they chose. It pushed many of them to later use their celebrity to advance the cause of people with disabilities, particularly intellectual ones. Rosemary could not consciously influence the public lives of Kennedys, but unintentionally her influence on their understanding of disability would have lasting consequences for the country, across borders and for decades to come.

Next born after Rosemary was Kathleen, or "Kick," less than three years younger than Jack but precocious enough to become a peer as they matured together in the 1930s. Given Rosemary's state, Kick was regarded as the eldest daughter. By the time she was thirteen, Kick's parents were growing concerned about the extraordinary attentiveness of every boy who met her. Constantly on the phone, she was pretty, not beautiful, dressed in the conservative style cultivated at convent schools that in her case made her no less desirable. Boys were drawn by her unreservedness tempered by aloof sophistication, her graceful assertiveness that did not diminish her femininity. Her quick wit and cleverness helped her filter out all but the brightest of the handsomest boys. She would not be intimidated by any of them. Her high-speed repartee with Jack, their duel of quips, made them inseparable at times, frustrating to many hoping to keep up the conversational pace. At Jack's side in social settings, her electric presence was the perfect complement to his youthful shyness with strangers. It was said, "Every friend Jack brought home from Harvard without exception fell in love with her."[1] Said another who knew her then, "I think she probably had more sex appeal than any girl I've ever met in my life. She wasn't especially pretty, but she just had this appeal."[2]

Dinah Bridge, who befriended the Kennedys later in London and Georgetown, said of Kick, "I'd characterize her as being sort of sunshine really. Everybody she saw she always made feel terribly happy and gay. She always came into a room and everybody seemed to sort of lighten up. She was that sort of a character."

Eunice, born in 1921, four years after Jack, was thin with some of the same then-undiagnosed health problems Jack had, including Addison's, whose symptoms include fatigue, weight loss, and muscle weakness. She nonetheless managed to be among the most athletic of the girls. She was the best female sailor in the family, better than one or two of her brothers perhaps, and at least one 1930s newspaper account of local regattas put her among the top finishers with male competitors.[3] She was also closest to Rosemary, playing games that kept Rosemary active and engaged despite the widening intellectual distance between Rosemary and her maturing siblings.[4] More than her sisters, she was powerfully driven to achieve professionally. Eunice's sensitivity to Rosemary's condition and her forceful personality, later given a national stage with the help of her successful brothers, led her to so influence American understanding of intellectual disability that some say her lifetime contributions to social justice rival those of her brothers. She would one day receive from Ronald Reagan the Presidential Medal of Freedom, the nation's highest civilian honor, as would her future husband, R. Sargent Shriver, a founder of the Peace Corps and Head Start and the 1972 Democratic candidate for vice president. Had she been born in another era when political aspirations extended to females, one may justly wonder if Eunice might herself have become president.

Some thought the most beautiful Kennedy daughter was Patricia, born in 1924 and said to have inherited Rose's aristocratic airs. She was also intelligent, sophisticated, and athletic. But despite her gifts, she was the one Kennedy who in those years lacked the family's drive and thirst for competition. Her mother worried Patricia was squandering her opportunities.[5] In the 1950s Jack was only two years in the U.S. Senate when Patricia had already achieved a level of fame in her own right, though in her case it was fame of the Hollywood variety. She married film star Peter Lawford. They later gave a daughter the middle name "Frances," partly after Lawford's "Rat Pack" pal Frank Sinatra. In time, with the political rise of her brothers, Patricia also focused energy on public service, most notably on programs addressing mental disability and addiction.

Eight years separated Jack's birth from Bobby's in 1925. They really did not get to know each other well until much later. Though Bobby enjoyed sailing all his life, as a youngster he never was as competitive at that sport as his brothers or Eunice. He did not immerse himself in interests or show much enthusiasm for anything. This of course all dramatically changed by the time he and Jack became adult professionals and partners in politics. As a youngster he was prone to injury because he was so fearless at play, a trait that stuck into his adulthood of outdoor adventure.

Jean, born in February 1928, was quiet, perhaps a bit cowed when young by the assertiveness and decibel level of her older brothers and sisters. For years to come she was considered shy and guarded compared to her siblings.[6] Nonetheless, she developed friendship networks of her own, and as a college student introduced both her brothers Robert and Ted to the women they would marry. In the Clinton administration, as U.S. ambassador to Ireland, she took a more assertive role in the peace process in that country than most protocol-conscious diplomats would dare. She founded Very Special Arts, or VSA, a program now in sixty countries that promotes artistic achievement by people with disabilities, an achievement cited by President Barack Obama when he awarded her a Presidential Medal of Freedom. In 2010, when she was the last of her siblings still alive, she said, "all my brothers and sisters were my best friends."[7]

It is likely Joe and Rose anticipated no more children after Jean, for the family named their sailboat *Tenovus*. Ted's arrival in 1932 made it a family of eleven, four years after the birth of his youngest sibling, Jean. Ted, sixteen years younger than Joe Jr., saw his oldest brother more as father figure than brother, and the reverse was also true. Ted was a chubby boy with a perpetual smile and greeted his oldest brother by rushing into his arms and getting hoisted up. Ted's love of sailing pours out of his memoir, published just weeks after he died at age seventy-seven in 2009. Ted's long Shakespearean life journey ended with more years served in the U.S. Senate than all but three Americans. He became America's voice of liberalism as the "Lion of the Senate." It is unlikely any of the Kennedys spent as much time on *Victura*, or loved it as much as Ted, the boat's long association with Jack notwithstanding.

~ There was little indication in the 1930s of all that Kennedy children would achieve in their adult lives. After a year of study in London, Joe enrolled in Harvard in the fall of 1934. Jack studied briefly at the London School of Economics and at Princeton, but illness again interrupted and he left Princeton. He joined his brother at Harvard in the fall of 1936, a place close enough to Hyannis Port to allow occasional visits. A classmate remembered,

> I think the thing that impressed me most about the Kennedy family was the great affection that they had for each other and which was shown outwardly. Many, many times I've seen Joe Jr. or Jack pick up Bobby or Teddy and hug them just like a father would hug a youngster. And I also noted the great affection and outward display of it that they had for their sisters, especially of Kick, as we knew Kathleen in those days, and Eunice. This was evidenced even in law school when Eunice

came regularly to the apartment. The outward show of affection that Joe would evidence when she came into the apartment was amazing.[8]

As Joe and Jack grew older and their rivalry faded, Jack learned not to compare himself to his brother. He did not then project—or perhaps even aspire to have—the leadership traits for which his brother was known. Though Jack lacked the academic discipline of Joe, he showed signs of greater intellectual depth. Both wanted to be football players but neither made it very far, particularly the frailer, younger brother. Collegiate sailing may not have been the ticket to campus popularity that football was, but it was a Harvard sport where both could excel, and they did.

Wianno Seniors, beloved on the Cape's South Shore, were not sailed extensively elsewhere on the Atlantic coast. For Joe and Jack to advance to the next level of competition, they would have to race against a different kind of one-design sailboat. The boat to master was a Star, the first to be raced in the Olympics. During the 1930s Joe and Jack acquired two Stars. The first, *Flash*, was soon replaced with another dubbed by Jack *Flash II*. Robert would, in the 1950s, sail Stars too, though none of that class would win the enduring family loyalty of Wianno Seniors. Joe and Jack sailed in the Star-class Atlantic Coast Championships, with Joe skippering in 1934 and 1935, with the ongoing financial support of his father.[9] A 1934 telegram from Joe Jr. to his father states that he "Qualified for Atlantic Coast Championship. Should have new sails. Cost one hundred forty dollars. Is that OK? Please reply Western Union. Love, Joe."[10]

The summer before entering Harvard as a freshman, Jack skippered and won the last race of the 1936 Atlantic Coast series, also with paternal underwriting. Jack relayed through family aide Paul Murphy a request for a new jib sail "of light material for use in medium breezes." Telling Joe Sr. of Jack's request, Murphy revealed Jack's lofty nautical aspirations, adding that a trusted adviser recommended they buy not just a jib but "a complete set [of sails] now as he thinks this year will be a big one for racing. He feels that if you expect to make the Olympic tryouts, you must have good sails."[11] Family confidant Edward Moore further reported to Jack's brother Joe, "Jack did very well in Long Island getting in first, and as a matter of fact, first by 4½ minutes, and yesterday he won the Star boat race at Wianno." Moore's report wasn't entirely flattering however: "Yesterday I was standing on the wharf at Wianno watching Jack come in from the races. Captain Billings was standing on the after deck of the Star boat and Jack jibed and the sail caught the Captain half way between the fanny and ankles and he went overboard. Jack didn't know it until after he was in the water and yelling."[12] Jack's Nantucket Sound Star-Class Championship Cup from that year is now on display in a glass case at the John F. Kennedy Presidential Library and Museum, next to a Hyannis Port Yacht Club trophy he won racing *Victura* to Edgartown.

After 1936, now both at Harvard, Joe Jr. and Jack could team up in collegiate sailing. They did so with impressive results. The major sailing event of 1938 was the MacMillan Cup, where Harvard faced nine competitors, with Williams and Dartmouth as the teams to beat. Some of the best young sailors in the world competed in the MacMillan Cup. Sailing for Williams that year was Bob Bavier, who would go on to successfully defend America's Cup, sailing *Constellation* in 1964. By 1943 Bus Mosbacher would lead Dartmouth to two MacMillan Cup victories before culminating his nautical career by twice successfully defending America's Cup in 1962 and 1967, the former race witnessed by President Kennedy, watching from the deck of the USS *Joseph P. Kennedy, Jr.*

Despite the level of competition, Harvard carried the day. According to the *New York Times*, "The Crimson skippers out-sailed the Williams stars, their most dangerous rivals, in two contests which practically amounted to match races. . . . The helm for the Crimson was handled by the local Wianno boys, Jack and Joe Kennedy, sons of Ambassador Joseph P. Kennedy, and by Loring Reed of Marion."[13] Joe Jr.'s biographer maintains that the Kennedy role in that victory was overstated, but in 1940 the sailing team's captain, James Rousmaniere, reporting on the class of 1940's nautical victories, credited Jack and Reed as two from that class who "sailed Harvard to a victory" in 1938.

A point missing from almost every account of that race is the fact that the Kennedys had a competitive advantage. That year the race was held at the Wianno Yacht Club in the same unique Nantucket Sound waters Joe and Jack had spent years mastering. Moreover, the one-design boat chosen for the competition was the Wianno Senior.[14]

~ Jack's other athletic achievement at Harvard was, unsurprisingly, in another water sport. All those Cape swimming lessons—all that experience under sail with crew so often jumping over the rail—made Jack an excellent swimmer. For the Harvard swim team he mastered the backstroke and as a freshman helped his team beat Dartmouth in the three-hundred-yard relay. His coach called him "a fine kid, frail and not too strong, but always giving it everything he had." As had happened so often in the past, illness interfered in 1937, just before a big Yale meet. A friend helped him sneak out of the infirmary to practice his backstroke a few times, but his determination this time was insufficient to contribute to a win.[15]

~ Joe, Jack, and Kathleen were launched toward college and adulthood from the idyllic settings of New England boarding schools and Cape seaside summers. The younger children came of age in more worldly settings and then in wartime. Joe Sr.'s well-chosen investments spared them from personal experience of the Depression, but his involvement in politics and his support of President Franklin Roosevelt gave the children personal exposure to the political turmoil arising in Europe. In 1938 President Roosevelt appointed Joe Sr. U.S. ambassador to the Court of Saint James. That spring Rose, eighteen-year-old Kick, and the four youngest children joined their father in London. Kick commenced studies at Queen's College in London, while Joe and Jack remained at Harvard for a few weeks more. Joe graduated in June, and Jack traveled to London for the summer to work with his father in the U.S. Embassy, giving him an opportunity to experience the kind of intensely vibrant social life that older children of an ambassador are privy to. Back home, the family apparently let friends race *Victura*. The Hyannis Port Yacht Club team beat Wianno, with *Victura* winning both the day's races, skippered by "F. Syme" in the morning competition, and "J. Whitehead" in the afternoon.[16]

Members of the family spent those prewar years traveling between London, the continent, New York, and Massachusetts. Joe, Jack, and Kick were all single and highly eligible, achieving celebrity status as the children of the American ambassador at a time when much world attention was on London and the spreading war in Europe. Five years apart in age, the three were old enough to go out on dates. They watched out for one another and experienced popularity and the gaiety of the London social scene, all under a darkening war cloud and the distant sound of jackboots in Germany, Austria, Czechoslovakia, and Italy. Later recalling the summer of 1938, Jack wrote, "You had the feeling of an era ending, and everyone had a very good time at the end."[17]

In the fall of 1938 Jack took extra courses at Harvard so he could take a semester's leave in the spring to tour European capitals and conduct research for his honor's thesis. That trip apparently hastened the end of one of his first serious romantic relationships, with Francis Ann Cannon of the prominent textile family. As he departed on the ss *Queen Mary*, he received from her a telegram dated February 25, 1939: "GREAT GOLDEN TEARS TOO PLENTIFUL FOR VERY FAMOUS LAST WORDS. CAN ONLY SAY STAY WAY FROM THE HAY. GOODBYE DARLING. I LOVE YOU. FRANCES ANN."[18] Just fourteen months later Jack was a guest at her wedding to John Hersey, a twenty-six-year-old journalist whose path would soon cross Jack's again. Hersey was on his way toward developing a groundbreaking new form of journalism, writing nonfiction that employs the story-telling techniques of a novelist.

Jack's itinerary included Danzig, Warsaw, Leningrad, Moscow, Kiev, Bucharest, Turkey, Jerusalem, Beirut, Damascus, and Athens, visits made especially fruitful by the access his father gained for him with diplomats and other government officials. His travels extended in the summer of 1939, bringing him to England, France, Germany, Italy and even Nazi-occupied Prague, a front-row seat to the great unfolding drama of the twentieth century. Despite the seriousness of the times, he had an extraordinary social life along the way.

During that same summer Joe Jr. and Kick visited Spain. "It wasn't until the summer of '39," Kick wrote, "when he took me on a trip to Spain three months after the end of the Civil War that he became aware of me as a companion as well as a sister. What fun we had! I remember thinking then of how brave Joe was when different Spaniards told me how he, the only American there, used to walk the streets during the horrible, bloody days of the siege of Madrid."[19]

In September 1939 Hitler invaded Poland and the young Kennedys would travel no more on the continent. Britain declared war, and Joe Jr.,

Jack, and Kick accompanied their parents to watch Prime Minister Neville Chamberlain address Parliament to outline his nation's declaration of war on Germany. Joe Sr. called President Roosevelt and said, "It's the end of the world . . . the end of everything."[20]

Jack returned to Harvard for his final year and for the completion of his honor's thesis, heavily armed with research made possible by his father. His thesis came to 148 pages and had the title, "Appeasement at Munich," exploring the roots of England's inability to avoid another war so soon after the first Great War. His paper showed how England's democratic institutions may have slowed the country's response to Hitler. Harvard faculty judged it very good—not great—but Jack was nonetheless convinced to turn it into a book. Academics were judging scholarship, not marketability, and Jack could create a book on a timely topic of great worry to Americans, written by the son of the ambassador in the middle of everything. With editing, it became *Why England Slept*, brashly invoking Winston Churchill's book of two years earlier, *While England Slept*. Jack went on the road to promote it on radio and in newspapers, and it became a bestseller from an author just twenty-three years old.

Timely it was. In May 328,000 British and French troops were miraculously evacuated from the French port of Dunkirk, after being encircled by Germans. In June Churchill gave one of the century's great speeches: "we shall fight on the beaches, we shall fight on the landing grounds, we shall fight in the fields and in the streets, we shall fight in the hills; we shall never surrender."[21] Paris fell to the Nazis a few days later.

In Hyannis Port, the summer of 1940 was, at least on the surface, back to normal. The family had spent the previous summer in England and Europe. Much of the family, except for Joe Sr., was back in Hyannis Port, including Joe Jr., Jack, and Kick. Joe Jr. launched his long-contemplated political career, winning a delegate's seat in the 1940 Democratic Convention in Chicago.

Those immediate prewar summers at the Cape were the start of another phase that would distinguish the Kennedys—the love affair news photographers developed for the imagery of the Kennedys at play. It is hard to underestimate the role that *Life* magazine had in shaping the Kennedy image, more than once with *Victura* as a prop. One *Life* photographer visiting Hyannis Port then was Alfred Eisenstaedt, arguably the greatest news photographer of all time. He had already photographed Hitler meeting Mussolini in 1934 and captured Joseph Goebbels hauntingly scowling at Eisenstaedt's lens in 1933 after Goebbels learned the photographer was a Jew. Eisenstaedt went on to create famous images of Einstein, Oppenheimer, Hemingway, Marilyn Monroe, First Lady Jackie Kennedy, and, most memorably, of a sailor kissing a nurse in Times Square on V-J Day. In 1940, out on the water of Nantucket Sound, Eisenstaedt stood on the bow of *Victura* so he could point his Leica toward the stern and focus on Ambassador Kennedy's handsome family. Joe Jr. was at the helm, with Bobby holding the mainsheet and Rose, with a scarf on her head, sitting to Joe Jr.'s right. With them were three sisters and Ted in the midst of his young chubby phase.

Joe Jr., Jack, and Kathleen, at that time so full of promise and already accomplishing extraordinary things, all high on pedestals from the perspective of their younger siblings, have been described more than once as the "Golden Trio." One visitor that summer was in awe:

> I was fascinated by them. Jack was autographing copies of *Why England Slept* while Grandfather Fitzgerald was reading to him a political story from a newspaper. Young Joe was telling them something that happened to him in Russia. Mrs. Kennedy was talking on the phone with Cardinal Spellman. A tall and very attractive girl in a sweat shirt and dungarees turned out to be Pat, who was describing how a German Messerschmitt plane had crashed near her father's house outside London. Bobby was trying to get everybody to play charades. The next thing I knew all of us were choosing up sides for touch football and Kathleen was calling the plays in the huddle for the team I was on. There was something doing every minute. The conversation at the dinner table was wonderful, lively and entertaining, ranging from the war and Washington politics to books, sports and show business.[22]

Joe Sr. returned from London in October 1940 with an air-raid siren. He would use it at Hyannis Port, he said, as a signal to bring the children in for dinner from their sailboats in the Sound.[23]

~ In July of a summer not long before the war, before Joe Sr. became ambassador, a Boston newspaper gave an account of an oddity concerning *Victura*. The boat's ownership was attributed to Joe Jr. rather than to Jack, perhaps because Joe was so clearly the leader of that generation of Kennedys.

OSTERVILLE, July 11—During the freak storm early today a bolt of lightning split the mast and drilled a hole through the side of the Wianno Class sloop *Victura* owned by Joseph P. Kennedy Jr., son of the ex–Securities and Exchange Commission chairman who summers at Hyannisport. The yacht was hauled upon the ways for repairs this afternoon.[24]

CHAPTER 5

War and Destiny

≈≈≈ The family was together again at Hyannis Port in the early summer of 1941. But not for long. Both Joe Jr. and Jack in those months pursued enlistment in the armed services. The attack on Pearl Harbor was still months away, and the question of whether the United States should intervene against Hitler or any other aggressors was still a matter of great national debate. One wonders what Rose and Joe Sr. thought that summer as they looked out from their wide porch to the yard, the shore, and sea. What would come of their sons in such turbulent times?

From that porch they might have watched as Jack piloted *Victura* off into Nantucket Sound for a crossing he made one day that summer to Martha's Vineyard. As Jack finished the crossing and entered the harbor at Edgartown, he saw an impressive eighty-foot gray powerboat, brought over from Newport by the navy and put on exhibition. It was a new warship for the U.S. Navy, though the British and other navies had tried them in other conflicts. As he walked its deck, Jack was impressed. It was a Motor Torpedo Boat, PT boat for short.[1]

Jack tried to enlist that summer. But in the years before 1941 his undiagnosed maladies had developed into intestinal disorders that kept him undernourished, and he started having back pain, for which he consulted an orthopedist.[2] Thus, for health reasons Jack was rejected by both the army and navy. He devoted that Cape summer to getting in shape and improving his diet.

Joe Jr. was more successful and was accepted for Naval Aviation Cadet training in May 1941. Joe Jr. started his military service at Squantum Naval Air Station, then located south of Boston, about a mile south across the bay from the site where *Victura* today is displayed on the lawn of the JFK Library and Museum. There Joe learned to fly and had his first solo in an open-cockpit yellow Stearman biplane.[3] A Stearman is controlled with a stick, which might have felt familiar, like a sailboat's tiller. Proximity to Cape Cod gave him an opportunity to return on leave to race *Victura* in a July 10 race over an eight-mile course.

Two months later the family reassembled at Hyannis Port for Joe Sr.'s fifty-third birthday, but Joe Jr. was absent. The navy had sent him to the Jacksonville Naval Air Station in Florida, to learn to fly PBM Mariners, an ungainly looking "flying boat." Next he went south to Banana River, where Cape Canaveral and the Kennedy Space Center would later be situated. On May 6, 1942, Joe Jr. received his naval wings in his father's presence. He spent the rest of 1942 as a flight instructor, a role he thought could get him the flight hours necessary to command a plane's crew. The gambit worked and by January 1943 he was in Puerto Rico, and then Norfolk, Virginia, leading patrol missions in search of U-boats. No one knew with certainty that U-boats on the American side of the Atlantic were a rarity. None were found until June 1943, when another plane's crew in Joe's squadron made a sighting one hundred miles east of Norfolk. They dropped depth charges, but the sub slipped away.[4] If that was all the action there was, Joe was ready to cross the Atlantic.

Jack was finally accepted into the navy. "I'd spent a lot of time in boats," Jack said later. "Therefore, when it looked as if the war was coming, I was interested in joining the navy. My brother was in the navy, too. I think everyone who could headed in that direction, and I joined in September 1941."[5]

He got in the navy through a side door—the Office of Naval Intelligence, where physical requirements were less demanding and medical scrutiny less strict. To get the necessary security clearance he needed endorsement letters, one of which came from Cape Cod neighbor Jack Daly, who said Jack had a "very active mind" and was a "damn good sailor."[6] Jack was assigned to a desk job in Washington DC, writing briefing papers and memos, unsatisfying work for men like Jack, who thought only combat duty met the nation's needs. At around the same time Kick took a job at the *Washington Times-Herald*, so Jack had his sister and his buddy Lem Billings in Washington with him.

Jack's day job might not have been much, but the after-hours social life was good. Kick introduced Jack to Inga Arvad, a columnist she met from her newspaper job, leading to what was surely Jack's most exotic romantic relationship as a bachelor. She was Danish, had acted in two Danish films, and had been a freelance reporter covering news of high-ranking Nazis in Germany in 1935–36. She interviewed Hitler and was invited to sit in the Fuhrer's box at the 1936 Olympics.[7] Four years older than Jack, she was already twice married and ending her second marriage when she took up with Jack. When the FBI got wind of the ambassador's son's relationship, they wondered if she was some kind of Mata Hari. The navy reassigned Jack to new duty in Charleston. Some, including Jack, have speculated that it was to separate him from the suspicious "Inga Binga," as he called her. They still managed to visit each other and continued to correspond through his tour of duty in the South Pacific.

In July 1942, seven months after Pearl Harbor, Jack's desire to see more action was set in motion when he transferred to officer training at Northwestern University, on the lakefront just north of Chicago. As a junior officer, Jack now militarily outranked his brother Joe, a circumstance of no small emotional significance, given how intensely competitive the two had always been.[8] During Jack's time at Northwestern, a group of PT boat service recruiters arrived with Lt. John D. Bulkeley, an early hero of the war and Medal of Honor recipient. He had evacuated General MacArthur from the Philippines and sank a Japanese cruiser in Subic Bay, turning PT boat service into something glamorous back home.

Jack was among the candidates Bulkeley interviewed. Jack's sailing experience and race credentials made him a strong candidate for torpedo boat school, whose recruiters prized seamanship, small boat experience, and knowledge of ship deck teamwork. In fact, torpedo boat recruiting drew heavily on the Ivy League set, which disproportionately contained men who grew up around Atlantic Coast yacht clubs.[9]

Jack spent much of 1942 at the Motor Torpedo Boat Squadron Training Center in Melville, Rhode Island. His friend Torby Macdonald shared a Quonset hut with him. Practice runs in Narragansett Bay were only about a fifty-mile crow's flight from Hyannis Port, and they sometimes traveled the same waters he sailed in *Victura*, weather notwithstanding. "Jack phoned us tonight," wrote Bobby, "and said he had just taken a trip in his PT Boat and had gone to Edgartown where the temperature was

10 below zero, which I'm sure must have been delightful. He is very proud of himself at the present because Torb, because of the trip, is flat on his back with the grip while he is still moving around."[10]

Cape Cod as a whole was transformed that year for the war effort:

Beside huge sprawling Camp Edwards, there was a vastly expanded Coast Guard detachment operating between Sandwich and Province- town; a naval base at Woods Hole; an antiaircraft training center at Scorton Neck Beach, and two amphibian commando training units at Camp Can-Do-It in sleepy unspoiled Cotuit and in Waquoit, adja- cent to Falmouth. Hyannis Airport had been activated as a simulated flattop for the training of Naval Air Corps cadets; later it became an Army Cir Corps antisubmarine base. A mock German village of fif- teen buildings, complete in every detail from German signs to flower boxes and birdhouses, was erected . . . to prepare soldiers-in-training with actual village warfare conditions.[11]

Blackouts were held in July in preparation for possible attacks.

Nonetheless, from time to time Jack could return to Hyannis Port on leave and reclaim a bit of home life. He raced *Victura* to a third-place fin- ish in June. Less successfully, Robert was near the back of the pack in a major Wianno Senior regatta, moved to Lewis Bay from Wianno to ac- commodate army training maneuvers. A three-boat contest of Wianno Juniors was held, with Pat and Eunice sailing in *Tenovus* and *One More*, but the non-Kennedy boat won.[12]

At times during Jack's navy service, he would use his family's shared ex- periences sailing at the Cape to illustrate what he was experiencing in the navy. "Received a letter from Jack before he left for Florida and he didn't seem too sure he was going to make it seeing that he couldn't even find the right buoys off Hyannis Port," Robert reported to his parents.[13] Jack's references to sailing put his family in his shoes and perhaps betrayed some homesickness. The references to home port would come up again in his letters from the South Pacific.

His father told Joe Jr. that summer, "Jack came home and between you and me is having terrific trouble with his back." Jack valiantly concealed his recurrent back trouble from his military superiors. A nagging concern for his family, and perhaps a source of some self-doubt for Jack, was how his back would handle the wave pounding of a PT.

Jack shipped out of San Francisco and arrived in the South Pacific in April 1943. His PT boat squadron was based at Tulagi in the Solomon Islands. The Solomons are an extraordinary scattering of almost a thousand islands stretching along a 930-mile-long line of ocean east of Papua New Guinea and northeast of Australia. Tulagi was 20 miles north of the biggest island, Guadalcanal. Eight months earlier the island of Tulagi, two miles long and half a mile wide, had been occupied by five hundred Japanese soldiers. The August 1942 invasion of Tulagi by U.S. Marines involved intensive fighting that cost the lives of almost all the Japanese and about forty-five Americans. The much larger battle for Guadalcanal started the same month but took longer and was a costlier enterprise, starting with a shore landing of eleven thousand marines, the first major Allied offensive in the Pacific theater. The Japanese enjoyed significant naval power superiority, especially in nighttime operations, but the allies prevailed and the enemy finally evacuated Guadalcanal in February, two months before Jack's arrival at Tulagi. The naval confrontations were so intense that nearby waters were dubbed "Iron Bottom Sound."[14]

Settling in at camp on Tulagi and adjusting to the routine of life near the naval front, Jack wrote a letter to Kick expressing homesickness and other mixed feelings typical of sailors at war: "Thank you for your last letter—but how about cutting down on terse telegram communiqués—and sitting down and writing a letter. You should be able to do it—Sissie was paying you 40 clams a week for that cool limpid style. . . . That bubble I had about lying on a cool pacific island with a warm pacific maiden hunting bananas for me is definitely a bubble that has burst."

Jack said he ran into an old friend:

I took him over to the officers club and gave him some of my liquor chits and he polished off five scotches with no visible effect except he could hardly stand by the time I got him out. He was due to take his boat out that night, but as it's a boat that is supposed to go up on beaches, he couldn't go wrong. . . . He speaks very fondly of married life, but then they all do out here. . . . You've got no idea of the monotony of some of the jobs which fellows have to do with no recognition or even the occasional stimulant of getting your pants scared off. As a matter of fact this job is somewhat like sailing, in that we spend most of our time trying to get the boat running faster—although it isn't just to beat Daly for the Kennedy Cup—it's the Kennedy tail this time.[15]

Jack was referring to "Black Jack" Daly, a favorite Wianno Senior racing rival back home.

Jack's letter also mentioned a May 1943 *Life* magazine portrayal of PT boat crews, written by John Hersey, the very journalist who married his ex-girlfriend Francis Ann Cannon, just fourteen months after she and Jack split up. "Speaking of John Hersey, I see his new book, 'Into the Valley' is doing well. He's sitting on top of the hill at this point—a best seller—my girl—two kids—big man on Time [magazine]—while I'm the one that's down in the god damned valley. That I suppose is life in addition to fortune knows God, say I."[16]

For the well-to-do East Coast Ivy Leaguers like Jack, the war was often the first time they made friends with working-class Americans who never knew boarding schools, yachting, or summer homes—farmers, Midwesterners, middle-class kids. Hersey was describing men like Jack when he wrote his piece for *Life*. It told of PT boat crew members feeling left out of the larger war effort, relegated to merely harassing the enemy rather than winning tide-turning battles. Writing from the perspective of three PT boat captains in the first-person plural, a narrative device foreshadowing his later innovations in journalism, Hersey wrote,

But bitter as we were when we left [PT boat duty], we were at least friends. For the boat captains, at any rate, that was worth all the horrible things. We boat captains mostly went to Ivy League colleges. We had led sheltered lives. Another way of saying, that is, that we were snobs. To discover what the men in our boats were like was the best thing that could have happened to us.

The enlisted men on the PTs don't get much glory these days but we couldn't have done a thing without them. We value their loyalty and friendship. [One captain said] that the thing that pleased him most out there was not sinking a destroyer, not getting his Silver Star. It was having one of his men come up one day and say: "Skipper, don't mind if I say this, but I hope to Christ we'll have a chance to go out on a binge together someday." They have.[17]

Crewing together on a sailboat off Cape Cod may have been a fine way to make friends, but crewing together on a warship is, of course, something altogether different. In the South Pacific Jack would win the loyalty of his comrades and crew when tested, and they became lifelong friends. He got off to a good start when he first arrived, getting his hands dirty with his crew, scraping, painting, and repairing the sorry-looking boat he was given to command—PT-109. The enlisted men probably had low expectations of an Ivy League yachtsman from a famous family, but Jack had a knack for treating everybody the same and never made too much of his rank or social status. He was a regular guy. As they scraped and sanded and rid the boat of rats and cockroaches, Jack told them it reminded him of home, of getting *Victura* ready for the season.

But being on night patrols on a relatively small wood navy powerboat at the frontline in war, torpedoes strapped starboard and port, juxtaposed the beauty of the South Pacific Sea with the horrors of confronting the Japanese. Jack wrote his parents, "On good nights it's beautiful—the water is amazingly phosphorescent—flying fishes which shine like lights are zooming around and you usually get two or three porpoises who lodge right under the bow and no matter how fast the boat goes keep just about six inches ahead of the boat."[18] Such good nights may not have been the norm, but it reassured his parents.

On PT boats Jack made friendships of a different kind for him, folks he would never have met in his boarding schools or seaside estates. Horrible as the war was, the slow erosion of class distinctions was at least making halting progress with people like Jack. True, it only went so far, for there were no African American sailors on PT crews. The navy was particularly segregated. Back home that very summer, on a Detroit assembly line manufacturing PT boat engines, white employees shut down the line rather than work alongside black workers.[19]

"PT boats ought to be manned by cats," Hersey wrote.[20] They always patrolled at night watching for enemy ships exploiting the cover of darkness. Boats doused lights, leaving only the moon, stars, and reflections from shore to give silhouettes that might be friend, foe, or nothing at all. They were surrounded by small islands, some occupied by the enemy, some by allies, many deserted. Jack was reminded of sailing at night at home and looked at the sky for familiar constellations, points of light all humanity shared, all through time, in all countries.

The South Pacific was no place for recreational racing, but Jack did let his need for speed and competitive instinct get the better of him. Rushing his PT boat back to a dock, he had a habit of leaving the throttle well forward until the last moment, then throwing the engines into reverse to brake it to a quick stop. This was not advised for PT boats. The engines were so unreliable that a maneuver like that could kill the engine and leave it like a racing car without brakes. That was precisely how Jack accidentally rammed a dock, causing no small damage. He might have been severely disciplined, but the authorities were apparently too distracted by other concerns to make a big issue of it.

The PT boats with which Jack served were on the lookout for the Tokyo Express—racing destroyers that the Japanese used for rapid troop movement. PT boats watched for them at night and sought to intercept, harass, terrorize, and torpedo them. One August night was too dark even for silhouettes; it was like being "in a closet with the door shut," recalled one of Jack's crew.[21] Said Jack, "It was one of those tropical black nights without a star or the moon and the Japs were taking advantage of the darkness to try to relieve their garrison at Kolombangara. The job of our boats was to stop them from doing so."[22]

Jack's PT-109 had a crew of thirteen, several of them helping to keep watch. Boats ran slow to minimize the phosphorescent wake that helped enemy aircraft spot targets. Jack, at the wheel, had just one of his three engines in gear, a common practice. A crewman saw a distant dark shape, but no one's straining eyes could tell what it was.

"Ship at two o'clock!" someone shouted. Boats, whether powered by wind or engine, respond to steering with agonizing sluggishness when underpowered, and Jack had just the one engine engaged. He spun the wheel. Minimal response. There has been some speculation that Jack might have too quickly thrust his three throttles forward, stalling the engines. Whatever the case, he had an unresponsive PT boat and no time to get it moving.

"Sound general quarters!" Jack yelled. By then they saw the Japanese destroyer doing perhaps forty knots right at them, growing giant as seconds passed. It sliced through the water, then sliced right through PT-109's wooden hull. Two members of the crew, Harold Marney and Andrew Jackson Kirksey, were probably killed at once. Jack was thrown against the cockpit wall; only the angle of impact saved him from being crushed too. Patrick McMahon was in the engine room with no knowledge of what was happening. At one moment he was checking gauges on an idling motor, the next he was surrounded by flames and then underwater. His face and hands were badly burned. Charles "Bucky" Harris, alarmed by a crewmate's shout, looked up, saw the destroyer's bow heading right at him, and leapt. Still in the air on impact, something rose up and struck him hard in the thigh. He wound up in the water. William Johnston was thrown in the water too and could watch, as did Jack, as the huge hull powered through the wreckage. Johnston could see the destroyer's crew, but then he was suddenly caught in the propeller's wake and sucked underwater. Like McMahon, he finally made it to the surface, beating away flames to breathe.

Another PT boat's crew saw the impact from a distance. The record isn't entirely clear, but they apparently thought PT-109's explosion so horrendous that the chance of finding survivors was too small to risk staying behind with Japanese destroyers racing about. Survivors there were, however, and Jack and three other crew were still on what remained of the PT boat's bow. Watertight chambers below kept the wreck afloat. "Everybody into the water," Jack yelled to those still on board. With flames all around he was afraid the boat would explode. The destroyer's wake cleared enough of the flames aside to give them a place to jump. PT-109 had a crew of thirteen that day, but floating with Jack were only two, John Maguire and Edgar Mauer. As the flames subsided so did the apparent danger of an explosion. The three climbed back aboard and used a light to signal the others in case any were swimming in search of the boat.

They heard a voice and Maguire went back in the water, despite the choking fumes all around, and helped three additional crew back to the boat. Other voices called for help, and this time Jack swam to them. By now the flames were doused completely and the pitch-black night was the new threat. "I'm over here . . . where are you?" Jack called out. "This way," they responded. Jack made it to them, but McMahon, who had been in the engine room, was too badly injured to swim, though he had a flotation vest. The other man, Harris, had an injured leg but seemed in better shape. Jack slowly towed McMahon back to the boat, guided there by the calls from the crew. Harris started falling behind, his left leg failing him and drowsiness taking over. Jack tried urging him on, and Harris swam a little more, then quit. With McMahon returned to the boat, Jack returned to Harris, calling his name until he found him.

Jack, frustrated, said, "For a guy from Boston, you're certainly putting up a great exhibition out here, Harris." Harris cursed Jack for making light of his situation, then got Jack to help him pull a heavy sweater and jacket off. With a lighter load, Harris could paddle back. Johnston needed help too, his lungs and stomach filled with heat and fumes, coughing violently and vomiting. Leonard Thom pulled him back to the wreck. The last of the missing survivors was Raymond Starkey, who drifted alone, unsure what to do. Eventually he spotted the boat and swam to it. That left two still missing, fate unknown. They drifted there in the blackness for the rest of the night, calling out, "Kirksey . . . Marney," every now and then. "Kirksey . . . Marney," repeated through the night. The collision caused a ringing in their heads that slowly waned. So too did their discussion about what to do next. The sound of the night sea's silence and their vulnerability occupied their minds until dawn.

~ Daylight brought more discussion of what to do. Jack, the skipper, abandoned rank. "There's nothing in the book about a situation like this. Seems to me we're not a military organization any more. Let's just talk this over," said Jack.[23]

They knew where they were geographically, but situationally they were adrift, exposed in broad daylight, surrounded by islands, some occupied by Japanese, some perhaps not. They had wet side arms that may or may not fire, some knives, and no first aid kit. By midday, to ensure they had enough daylight left, they took what meager supplies and weapons they had and slipped back into the water. They all had flotation vests. Jack said he would take the badly injured McMahon, and the others wrapped their arms around a wooden plank to stay together. They picked a destination they thought close enough to PT boat cruising areas and started paddling.

The definitive account of PT-109 comes from Robert J. Donovan, whose 1961 book recounts Jack and McMahon's venture, with the rest of the crew swimming separately:

> McMahon, sure that death was only a matter of time, remained silent when Kennedy helped him into the water, which stung his burns cruelly. In the back of his kapok a three-foot-long strap ran from the top to a buckle near the bottom. Kennedy swam around behind him and tried to unbuckle it, but the strap had grown so stiff from the immersion that it wouldn't slide through. McMahon was surprised at the matter-of-fact way Kennedy went about it all. It was as if he did this sort of thing every day. After tugging the strap a few times Kennedy took out his knife and cut it. Then he clamped the loose end in his teeth and began swimming the breast stroke. He and McMahon were back to back. Kennedy was low in the water under McMahon, who was floating along on his back with his head behind Kennedy's.[24]

For hours Jack swam, swallowing water, jaw aching from the pull of the strap. When he periodically stopped to rest, McMahon would ask, "How far do we have to go?" Jack's reply was always along the lines of "We're going good, how do you feel, Mac?" McMahon's reply was always, "I'm OK, Mr. Kennedy. How about you?"[25]

It took them some five hours to cross three and a half miles of water to reach Plum Pudding Island, a hundred yards in diameter with enough foliage to provide hiding space. Since the collision Jack had been in the water for more than fifteen hours except for short intervals floating on the PT wreckage. They were completely exhausted. They weighed options and came to agree their only chance would be to somehow signal a PT boat on night patrol in Ferguson Passage, two or three miles away. They had a ship's light and a pistol they hoped would work. Despite his exhaustion, Jack told the men he would go. The others thought Jack's chances too slim and tried to talk him out of it. After nightfall, he went anyway. He stripped to his undershorts, shoes, and a flotation belt and carried the light and pistol. He made his way though water mostly shallow enough to allow him to stumble along an uneven coral bottom, made harder by the darkness. Sometimes it was deeper and he had to swim. He saw the shapes of large fish and mostly did not know what he was stepping on or swimming through.

It took hours to get to Ferguson Passage. He floated far offshore to where he hoped he might intercept a passing PT boat. He floated there in darkness for hours more. He saw lights and boat movement miles in the distance, but this night no one came through the passage. Eventually he allowed the realization to set in that the boats were taking another route, patrolling another area, the first time they had done that in many days. They sent no boats or planes to search for the crew of PT-109, and now they did not even patrol the same waters as they had the previous days. Hours of pulling McMahon, hours making his way to Ferguson Passage and waiting, treading water there, exhausted him further.

Jack gave up. He tried to make his way back toward the island and his crew, but now a current pulled him in another direction and he hadn't the strength to fight it. "He thought he had never known such deep trouble," said one account, based on an interview with Jack a few months later:

He stopped trying to swim. He seemed to stop caring. His body drifted through the wet hours, and he was very cold. His mind was a jumble. A few hours before he had wanted desperately to get to the base at Rendova. Now he only wanted to get back to the little island he had left that night, but he didn't try to get there; he just wanted to. His mind seemed to float away from his body. Darkness and time took the place of a mind in his skull. For a long time he slept, or was crazy, or floated in a chill trance.[26]

He drifted that way until dawn and with light returned consciousness. Amazingly, he was still roughly where he was the night before, within swimming distance of a little island close to his crew's island. The currents in the islands were not all linear; some took circular routes. He made it ashore and fell hard asleep.

~ The men feared Jack was lost. But late that morning Maguire looked out and saw a figure in the water approaching their island. As the figure drew closer they were happy that it was Jack, but he looked awful. They helped him to the bushes and soon he fell asleep. Before he did he looked at George "Barney" Ross and said, "Barney, you try it tonight." Ross never liked the plan, but if Kennedy could do it he could. He was somewhat better rested than Jack had been when he set out, and he had Jack's advice on how to get out to the passage. He tried it, but again the night passed without PT boats. Ross went back ashore on the same small island Jack had found and slept, returning to the men late that morning. The men were disheartened, hungry, and thirsty; small amounts of coconut juice were all they had to drink. McMahon's burn injuries needed treatment. It was clear they were given up for dead by the men at the base. They did not know that a memorial service had already been held for their lost souls, and one officer wrote his own mother that George Ross and Jack were dead. "Jack Kennedy, the Ambassador's son, was on the same boat [as George] and also lost his life. The man that said the cream of a nation is lost in war can never be accused of making an overstatement of a very cruel fact."[27]

They decided to move to Olasana Island, closer to Ferguson Passage and about one and three-quarter miles away. Again, Jack towed McMahon and the rest swam together with the plank of wood. Luckily they encountered no Japanese on their new island, but they did find more coconut trees. They spent the night there but did not make another attempt at swimming into Ferguson Passage. It rained and they licked rainwater from leaves.

The collision with the destroyer happened at two thirty in the morning of Monday, August 2. It was now Thursday morning. At a loss for options, Jack looked across the water at another small island called Naru, half a mile away. With no clear purpose in mind, Jack asked Ross to join him for the swim to Naru so they could explore. Once ashore, they crossed to the opposite side, which directly faced Ferguson Passage, a location that made it a risk for the presence of Japanese. They walked the shore and saw the wreck of a small ship, then a crate on the beach that contained hard candy. Then what must have seemed a miracle: they found a dugout canoe with a tin of rainwater. This offered all kinds of possibilities. Jack and Ross drank from the tin.

Back in Hyannis Port, Joe Sr. was informed by friends that his son was missing in the South Pacific. For days he told neither Rose nor anyone else in the family.

~ Up to 1943, as Japanese forces occupied an ever-expanding region of the Pacific, there was a very real fear that even Australia and New Zealand were threatened by invasion. In the island territories occupied by the Japanese, they faced resistance from two peoples. One consisted of Australian expatriates who served as "coast watchers," using secret observation posts to collect and relay to Allied forces intelligence about Japanese ship and troop movements. The other pocket of resistance consisted of the aboriginal native population, many of whom to this day live in traditional huts without electricity and whose diet consists of coconuts, other gathered foods, and fish caught using dugout canoes and spears. They are the descendents of an ancient people who, over tens of thousands of years, gradually introduced human habitation to new islands in the South Pacific, migrating from one island to the next in their little dugouts.

Among these aboriginal peoples were great seafarers, crossing vast oceans in canoes outfitted with sails, navigating in ways still unknown, to impossibly remote islands. There are today still pockets of islanders who speak ancient languages that predate not just the arrival of Europeans in the sixteenth century but even the arrival four thousand years ago of speakers of the Austronesian language. Their small villages formed communities that for centuries stayed largely autonomous, preserving distinct tongues, so that Melanesia still has the world's largest diversity of languages concentrated in the smallest area. More than 1,300 distinct languages are spoken on the islands that arc across the northeast coast of Australia.[28] They are one of the few dark-skinned people in the world who are sometimes born with blond hair not genetically traceable to Europeans. The Japanese invaders treated them brutally, driving many to the side of the Allies.

Two native scouts for the Allied forces were named Biuku Gasa and Eroni Kumana. They worked closely with an Australian named Reginald

Evans, a sublieutenant who occupied a secret lookout on a volcano on the Japanese-occupied island of Kolombangara, a peak that rose above Blackett Strait, where PT-109 was sunk. Gasa and Kumana paddled from island to island in their dugouts, reporting on Japanese movements to Evans, who relayed the information on his radio. One night the two Melanesians heard an explosion offshore and saw big flames rising from a boat. Evans saw it too and in the morning saw wreckage afloat. He sent the scouts to investigate and perhaps look for survivors. They found nothing. Four more days went by. They paddled by the island of Naru and saw the wreckage of a Japanese ship in a reef just offshore. They climbed onto the wreckage and poked around, looking for anything salvageable. Suddenly, a mile away on the beach they saw two light-skinned men who they assumed were Japanese. Gasa and Kumana ran to their canoe and fled. The two light-skinned men were Jack and Ross, and they saw the natives too. From that distance Jack and Ross thought Gasa and Kumana were Japanese. Jack and Ross fled too.

As Gasa and Kumana paddled away from Naru, they grew thirsty and stopped for coconuts on Olasana Island. Once ashore, they spotted another light-skinned man and turned to run. By chance, they had come upon the rest of the crew of PT-109. The crew did not know what to make of the two black men. Lenny Thom took a gamble and approached them.

"Navy, navy," he yelled. "Americans, Americans."

Gasa and Kumana spoke almost no English and did not trust this man.

"Me no Jap." Then Thom pointed to the sky. "White star, white star." For some reason this clicked. The natives knew white stars were painted on the wings of American aircraft. Eventually, Gasa and Kumana were confident enough to pull their canoe ashore and hide it in the bushes near the crew. Later, Jack returned to Olasana in the other canoe and discovered his smiling crew with two new friends.

The famous idea of using the two natives as messengers did not immediately occur to them. With two canoes at their disposal, they must have been reluctant to send one of them off. Instead, Jack asked Ross to join him in paddling a canoe out into Ferguson Passage for one more attempt at hailing a PT boat. The weather had taken a turn, however, and the waves beyond the reef were too big for a canoe. Jack was more accus-

tomed to braving extreme weather, but Ross objected. They tried anyway
and capsized.

"Sorry I got you out here, Barney," said Jack, as they struggled with the
boat and waves.

"This would be a great time to say I told you so, but I won't," he
answered.

The next day Jack took Gasa with him to Naru for yet another look at
Ferguson Passage. At around the same time Jack on Naru and Thom on
Olasana had the same idea. Send for help with the natives as messengers.
Jack could find nothing to write on, so he took a coconut and used his
knife to carve a note:

NAURO ISL.

NATIVE KNOWS POSIT

HE CAN PILOT 11 ALIVE. NEED

SMALL BOAT

KENNEDY

Thom wrote a similar note but he had paper and pencil to write it
on. When the crew was reunited, both messages were given to Gasa and
Kumana, and they were asked to take their dugouts to the PT boat naval
base on Rendova Harbor, a distance fully thirty-eight miles east. The natives left but, fortunately, chose to make a stop along the way to first de-
liver their message verbally. Word reached the Australian coast watcher
Evans, who the next day sent seven scouts in a "war canoe" to Naru. They
fetched Jack first, hiding him under palm fronds, where he listened as the
natives paddled and, between strokes, tapped oars in rhythm against the
side. He was brought to Evans, and that evening, just before midnight,
Saturday, August 7, six days after the crash of PT-109, Jack arrived at Olasana Island with two PT boats.[29]

Years later Ted Kennedy was interviewed on the subject of Cape Cod
sailboat races, and he brought up PT-109. "No question in my mind that
the fact of his [Jack's] association both with sailing [Wianno] Seniors,
the competition that he had with that, the knowledge of the sea, was absolutely indispensable in saving his life in the Pacific when his ship was
sunk by the Japanese, and he was able to save directly the two men who

he dragged to shore, [and] save the rest of his crew as well. And I am absolutely convinced it was those lessons that he learned on the *Victura* and
racing Seniors that made such a big difference."[30]

~ Joseph P. Kennedy Sr. was driving his car home from a trip to Osterville with the radio on. Suddenly he heard his son's name. John F. Kennedy
had survived six days lost in the South Pacific after his boat was rammed
by a destroyer. It so stunned Joe that he drove off the road.[31] Joe still had
told no one at home that Jack was missing. Sometime after he returned to
the house, Rose came running to him, crying. She too had the radio on.
"They say Jack's been saved. Saved from what?"[32] Eleven-year-old Teddy
and his sister and friends rode bicycles to a newsstand to buy papers for
their parents. There a front-page story caught Teddy's eye. The *Boston
Herald* had a drawing of a PT boat being rammed by a much bigger ship,
accompanied by a story of Jack's crew.[33]

"I was dumbfounded," Ted said. "I hadn't been told anything about
it."[34]

Some have said that Jack's older brother, Joe, while certainly happy for
his brother's survival, grew jealous of his sudden fame. He was still flying
missions from bases in the United States when he got the news. When
the family heard nothing from Joe, their father wrote him to express his
disappointment in his lack of curiosity about Jack's well-being. When
Joe Jr. finally wrote home on August 29, he made light of everything:
"With the great quantity of reading material coming in on the actions of
the Kennedys in various parts of the world, and the countless number of
paper clippings about our young hero—the battler of the wars of Banana
River, San Juan and Virginia Beach . . . will now step to the microphone
and give out with a few words of his own activities."[35]

Later that summer, Joe had time on leave to visit Hyannis Port for his
father's birthday. During that furlough, Joe Jr. took *Victura* out for a sail in
the waters in front of the big house. He also demonstrated his new skills
as a pilot by borrowing a training plane from the Hyannis Airport and
buzzing the harbor and waterfront. Airport authorities soon told him to
cut it out; several people had called to complain.[36] At a party for Joe Sr.,
the police commissioner, Joe Timilty, gave a toast: "To Ambassador Joe

Kennedy, father of our hero, our *own* hero, Lieutenant John F. Kennedy of the United States Navy." Unmentioned in the toast, Joe Jr. apparently could not hide the offense taken. Timilty that night took a guest bed in a room shared with Joe Jr. and claims he heard Joe cry.[37]

Joe Jr. got up the next morning, glanced at the house and at Nantucket Sound, and left to report for duty in Norfolk. He would never return to Hyannis Port.

~ With the crew of PT-109 safely returned to Tulagi and on the mend, Jack had a debriefing with authorities to anticipate. He was a hero to his crew, and reporters were on hand for their return to base, so their survival story was quickly told across the country back home. But Jack had to wonder how his loss of the boat and two crew would be viewed by his superiors. Engaging the enemy is one thing; unintentionally idling right into the path of a speeding Japanese destroyer, one he was supposed to instead be attacking with torpedoes, was something else. His snide brother Joe later asked Jack questions Jack's superiors might ask. "What I really want to know is where the hell were you when the destroyer hove into sight, and exactly what were your moves, and where the hell was your radar?"[38] It all left Jack feeling guilty. He was skipper and at the wheel when the collision killed two of his crew. For a long time afterward, when asked about his heroism, he replied, "It was involuntary—they sank my boat." His survival also left him thirsty for revenge against the Japanese, more risk prone and impulsive, willing to volunteer for dangerous missions when others in his place might have felt they had done their duty.

It was what Jack did to save his crew after the collision that impressed everyone most. He and Thom both received promotions, command of new PT boats, and the Navy and Marine Corps Medal. Jack also earned a Purple Heart for his injuries. His father tried to get him home, but Jack wanted to stay and sought command of a new boat. This he received— PT-59—and some of his PT-109 crew volunteered to serve with him again, even though their "new" boat was old and retrofitted as a gunboat without torpedoes. With Jack at the wheel, it saw a lot of action evacuating marines. On one occasion, again as always on a night mission, Jack had to expose PT-59 to enemy fire from shore to rescue about forty-five marines from a damaged boat they were unsuccessfully trying to use for their escape. The marines clamored onto Jack's boat, occupying every square foot of its deck. The worst-injured marine, Corp. Edward James Schnell of Wilmette, Illinois, was carried below and laid in Jack's bunk. PT-59 delivered the marines to yet another boat for their final voyage to safety, but they kept Schnell aboard so they could rush him to where he could get emergency medical attention. As they pressed on, Jack checked on Schnell from time to time. He grew worse. Before they could reach their destination, Schnell died in Jack's bunk.

In September, the sinking of his ship fresh in mind, Jack wrote to tell his father that Bobby was still too young for Pacific duty. "To try to come steaming out here at 18 is no good. . . . It's just that the fun goes out of war in a fairly short time and I don't think Bobby is ready to come out yet. I also think Joe is nuts to come. He's doing more than his share by merely flying."[39]

He wrote a war-weary letter to Inga too, expressing emotions he wouldn't convey to a brother or sister, and perhaps also tugging strings for sympathy from a woman he hoped to see again. Perhaps, too, he was thinking of her status as a journalist who would appreciate his perspective from the front.

> The war goes slowly here, slower than you can ever imagine from reading the papers at home. The only way you can get the proper perspective on its progress is to put away the headlines for a month and watch us move on the map. It's deathly slow. The Japs have dug deep, and with the possible exception of a couple of marine divisions are the greatest jungle fighters in the world. Their willingness to die for a place like Munda gives them a tremendous advantage over us. We, in aggregate, just don't have the willingness. Of course, at times, an individual will rise up to it, but in total, no. . . . Munda or any of those spots are just God damned hot stinking corners of small islands in a group of islands in a part of the ocean we all hope to never see again. . . .
>
> We are at a great disadvantage—the Russians could see their country invaded, the Chinese the same. The British were bombed, but we

are fighting on some islands belonging to the Lever Company, a British concern making soap. . . . I suppose if we were stockholders we would perhaps be doing better, but to see that by dying at Munda you are helping to secure peace in our time takes a larger imagination than most possess. . . .

The Japs have this advantage: because of their feeling about Hirohito, they merely wish to kill. An American's energies are divided: he wants to kill but he also is trying desperately to prevent himself from being killed. . . .

The war is dirty business. It's very easy to talk about the war and beating the Japs if it takes years and a million men, but anyone who talks like that should consider well his words. We get so used to talking about billions of dollars and millions of soldiers, that thousands of casualties sound like drops in the bucket. But if those thousands want to live as much as the ten I saw, the people deciding the whys and wherefores had better make mighty sure that all this effort is headed for some definite goal, and that when we reach that goal we may say it was worth it, for if it isn't, the whole thing will turn to ashes, and we will face great trouble in the years to come after the war. . . .

I received a letter today from the wife of my engineer, who was so badly burnt that his face and hands were just flesh, and he was that way for six days. He couldn't swim, and I was able to help him, and his wife thanked me, and in her letter she said, "I suppose to you it was just part of your job, but Mr. McMahon was part of my life and if he had died I don't think I would have wanted to go on living."

There are many McMahons that don't come through. There was a boy on my boat, only twenty-four, had three kids, one night, two bombs straddled our boat and two of the men were hit, one standing right next to me. He never got over it. He hardly ever spoke after that. He told me one night he thought he was going to be killed. I wanted to put him ashore to work. I wish I had. He was in the forward gun turret where the destroyer hit us. . . .

I don't know what it all adds up to, nothing I guess, but you said that you figured I'd go to Texas and write my experiences—I wouldn't go near a book like that. This thing is so stupid, that while it has a sickening fascination for some of us, myself included, I want to leave it far behind when I go.

Inga Binga, I'll be glad to see [you] again. I'm tired now. We were riding every night, and the sleeping is tough in the daytime but I've been told they are sending some of us home to form a new squadron in a couple of months. I've had a great time here, everything considered, but I'll be just glad to get away from it for a while. I used to have the feeling that no matter what happened I'd get through. . . .

It's a funny thing that as you have that feeling you seem to get through. I've lost that feeling lately but as a matter of fact I don't feel badly about it. If anything happens to me I have this knowledge that if I had lived to be a hundred it could only have improved the quantity of my life, not the quality. This sounds gloomy as hell. . . . I'll cut it. . . . You are the only person I'd say it to anyway. As a matter of fact knowing you has been the brightest point in an extremely bright twenty-six years.[40]

~ Prolonged PT boat duty was physically punishing for a man who had battled illness, stomach maladies, and a bad back since childhood. Jack's symptoms of ill health returned and multiplied. His skin was yellow, a navy doctor said he had a duodenal ulcer, and back pains returned. His weight dropped to 120 pounds. X-rays led a doctor at Tulagi to diagnose "chronic disc disease."[41] Nine months after arriving in the Solomon Islands, Jack was ordered home. He missed getting home for Christmas, arriving in San Francisco on January 7, 1944.

He made it to Los Angeles and saw Inga. No doubt he still had feelings for her; what homesick warrior returning home to a beautiful girlfriend would not hope for the warmest kind of reunion. But it appears she had a new beau, and their reunion was as friends. She was still a working journalist too, and their talk shifted from conversation to interview. Inga, apparently unconcerned about her capacity for objective journalism, wrote a glowing account of Jack's heroism that was picked up within a week of Jack's stateside return by the *Boston Globe*, the *Pittsburgh Post-Gazette*, and other newspapers. Her account began in part, "This is the story . . . about the skipper hero, 26-year-old Lt. John F. Kennedy, son of Joseph P. Kennedy, former U.S. ambassador to Great Britain, now home on leave, who though he saved three lives and swam for long hours in shark-infested waters to rescue his men, today says, 'None of the hero stuff about me . . .'"

For her article Inga interviewed the wife of the crewmate Jack had towed to safety by pulling his strap with his teeth. "With tears in her eyes and a shaky voice she said, 'when my husband wrote home, he told me that Lt. Kennedy saved the lives of all the men and everybody at the base admired him greatly. I wrote and told Lt. Kennedy that "I suppose to you it was just part of your job, but Mr. McMahon was part of my life and if he had died I don't think I would have wanted to go on living.""[42] That was the sentence Jack quoted in his letter to Inga.

Only days later, yet another of Jack's former romantic attachments had a hand in yet another major news account of Jack's heroism, though this time the girlfriend's role was indirect. Visiting New York, Jack paid a visit to an old flame, Frances Ann Cannon, and her new husband, John Hersey. Listening to Jack's PT-109 experience, Hersey thought it would make a good subject for an article he would pitch to *Life* magazine. Hersey then wrote a gripping account with Jack as the central character that began, "Our men in the South Pacific fight nature, when they are pitted against her, with a greater fierceness than they could ever expend on an enemy." Hersey wrote, "I asked Kennedy if I might write the story down. He asked me if I wouldn't talk first with some of his crew." Hersey interviewed three crewmen, and all spoke glowingly of their commander. Then, afterward, Hersey interviewed Jack, who was by then recovering from back surgery in a Boston hospital. Although Hersey was at the start of a successful career, winning a Pulitzer Prize that very year for the novel *A Bell for Adano*, his account of PT-109 was rejected by *Life* as too long. It was published instead in the June 17 *New Yorker* and titled "Survival." Though pleased by the article, the Kennedys would have preferred *Life*'s larger circulation. Never one to accept less than a complete success, Joe used his influence to persuade *Reader's Digest* to run a condensed version of "Survival" in August. *Reader's Digest* had an even bigger circulation than *Life*, and Joe still had 150,000 additional reprints made. The story of PT-109 was becoming seafaring legend.

~ In the summer of 1944, Jack was at home in Hyannis Port recuperating from surgeries on his back and rectum, neither of which were successful. He rested much of the time on a wicker chair on the veranda, watching boats sail in and out of the harbor. Bob, now nineteen, enlisted in the Naval Reserve and set to enter Harvard in the fall, was sailing *Victura* in Jack's stead, though not particularly well. He placed last in the Edgartown Regatta the previous year, still not mastering the sport the way his brothers did. At least he enjoyed himself. It might have been a happy time, especially with Jack safe, home and enjoying new fame as a war hero. Instead, the five months from May to September 1944 proved to be one of the most crushing and trying periods ever for the Kennedys, a family known for its large share of trials.

A year earlier in the summer of 1943, Kick had returned to London and was working for the Red Cross. In addition to serving the war effort, it was an opportunity to return to England, which she had come to love during the ambassadorial years. It also became an opportunity to rekindle a relationship with Billy Cavendish, Marquis of Hartington, heir to the Duke of Devonshire and one of England's most eligible bachelors. They had been an item before, and their renewed appearances together sparked much gossip, particularly because he was Protestant and she Irish Catholic.

Joe Jr. was also assigned to duty in England and arrived not long after Kick, bearing a gift for her from Hyannis Port. On the way over he teased a fellow pilot that—engine problems notwithstanding—there would be no delay in landing. "I can't stick around and circle. I've got a crate of eggs for my sister."[43] Given that eggs were rationed in England, it was exceptionally precious cargo. Later, a member of Joe's crew told Kathleen, "I certainly hope you enjoyed those eggs. There wasn't anything Mr. Kennedy didn't make our plane do on the excuse that those eggs should arrive fresh and unbroken."[44] On arrival he was stationed some distance from London, but Joe and Kathleen spoke by phone two or three times a week, and when he visited London he made sure to see her every day. They also enjoyed an enviable social life together. They dined at the Savoy with war correspondent William Randolph Hearst, and when Kick threw a party for Joe, Irving Berlin showed up to play the piano and lead the guests in song.

By early 1944 Kick and Billy Cavendish grew serious. Informed by Kick of their intent to wed, Joe and Rose expressed firm opposition, especially Rose. A Catholic does not abandon faith in God, Rose believed, merely for the love of a man. Rose's telegram to Kick said, "Heartbroken. . . . Feel you have been wrongly influenced—sending Arch Spellman's friend [Archbishop Godfrey] to talk to you. Anything done for our Lord will be rewarded hundred fold."[45] They sought a way to structure a marriage or raise children in some way acceptable to religious authorities, but there was no Catholic, Protestant, or Anglican solution satisfactory to all sides. They hoped Joe Sr. might pull strings, but that was not to be. With the invasion of Europe looming and Billy headed into battle, they wanted to act fast. They announced their engagement on May 4, 1944, and were joined in a civil ceremony two days later, Joe Jr. the only Kennedy family member in attendance.

Joe Jr.'s communiqués home kept the family informed about the marital negotiations, and he helped Kick arrive at legal settlements necessary to become a Cavendish. Joe Sr. had earlier chastised his eldest son for not communicating after Jack's PT-109 incident; now the table was turned. Joe wired his father: "The power of silence is great." Their father sent Kick a telegram: "With your faith in God you can't make a mistake. Remember you are still and always will be tops with me. Love Dad."[46] Rose still communicated nothing. Worsening the situation, the drama of Kick's romance played out in the press on both sides of the Atlantic. It was too good a personification of the ongoing drama of American-British cooperation in the war effort at the time of D-Day.

Kick later said of her brother,

Never did anyone have such a pillar of strength as I had in Joe in those difficult days before my marriage. From the beginning he gave me wise, helpful advice. When he felt that I had made up my mind, he stood by me always. He constantly reassured me and gave me renewed confidence in my own decision. Moral courage he had in abundance and once he felt that a step was right for me, he never faltered, although he might be held largely responsible for my decision. He could not have been more helpful and in every way he was the perfect brother doing, according to his own light, the best for his sister with the hope that in the end it would be the best for the family. How right he was![47]

One after another, the days of June ticked off moments of lasting consequence for the Kennedys. Kick and Billy were married only a month when D-Day occurred on June 6. On June 13 the Germans first targeted a new weapon on London—the v-1, or buzz bomb, a winged, pilotless, jet-powered flying bomb that was as terrifying as it was destructive. A dangerous mission to destroy the v-1's launching facilities near Calais, France, using another experimental flying weapon conjured up by the Americans, would be piloted by Joe in a few weeks' time. On June 17, as Jack recuperated at Hyannis Port, the *New Yorker* article about PT-109 appeared. Billy's company was called to duty June 20.

~ Joe Jr., groomed to lead and ambitious all his life, by now felt surpassed by Jack. Joe won his promotion to full lieutenant, but Jack had achieved that faster. Jack was now a champion sailor, a Harvard scholar–turned-author, and a celebrity war hero. Joe might have wondered if he could ever be that good, but they all learned from racing sailboats that just because you are behind at any given time, does not mean the wind and current will not favor you in the final leg. It would be easy to attribute Joe's motivation to jealousy and sibling rivalry. Ascribing such feelings to him unjustly oversimplifies Joe's motives for volunteering for every dangerous mission offered him. Joe was unquestionably brave. He stepped forward when duty called. Doing that, no matter the motivation, defines a hero.

Joe's roommate in the squadron, Louis Pappas, said, "There was never an occasion for a mission that meant extra hazard that Joe did not volunteer for. He had everybody's unlimited admiration and respect for his courage, zeal and willingness to undertake the most dangerous mission."[48]

It has also been suggested that Joe, bred to win, was driven by an excessive need to please his father. But their father was clearly worried about his children and had no desire to see them in harm's way. When Joe wrote in March that he might have to fly ten more missions beyond the thirty that

made him eligible to be relieved, his father replied, "I sincerely hope that
they'll call it a day at 30."[49] On July 26 Joe wrote his parents, "I am going
to be doing something different for the next three weeks. It is secret, and I
am not allowed to say what it is, but it isn't dangerous so don't worry. So
probably I won't be home till sometime in September."[50] Joe Sr. replied, "I
can quite understand how you feel about staying there . . . but don't force
your luck too much."[51]

~ At their peak v-1 buzz bombs, "doodlebugs," as they were also known,
were falling at a rate of a hundred a day on London and southeast England. In her diary Kick wrote of them and of "the inability to hit back
at a human target." Kick continued, "People are absolutely terrified and
one senses that they are always listening first for them to arrive and next
for the sound that the dreaded engine has stopped," signaling it would fall
and explode somewhere near.[52] Joe Jr. told his parents that Kick "is terrified of the Doodles as is everyone else, and I think she is smart not to
work in London."[53]

The v-1 was developed at a secret rocket research facility near Peenemunde, Germany, on the Baltic Sea. Along with the v-1, scientists there
also created the v-2 ballistic missile, fired at London for the first time on
September 8, 1944. The v-2 looked like something out of early science
fiction and rocketed at multiples of the speed of sound. Though not an
effective weapon for the Germans, the liquid-fueled v-2 was the precursor
to all the Cold War ballistic missiles that came in the following decades,
including those that could carry nuclear weapons across continents and
men into space.

A principal Peenemunde scientist and v-2 engineer was Wernher von
Braun. When the Allies finally entered Germany, von Braun surrendered
himself and many of his fellow rocket scientists to American soldiers. Before long, they were building rockets for the United States and, in time,
von Braun became a central figure in the space race to the moon that Jack
would initiate. But von Braun's days as one of President Kennedy's chief
rocket engineers were two decades ahead. At the time of Joe's service in
England, von Braun was filling that role for Adolf Hitler.

~ There were several v-1 launch sites along the coast of France, and Allied forces diverted enormous resources to bombing missions aimed at taking them out. Heavily fortified, they were hard to destroy using conventional aerial bombing or artillery. Thus, Operation Aphrodite was conceived, a project for which Joe volunteered. Old, war-worn B-17 Flying Fortresses and PB4Y bombers were stripped of all weight except that which was necessary to get airborne. The planes were then packed solid with twelve or more tons of Torpex explosive, 50 percent more powerful than TNT. Rather than drop bombs, the planes were themselves a single enormous missile that would be flown by radio control directly into their targets.

Its crew canopy was removed so that two men—a pilot and engineer —could get it airborne before parachuting to safety while still over England. Control devices on the pilotless plane would afterward keep it on its path, radio controlled by a remote pilot on a trailing plane. The drone had two television cameras so the remote pilot could see its instrument panel and view of the ground. The top of the plane was painted white to make it more easily seen from above against the background of the earth below.

Piloting these flying bombs was strictly voluntary. Only half a dozen attempts at these missions had been tried, most dismal failures, none of them deemed entirely successful, two of which were fatal to their pilots. Joe signed on nonetheless and his turn as pilot came on August 12, 1944. The day before he was to fly he called William Randolph Hearst's wife, Lorelle, in London and told her, "I'm about to go into my act. If I don't come back, tell my dad—despite our differences—that I love him very much."[54]

~ On the evening before his mission, Joe rode his Raleigh bicycle to make a final inspection of his plane, according to Doris Kearns Goodwin. "The bomber . . . sat, huge and clumsy, on the field, her body already so crammed with explosives that she seemed about to squash her tires. . . . He pedaled back to base, scrambled some eggs for his roommate and himself, and then, as he always did before turning in, he knelt on the floor to pray."[55]

The mission was to be flown in the early evening, and it was not until two in the afternoon that Joe was told the secret of his target. It was to be a v-1 launch site at tiny Mimoyecques, eight miles southwest of Calais. Of all the v-1 sites, this was closest to London.

Three planes would accompany Joe's, one of which serendipitously carried Franklin Roosevelt's son Elliott, an "Iliad-level" detail of the story, as one writer called it, referring to the son of one president flying with the son of the father of another president.[56] Elliott planned to photograph the crew's bailout.

Ensign James Simpson helped Joe get his plane ready for departure: "I was in the plane testing and double checking three minutes before takeoff. I shook hands with Joe and said, 'So long and good luck, Joe. I only wish I were going with you.' He answered, 'Thanks Jim, don't forget you're going to make the next one with me. Say, by the way, if I don't come back, you fellows can have the rest of my eggs.'"[57]

Shortly before 6 p.m. Joe's plane made its lumberous way down the airstrip, left the ground, and responded sluggishly to his steering, compared to what he was accustomed to in PB4YS not so laden with heavy explosives. Joe banked, pointed the plane toward Calais, and reached two thousand feet, the planned maximum altitude to stay below German radar. The target was only an hour away. Into the microphone Joe said, "spade flush," code words signaling the remote pilot to take control of his plane. Control was successfully transferred, and the TV cameras were transmitting a signal adequate for the remote pilot to see by. As the plane approached Newdelight Wood, at 6:20, a radio command was sent to bank the plane slightly left. At that instant the plane erupted with two enormous blasts, each a second apart.

Elliott Roosevelt saw it happen, then felt the shock wave violently hit his twin-engine Mosquito aircraft. Control of a nearby B-17 was almost lost, and its crew considered bailing out. One thought it was the biggest explosion he'd ever seen, other than later pictures of the atomic bomb. Joe vanished.

~ At Hyannis Port, the afternoon of Sunday, August 13, was warm and sunny enough for lunch on the porch, picnic style. Afterward, as was his habit, Joe Sr. went upstairs for a nap while the children gathered in the sunroom, softening their voices to avoid disturbing their father, listening to a recording of Bing Crosby singing, "I'll Be Seeing You." Gathered there were Jack, Ted, cousin Joey Gargan, Jean, Eunice, and a friend of Eunice's. There was a knock at the door, and Rose saw two Catholic priests on her porch. They asked to see Joe Sr. Such visits by clergy were not out of the ordinary, so Rose explained that her husband was resting and asked if they could join the family in the living room until Joe returned downstairs. Their message was urgent, they said, and could not wait. It concerned Joe Jr. They said Joe Jr. was reported missing in action the day before.

"I flew upstairs, hesitated, stumbled," Rose said, and told Joe about the visitors and their news. The children had overheard words such as "missing" and "lost." Joe and Rose invited the priests into a room where they could talk privately. There they were given fuller details, as much as could be said about a secret mission. There was no hope; Joe was dead.[58]

The children waited, sensing something awful was happening. Joe opened the door and his face conveyed as much as his voice. Tears in his eyes, he said, "Children, your brother Joe has been lost. He died flying a volunteer mission." Then he added, "I want you all to be particularly good to your mother."[59] Joe stumbled upstairs and there followed several minutes of children sobbing.

On any other Sunday afternoon, the children would race their sailboats. On this Sunday there are two versions of what happened next. Some have said that Joe told them they should keep their plans and sail, which they did, though Jack went instead for a solitary walk on the beach. The alternate account told separately by both Joey and Ted is that it was Jack who said, "Joe wouldn't want us sitting here crying. He would want us to go sailing."[60] In both versions Kennedy children headed out into the Sound on a sailboat, most likely *Victura*.

Timothy Reardon, Joe Jr.'s Harvard roommate and close friend for years afterward, finished a posthumous tribute to Joe with the words, "Were I a painter, I would conclude with a portrait of Joe as I like best to think of him—stripped to the waist, his body brown and strong, his hair lightened by the sun, his eyes sparkling and his lips parted in a full smile, at the rudder of a white sailboat against a background of blue skies and the blue-green ocean. And under it I would write simply, 'A True Man—A Great Friend.'"[61]

Goodwin observed that had Joe's mission been successful, his heroism would likely have been judged greater than Jack's, for he entered into it in full knowledge of its danger, knowing others had died trying it before. He risked his life trying to destroy a key component of Germany's ability to bomb and terrorize England. But that outcome was not to be.[62]

~ Three weeks after Joe's death, for Labor Day weekend Jack hosted a reunion of his PT boat comrades at Hyannis Port. In attendance were Red Fay, Jim Reed, Lenny Thom, and Barney Ross. The joy of being with old friends and survivors must have been a relief from days of grieving, and the men enjoyed old stories and teased one another. It was too much for Joe, though, who shouted from an upstairs window, "Jack, don't you and your friends have any respect for your dead brother?"[63] For years to come Joe found it all but impossible to talk about his eldest son without tearing up. Jack later privately published a collection of tributes, called *As We Remember Joe*, but the pain was so great that Joe Sr. could never bring himself to read it.

~ The USS *Warrington*, a Somers-class navy destroyer with a crew of more than three hundred, saw duty in the Solomon Islands and other South Pacific ports of call at the same time Jack served on PT-109. Like Jack, the *Warrington* headed home in 1944, making its way north past Bora Bora, then through the Panama Canal, arriving for repairs on July 15 at the New York Navy Yard. The following month it moved to the Norfolk Navy Yard for more alterations. On September 10 it set out for an assignment in the Caribbean.

On September 9 a hurricane in full fury, heading northwest toward the United States, was first spotted by reconnaissance flight crews northeast of Puerto Rico. Two days out of Norfolk, the USS *Warrington*, now with a crew of 321, was warned that it was headed straight toward a storm that, it was later said, generated 150-knot winds and seventy-foot waves. They rode it out through the night, but on the morning of the thirteenth, about

450 miles east of the Florida coast, the *Warrington* began losing headway. It took on water through vents. Electrical power was lost, then the main engine. Another engine that powered steering shut down. Distress calls were issued to any ship able to provide assistance. The ship took on more water and the captain ordered it abandoned. Almost immediately after the men entered the hellish waters, the *Warrington* went down. Of the 321 aboard, all but 73 were lost.[64]

Hurricanes in those days were not given names, but the intensity of this one prompted weather emergency authorities to dub it the Great Atlantic Hurricane. It continued on its path to the coast. As it made its way, a 136-foot minesweeper, the USS *YMS-409* foundered and was sunk, all 33 aboard lost. The storm continued on a path toward the Outer Banks, Rhode Island, and Cape Cod. Two coast guard cutters, the *Bedloe* and the *Jackson*, were destroyed and the coal-cargo steamer ss *Thomas Tracy* ran aground at a beach in Delaware.[65]

On the evening of September 14, as the Great Atlantic Hurricane approached Cape Cod, a 123-foot Lightship, the *Vineyard Sound*, was at its mooring, marking the entrance to Buzzards Bay and Vineyard Sound, about thirty-five miles southwest of Hyannis Port and just ten miles west of Martha's Vineyard. It sank with all 12 aboard lost.[66]

Jack was at home in Hyannis Port, recovering from surgery undertaken a month earlier to relieve lower abdominal pain.[67] "On leave" from Chelsea Naval Hospital, Jack got in his Buick to check the harbor where *Victura* was moored. The storm "swept Hyannis Port's harbor clear of boats, and many of those that came ashore were smashed to pieces on the beach." It destroyed several buildings along the waterfront and harbor; the surge washed a pier and a yacht club building away. Porches were ripped off homes and trees uprooted. The Kennedy home sustained some water damage but was relatively unharmed. At the harbor Jack somehow managed to secure the two-ton *Victura* on the beach, protected from pounding waves and the surge. *Victura*'s damage was thus minimal compared to many others.

When Jack later returned to his car, he found himself stranded, the road to Hyannis Port flooded by the storm surge. He climbed in his car and waited out the storm until the waters receded, in the meantime declining a passerby's offer of coffee and a place "to get out of the storm."

The next afternoon, the storm over, national guardsmen were in the Hyannis Main Street business district, protecting storefronts with broken windows and assisting with clean up. Two young sisters spotted Jack and another man picking their way through the wreckage of other sailboats and waterfront debris. Befitting an emerging pattern in Jack's life, he had befriended a *Life* magazine staffer, in town to write photo captions. Jack—in a blue baseball cap, open-collared white shirt, khakis, and sneakers—approached the two sisters and made introductions.

"He looked ill," said one of the sisters later. "But he certainly didn't act it. And he had the most charming smile." She was also surprised at how young he looked for a man of twenty-seven. After awhile, with some coaxing, Jack persuaded the girls to join his new journalist friend and him for lunch. Later, he took them to the family's house, where he changed into a "rumpled and unpressed" navy uniform so they could go to dinner. After dancing they agreed to meet the following day and go to the Center Theater in Hyannis. They were going to go out on the third evening too, but at the last minute Jack had to cancel his plans. There was a family emergency and he needed to go to New York.[68]

~ In the space of five months from May to September 1944, Kathleen married out of the church and broke her mother's heart; Jack went through two painful, less-than-successful surgeries while simultaneously gaining war hero fame in magazines and newspapers; doodlebugs and v-2 rockets started falling on London; and the Allied D-Day invasion occurred with Joe Jr. and Kick's husband in the thick of the fighting. Then Joe Jr., the anointed son, was killed. After that, one of the worst hurricanes in New England history was visited on Hyannis Port.

On September 9, on the same day the Great Atlantic Hurricane was first spotted in the Caribbean, a German sniper in Belgium pointed his rifle's barrel at a British army soldier and squeezed the trigger. His bullet went straight through the heart of Billy Cavendish. He and Kick had been married for just four months and had spent just five weeks together as a married couple. Joe Jr. had been dead less than a month. Kick did not get the news of her husband's death until a week later, when she and some of the Kennedy clan were in New York City.

"So ends the story of Billy and Kick," Kick wrote in her diary a few days later. To her parents she wrote, "If Eunice, Pat & Jean marry nice guys for fifty years they'll be lucky if they have five weeks like I did — Tell Jack not to get married for a long time. I'll keep house for him."[69]

In a letter to Jack's friend Lem Billings, Kick quoted a friend who told her, "One thing you can be sure of life holds no fears for someone who has faced love, marriage and death before the age of 25."[70]

"Luckily I am a Kennedy," Kick continued. "I have a very strong feeling that that makes a big difference about how to take things. I saw Daddy and Mother about Joe and I know that we've all got the ability to not be got down. There are lots of years ahead and lots of happiness left in the world though sometimes nowadays that's hard to believe."[71]

BOOK II

Changing Course

CHAPTER 6

Jack

> God doesn't care who wins this race
> And neither do you or I.
> There are bigger things to care about
> Like the wind and the sea and the sky.
>
> ~ From "Windy Song," a poem about sailing by Jacqueline Bouvier,
> age fourteen. Written in 1943, the year of the sinking of PT-109, the
> original is today on public display at the JFK Library and Museum
> with her margin illustrations of anchors, lighthouses, and gaff-rigged
> sailboats. Ten years after writing it she married John F. Kennedy.

"Well, after I came home and was released from the navy, I went to work for a newspaper, the *Chicago Herald American*," Jack said, recounting his career after entering national politics. "And then I came home to Boston. I had an older brother who I thought would be a politician, but he was killed as a flyer in Europe. I never wanted to be in politics until really almost the time I ran. I was always interested in writing. I wanted to teach for a while. So that, really, the war changed my life, and I suppose if it hadn't been for that and what happened then, I would have went on with my original plans."[1]

The transformation of Jack Kennedy from cerebral second son to family political standard-bearer was not immediate or assumed. His father said Jack was "altogether different" from his older brother. Joe Jr. was "more dynamic, more sociable and easy going," said their father. "Jack in those days . . . was rather shy, withdrawn and quiet. His mother and I couldn't picture him as a politician. We were sure he'd be a teacher or a writer."[2]

Jack's career in journalism was brief but eventful, lasting from May to August 1945. Jack's father helped him win an assignment as a reporter for William Randolph Hearst's Chicago newspaper, which led to articles being published in other Hearst papers. He wrote from San Francisco about the formation of the United Nations and from London about parliamentary elections, where he showed better-than-average prescience for an American by predicting Winston Churchill's possible electoral defeat. He was exposed to, and in some cases met, numerous great political leaders of the era.

Jack soon came to believe that those who did great things were summoned to a higher calling than those who wrote about those who did great things. Reporting was not sufficiently satisfying.[3] Jack entered Harvard Law School.

When the incumbent occupant of a Boston congressional district forfeited that seat to run for mayor of Boston, Joe and Jack saw an opportunity for the son to try politics. In a district so overwhelmingly Democratic, the party primary mattered much more than November's general election. Joe poured money into the campaign, making a particularly noteworthy investment in advertising and public relations, politically innovative in its time, according to historian Michael O'Brien.[4] Though Jack had not lived in Boston since early childhood, his grandfather had been mayor and his father was rich and famous, so the Kennedy name was a strong asset.

He ran as a war hero and the story of PT-109 became a campaign narrative that would be repeated then and at every future step up in office. Copies of the condensed version of the John Hersey *New Yorker* article were sent to homes throughout the district. Advertising echoed the narrative, and a PT-109 crewmate issued an endorsement for the campaign.

His discomfort and avoidance of traditional Irish political glad-handing and back slapping conjured an image more dignified and less old-school. His skills and self-confidence at public speaking improved. With nine opponents, Jack received 42 percent of the vote in the primary and, effectively, the seat. A friend visiting at Hyannis Port looked out over the Sound and wondered aloud how a presidential yacht might look there.

The race was exhausting, and Jack retreated to Hyannis Port to rest. He still had campaigning to do for the general election and on behalf of other Massachusetts Democrats, but with the June primary behind him he could get in some sailing and reflect on where life circumstances were taking him. For that he had the help of a new friend, a recently ordained Catholic priest named Edward C. Duffy. They met at the unveiling of a new main altar at St. Francis Xavier Church in Hyannis, built with Kennedy family money and dedicated to the memory of Lt. Joseph P. Kennedy Jr. Several times that summer Jack invited Father Duffy to sail on *Victura*, just the two of them, cruising and talking. Jack confided more than once to the priest his insecurities about living a life in politics originally intended for his older brother.[5]

~ The Kennedys had servers when they dined at home, and a new one who started that summer was Joanna Barboza, age sixteen. She recalls Joe Sr. was not around much and when he was the children talked to him as though they were "reporting":

> These are the yachts that are in, these are the yachts that are out, and here's what people, and we, did, and so on and so on, and that kind of thing. There was a lot of that kind of conversation.
>
> There was nothing that told me that this thin man [Jack] with this huge mop of hair . . . would ever be president of the United States, would leave a mark on the lives of people around the world. . . . All I saw was this kind of blonde kid who raced around and was a very fine sailor. No, nothing. There was nothing there.

The following summer Barboza saw a change in Jack. Where the first summer he was reflective and had an intensity about him, "like smoke, you couldn't hold," the second summer after going to Congress he was more open and warm. "He personally had moved to another place emotionally."[6]

As Jack made his strong start in public life, and was enjoying it, across the Atlantic his sister Kick was recovering from her loss of Billy and starting a new life of her own. She had discovered a new love, Lord Peter Fitzwilliam. Peter was something of a composite of the three male Kennedys who were most important in her life—her father and brothers Joe and Jack. For his service in the war he was a recipient of the Distinguished Service Cross, Britain's second-highest honor, putting him on par with Jack and Joe Jr. for bravery. He was of a wealthy family, nine years older than Kathleen, roguish and an aggressive businessman, like her father. He was also loaded with charm. She was deeply in love and her happiness showed to those who knew of the relationship. Sadly, however, it was a happiness she could not share with her parents. He was a Protestant and married, working on a divorce. Though she confided in Jack, she knew her parents would deeply object.

Rose and Jack visited Kathleen in London, and then Rose accompanied her daughter on a shopping trip to Paris, leaving Jack behind in London. There Jack again took seriously ill. Finally he received the accurate diagnosis that had for so many years eluded his other doctors. The news he had Addison's disease was an awful blow because until the 1930s, victims tended to die within months of diagnosis. The good news was that by 1947 treatments were being found that prolonged life by replacing the hormonal deficiencies caused by the disease's diminishment of adrenal function. Life expectancy could be extended by a few years. It was still considered a death sentence, however.

He returned to the United States on the *Queen Mary*, borne off the ship on a stretcher. Reporters and supporters were told he was suffering from a recurrence of malaria, a tale that fit a pattern. When reporters described Jack's back problems as a consequence of the trauma of the PT-109 collision, they were not corrected, though the back problems long preceded his war service. Now the symptoms of Addison's disease were misrepresented as another consequence of his service to his country. For a time, Jack missed votes in the House and, some thought, showed less ambition.

In England Kathleen's relationship with Peter intensified, and after a few months she could wait no longer to tell her parents. Rose was appalled. If she married Peter, Rose said, Kick would be disowned by the family, dead to them. Kick's father, by his silence, assented.

Perhaps it was Joe's silence that convinced Kick he was persuadable. A few months later Joe made plans to travel to Paris on business. Hoping her father could be won over, Kathleen and Peter decided to travel there to meet him. They first flew to Cannes, with plans to spend a couple of days in the Riviera before going to Paris. Their eight-passenger plane encountered weather problems, and the pilot lost control. On May 13, 1948, the plane crashed into a mountainside and killed them all.[7]

~ Of the Golden Trio, Jack was now alone. He was the one who was always sick. The other two who were most healthy, vibrant, and alive, the two with personalities that lit rooms, who had the greatest potential, were gone. The family gathered at the house in Hyannis Port. Joe, in Paris, traveled to see her body, but then did not know what to do about her burial. Billy's family convinced Joe to have her buried in Chatsworth with her late husband, Billy.

The effect on Jack was profound. He had loved his older brother, but they kept their emotional distance. Not so with Kick. His friend Lem said Jack asked again and again, "why?" He could not sleep, kept awake by memories of the many nights he and Kick stayed awake into the night in long conversation. Growing up, practically every boy who met Kick fell in love with her, and even though Jack's was a brotherly love, he was charmed by the same traits the boys always saw in her personality and wit. Nobody else fell into such perfect intellectual and emotional sync with Jack.

~ The loss of a brother, sister, and brother-in-law, and the looming presence of his own mortality, made for a dark, dark time. Said Lem Billings, "He just figured there was no sense in planning ahead anymore." He lived for the moment, "treating each day as if it were his last, demanding of life constant intensity, adventure and pleasure."[8]

He might have asked himself, "what's the point of it all?" Instead, Jack was newly motivated. He would make the most of the time he had. Jack's enthusiasm for politics returned, and the way he articulated positions on issues and his speeches struck many as more bold and thoughtful. He even flirted with a run for governor of Massachusetts. His supporters circulated nominating petitions that demonstrated his potential for garnering support outside his congressional district. Though he withdrew his candidacy and stayed on in Congress, he had sent a signal of intent and capability for higher political office.

~ In a summer during those early years of Jack's service in Congress, sometime in the late 1940s before Ted finished boarding school and headed off to Harvard, Ted received a phone call from Jack. It was July, Ted was at the Cape house, and the Edgartown Regatta was to be the following weekend.

It was a race the Kennedys did not miss. Ted and his cousin Joey Gargan had signed on to enter *Victura* in the race. Jack told Ted he wanted to be aboard too but told him not to wait if he was running late.

Ted was thrilled at the prospect of racing with his navy war-hero big brother, now a member of Congress. Before the day of the race Ted sailed *Victura* over the 16.5-nautical-mile (19-statute-mile) distance from Hyannis Port across Nantucket Sound to Martha's Vineyard. On race day Ted and Joe got the boat ready and criss-crossed Edgartown harbor waiting for Jack, happy to risk a late start if it meant getting Jack on *Victura*. Only a few minutes remained before the race's start. Ted and Joe, looking for some sight of Jack's plane in the overcast sky, made out a single-engine plane. As it descended toward the grass landing strip nearby, they studied it more closely and there they saw Jack with a big smile waving at them. He must have quickly spotted his sail #94 among all the other boats.[9]

The Edgartown Regatta is the highlight of Cape Cod's sailing season, as big a social event as sport, and the pier area that year was crowded with friends and families of sailors. Jack had his taxi driver speed from the island's grass landing strip to the pier. On this day there were two classes of sailboats racing, twenty in each. The races were well organized, and the rules clearly stated and enforced. To join a crew, racers needed the official red tag to identify them as entrants. Jack had none. Wearing his blue suit and tie and carrying his briefcase, Jack made his way quickly through the crowd as Ted steered his boat to the end of the pier. When a race official realized what was going on, he cried, "Hey! You can't just pick people up here!" Jack jumped in anyway, just as the sound of the starting gun could be heard. The starting line was off in the distance, but they pointed *Victura* and trimmed sails. Jack went into the tiny cabin, made a quick change of clothes; then Ted handed him the tiller.[10]

It was drizzling as they crossed the starting line, and over the long course the mist made it hard to see the position of the other boats. Throwing the dice, Jack chose a route the other sailors had not. Some points of sail in relation to the wind are faster than others. A beam reach, for example, where the wind hits the boat at a ninety-degree angle to the boat's direction, is usually fastest. Before long, the wind shifted and suddenly *Victura* had the advantage. Maybe the others had to tack an extra time, slowing to turn through the wind. Perhaps the new point-of-sail helped. Whatever the reason, the gamble paid and Jack, Ted, and Joe won their division.

It was easy to get a soaking in a Wianno Senior, and Jack was drenched. He went below to change back into his suit, jumped off at the pier, and Ted soon saw his small plane climbing against the gray sky, the engine noise getting faint as it grew smaller in the distance.[11]

~ In 1948 the first clinical medical trials of cortisone were completed. Cortisone proved effective at first for rheumatoid arthritis, and its discoverers won a Nobel Prize for medicine in 1950. It soon became a key treatment for Addison's disease, and Jack began taking it orally by around 1951. The result was a dramatic improvement in his health. It is hard to imagine how he could have run for president in 1960, or perhaps even lived long enough, had cortisone not freed him from the recurring illnesses he had experienced in all his years prior to the new medicine's availability.

In October 1951, to beef up his foreign policy bona fides, Jack went on a tour of the Middle East and Eastern countries and brought along Bobby and Patricia. Bobby had just earned his law degree from the University of Virginia. The eight-year difference in age between Jack and Bobby meant that they really had not formed an adult relationship, but twenty-five thousand miles on the road changed that. The following year Jack asked Bobby to manage his campaign for the U.S. Senate against the incumbent, Henry Cabot Lodge, a product of Boston Brahmin upbringing. Jack won and thus began a tradition in which Kennedy siblings and close relatives graduated from racing sailboats together to racing for public office together. Many a future Kennedy campaign manager would be directly related to their candidate.

Jack ran for political office five times beginning in 1946 and made frequent use of aircraft in his campaigns, most famously in the 1960 presidential race, when a twin-engine Convair campaign airplane was called *Caroline*, after his daughter. It was the first use of a private plane in a presidential race. It was more common in those years to give airplanes names, just as we name boats, and according to the yachting writer Julius Fanta, before Caroline's birth in 1957, Jack flew in a campaign plane called *Victura*.[12]

~ For decades the Kennedys and the press had a relationship that was—depending on the circumstances—symbiotic, antagonistic, serendipitous, chummy, cloaked, calculated, complicated, and mutually admiring.

Under the category of "serendipitous" falls the *Washington Times-Herald*. The *Times-Herald*, which outsold the *Washington Post* in the postwar years, had a habit of hiring attractive young female reporters close to Jack. Kick was writing for it after her college years, while Jack was in Washington working for Naval Intelligence. There Kick met Inga Arvad, a fellow *Times-Herald* staff member, and introduced her to Jack, leading to one of Jack's most intense romantic relationships. In 1951 Arthur Krock, who had years earlier helped Jack publish *Why England Slept*, was at the Washington bureau of the *New York Times*. Krock, also a friend of the Auchincloss family, called the editor of the *Times-Herald* to recommend for employment an inexperienced Auchincloss step-daughter. "She's round-eyed, clever and wants to go into journalism." Her name was Jacqueline Bouvier.[13]

Jack and Jacqueline met in May 1951 at a Georgetown dinner party. After that, Jacqueline and her sister, Lee, went to Europe for six months. She returned in the fall, took the job as "Inquiring Photographer" at the *Times-Herald*, and began dating Jack with more seriousness.

"It was all spasmodic," Jacqueline said, "because he spent half of each week in Massachusetts. He'd call me from some oyster bar up there, with a great clinking of coins, to ask me out to the movies the following Wednesday in Washington. . . . He was not the candy-and-flowers type, so every now and then he'd give me a book."[14]

As they entered into 1952, they managed somehow to maintain their courtship while Jack campaigned for the Senate. That summer she started showing up at Jack's campaign speeches and teas. As it was summer, the couple paid visits to the Cape house at Hyannis Port.

Bobby's wife, Ethel, was the first to marry into the family, and she fit in remarkably well, sharing in common with the Kennedy sisters all their athleticism, informality, and assertive nature. While Ethel blended in, Jacqueline brought culture change. The Kennedy men enjoyed Jackie's presence, and she shrewdly charmed them, but the women were less than charitable toward her. The sisters referred to Jacqueline as "the deb" and noted that she preferred her name be pronounced "jack-leen." "Rhymes with 'queen,'" Ethel noted. For her part, Jacqueline confidentially referred to the sisters as the "toothy girls" or the "rah-rah girls."[15] In time, the shared experience, the extreme highs and lows of being a Kennedy, would bring them all close.

Jacqueline held her own, in her own style. Dinah Bridge, a British friend of the Kennedy family, visiting Cape Cod that summer, said, "I think I was probably one of the first people to see her in the Kennedy household." Bridge was with Bobby at his and Ethel's house.

> We were all sitting around having breakfast, and Jack was there, and Jean. And around the corner of the front door came this beautiful girl in riding clothes to pick up Jean to go riding. . . . And very shortly after that . . . she was invited to supper, and lots of games were played, and she was sort of put through her paces, I should think you would say. And she stood up extremely well to the Kennedy barrage of questions. . . . It was quite a barrage. You had to sort of know the form to keep up, you know, because the jokes went so fast, and the chitter chat. But she did extremely well, as I remember.[16]

The family for years had played "The Game," similar to charades, and to the extent it was a demonstration of intellect and cleverness, Jackie proved hard to beat. She was athletic enough to play touch football with the family, even if she did not know the rules at first, but once she proved to the family she was fit and sporting, she afterward could avoid Kennedy sports that were excessively physical.

The Kennedy sisters understood why Jackie had won Jack's heart but must have been taken aback by the speed at which Joe warmed to her. In an interview Doris Kearns Goodwin said Jackie, "told me that at the beginning she identified more with Old Joe, that she'd sit with Joe and listen to classical music, and he'd tell her not to worry about touch football and that he'd rather talk to her anyway. He really did love classical music and he was an interesting fellow, and probably he was much more interesting to talk to at that stage of her life than Rose would have been. He was worldly, he had adventures, he was a flirt. I can see that she would have liked him."[17]

Jack successfully ran statewide in November 1952, and Bobby as manager got a crash course in the higher-level politics of a U.S. Senate campaign. Soon after taking his new office he told the family of his intent to marry. Joe was delighted. The engagement was announced on June 24, 1953, robbing American women of "the golden boy, the most eligible bachelor in New England," as one female journalist described him, herself a target of his preengagement romantic advances.[18]

As had happened before, and would happen again, a media opportunity was not to be overlooked, and the engagement was a perfect opportunity. Once again *Life* magazine was the willing collaborator. Another talented photographer, Hy Peskin, whose work for *Sports Illustrated* included some of that magazine's most memorable early images, was dispatched by *Life* to Hyannis Port.

In 1953 only about half of American households had televisions. Radio, newspapers, and movie newsreels were major sources of news. So were magazines, and in the decade before TV images of any quality were broadcast, *Life* was one of the most popular ways to visually witness world events. *Life* hired the best photographers in the world and printed their pictures in a ten-by-fourteen-inch format, fully 50 percent larger than typical magazines, above which *Life* towered on the newsstand. By 1950 *Life* reached one American in five and it doubled that reach by 1960.

Published photos of the newly engaged couple inside the magazine showed Jackie on the Hyannis Port lawn doing an "end run" with a football and swinging a bat as Jack played catcher, her ambivalence for such sports set aside for the photo opportunity. One caption stated that Jackie "displays unorthodox but vigorous batter's style on broad, well-kept lawn of estate." Another caption beneath a group on the lawn read, "Kennedy sisters Jean and Eunice question Jackie, 'How did he propose?'" Jackie was given a full-page photo, sitting on the big house porch rail, legs swinging playfully upward, a big sun bonnet on her head, with the sweeping view of whitecaps on Nantucket Sound behind her. The caption stated that she "studied at Vassar, George Washington University and the Sorbonne in Paris. Her last assignment for her newspaper, the *Washington Times-Herald*, was the coronation last month of Queen Elizabeth II." It is hard to believe that men who remembered her just a year or two earlier found her looks unremarkable. By 1953, cameras loved her, and *Life* said she was smart and cultured too.[19]

But it was the cover of *Life* that was most striking. To the extent the

Kennedys intended it, it was an early masterpiece of twentieth-century political image making. Just as the family had done with *Life*'s Alfred Eisenstaedt thirteen years earlier, when his 1940 photograph showed Joe Jr. at the tiller with Jack not even in sight, now Jack and Jackie took Peskin out for sail, again on *Victura*. The resulting cover photo showed Jack and Jackie with beautiful smiles, forward on the bow, sails full of sunlight and air, the picture of youthful promise. *Victura* is heeling leeward about twenty-five degrees. Jack is handsome and relaxed, bare feet on the rail, shorts wet with seawater. He's in his element, confident on his boat. In no need of a handgrip, his hands drape casually over his knees. Jackie's short kinky hair is windblown, her collar flapping upward, her figure thin and girlish. Her legs are bent away from the rail and one hand tightly grips the mast while her other is apparently holding Jack. She's less accustomed to sailing, and she betrays perhaps just a hint of insecurity about the heel of the boat. "SENATOR KENNEDY GOES A-COURTING," says the cover blurb.

Jack Kennedy was new enough on the national scene that the article still needed to identify him as the son of the ambassador. If ever there was a single moment when the Kennedy brand was newly defined, it was on July 20, 1953, the date on the cover of *Life*. Journalists writing about Jack would soon no longer need to call him the son of an ambassador. Nothing could make Joe happier.

Later, after seeing the *Life* cover, a friend told Jackie that she must be quite a sailing enthusiast. "No, my husband is," she responded. "They just shoved me into that boat long enough to take the picture."[20]

~ Jack and Jackie married on September 12, 1953, with Bobby as best man, Jackie's sister, Lee, as matron of honor, and Ted as an usher. Jackie's parents would have preferred a smaller private wedding, but Joe insisted on a media event and he got his wish. While on their honeymoon, she wrote a poem about her new husband that her daughter, Caroline, many years later included in a published collection of Jackie's favorite poems, "although I know my mother would have felt slightly embarrassed to have her own poems included with the ones in this book that she so admired."[21] The volume included works by Homer, Shakespeare, Shelley, Keats, and Langston Hughes.

Jackie's 370-word poem, inspired by Stephen Vincent Benet's "John Brown's Body," was called "Meanwhile in Massachusetts" and spoke of Jack's New England upbringing, Irish heritage, and his calling to serve. She wrote of the family's main house, "There his brothers and sisters have laughed and played / And thrown themselves to rest in the shade." And she wrote of Jack's promising destiny: "All of the things he was going to be. / All of the things in the wind and the sea.["]22

Ted Sorensen, a political adviser and speechwriter who began working for Jack the year he married Jackie, said, "After their marriage, she interested him slightly in art and he interested her slightly in politics."23

Jackie loved poetry and read Proust and other French writers in their original language. She not only wrote but illustrated her own poetry. Jack loved books probably as much as any politician ever born, so here they found common interest. By the 1950s Jackie's influence, combined with the Harvard education that Jack, Bobby, and Ted had acquired, began to generate in the men a growing taste for poetry and literature. At Hyannis Port Jack and Jackie read poetry aloud to each other. Jackie later helped Bobby refine his knowledge of the classics, and he too grew fond of reading literature aloud. As Jack rose to national prominence, allusions to poetry and literature began appearing in more of his speeches.

Early in Jack's political career his speeches made reference to historic figures, and if there were quotes they might come from Jefferson, Madison, Lincoln, Churchill, or Clausewitz, noted Edward Klein, writing about the relationship between Jack and Jackie. Sorensen described the couple sprawled out on a rug at home, surrounded by piles of books. "Oh listen to this Jack," he recalled her saying. "This fits right into what you're trying to say." Sorensen said, "Jackie wasn't so much a researcher as she was this remarkable font of knowledge about literary matters."24

One of Jack's Senate staffers recalled, "What she would do is make suggestions to Jack—ideas on positions he might take, poetry he might recite, historical references. . . . And he would always incorporate her ideas into what he would say." Added another aide, Charlie Bartlett, "They were doing a hell of a lot of reading together and Jackie, who was very, very bright, would pick out quotes. . . . It was she who dug up a lot of the quotes that Jack started dropping in his speeches in the course of the [presidential] campaign."[25]

The imagery of the sea and sailing was a favorite, and Jackie, perhaps knowing Jack's fondness for the topic, fed his interest. "One poem that was special to both of them was Alfred Lord Tennyson's *Ulysses*," said Jack and Jackie's daughter, Caroline. "My mother had memorized it with her grandfather when she was ten years old. She introduced it to my father who often quoted from it in his speeches, and later the poem became identified with my uncle Bobby as well."[26] Ted also.

She showed Jack the poem shortly after they were married. It tells of an aging mariner king, known to the Greeks as Odysseus of Homeric legend, who as a young man rose to greatness through epic sea voyages and naval escapades. Older and not content with a king's idle life on a throne, Ulysses implores his aging comrades to reclaim their glorious past and seek greatness anew. He longs to journey out to sea again. It is fascinating to picture the young Jackie, all of twenty-five, sitting near the shore of Cape Cod, looking out across the Sound with Jack, so delighting him with this gem of a poem that he would use it in future speeches, as would his two brothers after him. The closing lines were their favorites:

> Come, my friends,
> 'Tis not too late to seek a newer world.
> Push off, and sitting well in order smite
> The sounding furrows; for my purpose holds
> To sail beyond the sunset, and the baths
> Of all the western stars, until I die.
> It may be that the gulfs will wash us down:
> It may be we shall touch the Happy Isles,
> And see the great Achilles, whom we knew.
> Tho' much is taken, much abides; and tho'
> We are not now that strength which in old days
> Moved earth and heaven; that which we are, we are;
> One equal temper of heroic hearts,
> Made weak by time and fate, but strong in will
> To strive, to seek, to find, and not to yield.

~ During the 1950s the sisters—Eunice, Patricia, and Jean—were coming into their own too. In the thirteen-month period that started in May 1953, Jack and two of his four surviving sisters all married. Jean married in 1956. All the men thus brought into the Kennedy fold through marriage would have important roles to play in both the personal and political lives of Kennedys.

The first of those sisters to marry was Eunice. Her husband was R. Sargent Shriver, whom she met through her father. Like Jack, Shriver had been a navy lieutenant who saw action in the Solomon Islands, specifically Guadalcanal. After the war he was hired by Joe to manage the Merchandise Mart in Chicago. He would go on to play crucial roles in the Kennedy administration and would even run for president himself.

The Kennedy sisters are commonly thought to have arrived at lives in public service as a result of Jack's elevation to the presidency. In fact, Eunice was headed there with greater alacrity than Jack at first. Nor did Patricia need Jack's help to get places. Patricia's 1954 wedding to the Hollywood actor Peter Lawford was as big a social event as Jack and Jackie's. Both weddings drew similar-sized crowds of more than three thousand spectators.[27] Lawford was more famous than Jack at that time, having been a Hollywood leading man since the 1940s. At the height of his career he received thousands of fan mail letters weekly. In 1953 he starred in roles on the TV anthology, General Electric Theater, hosted by Ronald Reagan. By 1959 he was a full member of Frank Sinatra's "Rat Pack." Sinatra became an important Kennedy backer, a part of a Kennedy process of blurring the lines between celebrity and politics, something impossible to imagine from Ike or Harry Truman before him, or Richard Nixon after.

Jean kept a lower profile for many years, but her marriage to Stephen Edward Smith brought to the clan his financial acumen and skills as a political strategist. He managed Kennedy family finances for many years, was managing Jack's reelection campaign until the assassination in 1963, and then managed Bobby's 1968 campaign for the presidency until that too was stopped by an assassin.

~ In 1954 Jack's back gave him so much trouble that for weeks he needed crutches to walk. The advice he sought from a team of doctors came without unanimity about the advisability of surgery, particularly because his Addison's disease exposed him to risk of potentially fatal infections. He became convinced that his choice was between a life in pain on crutches or a chance at fixing the back that had been failing him since childhood. "I'd rather die than spend the rest of my life on these things," he said, punching his crutches with a fist.[28]

The surgical option was to involve a double fusion of spinal disks. He went through it in October 1954. Just as his Addison's disease was kept secret, so too was the outcome of the surgery, which very nearly killed him, according to various accounts. The Kennedy family had another seaside home in Palm Beach, Florida, where Jack went for convalescence, but he was confined to bed and in constant pain. In February 1955 he returned to New York for yet another spinal operation, then returned to Palm Beach to resume his recovery. Jackie spent many days nursing him, and she and friends read to him to take his mind off the pain. Finally, on March 1 he walked without crutches for the first time in weeks. The next day he put on shorts and a baseball cap and, with help from Jackie and a longtime friend and aide, Dave Powers, made his way to the beach. "He stood there feeling the warm salt water on his bare feet and broke into a big smile," Powers said.[29]

Before his surgeries he and his aide Ted Sorensen had discussed an idea for a book that would collect the stories of a small number of American politicians who had in common the bravery to put politics and popularity aside to take a bold stand on an issue. Knowing his convalescence would be a long one, he and Sorensen had time to begin work on what would be called *Profiles in Courage*. As he increasingly could get up and move around, Jack sat by the Palm Beach oceanfront to work on the book and on Senate office matters.

His mother, Rose, remembered seeing him at work:

There is a little promontory, about the size of a big bay window and shaped like one, that protrudes from the wall, with beach and ocean on three sides. On calm sunny days this was an office and studio for him. . . . I remember looking out from the house across our sturdy green lawn and past the tall royal palms toward the tropical sea, the aquamarine white-capped ocean and blue sky and passing clouds and ships in the distance, and here was Jack in his sea-wall alcove with his writing board and thick writing pad clamped to it, and a folding table or two piled with books and notebooks and file folders—paperweights or perhaps some rocks from the beach to hold things down against the sea breezes—and his head would be forward and he would be writing away on that book. From full heart, mind and spirit.[30]

Profiles in Courage was awarded a Pulitzer Prize in 1956, and the journalists who covered Jack's career must have envied him for that more than just about anything else Jack did. For *Profiles in Courage* Jack had a lot of help—so much that the true extent of his authorship has been a subject of debate. Skeptics claimed it was really Sorensen's work. In his preface Kennedy credited many with advising him, but none more than Sorenson, to whom he said, "the greatest debt is owed." He meant that almost literally because Sorensen even received a share of the royalties. At a minimum surely Jack closely supervised the project, and the quality of the resulting book far surpasses that of the thousands of other books politicians have written over the years with considerable assistance from ghostwriters, editors, and researchers. Jack had experience with courage, and as he sat on his windswept promontory looking out across the sea, he had plenty of time to contemplate the meaning of political courage.

~ Despite having the financial means to live on their own, Jack and Jackie spent the early months of their marriage living with family, much of the time at Hyannis Port. In 1955 they acquired Hickory Hill, a Virginia mansion across the Potomac from Washington.

Jack, fully recovered and looking healthier than ever, fell onto Adlai Stevenson's short list for a running mate in his 1956 run for the White House. Meanwhile, Jack and Jackie were trying to have a baby. Jackie had a miscarriage during their first year of marriage and was pregnant again that summer of 1956 when they traveled to Chicago, where she carried out the demanding schedule of a wife of a rising star at a national political convention.

Stevenson had an early lock on the nomination to be the Democratic Party's choice to run against President Eisenhower, so much attention was focused on the competition to be his running mate. Kennedy, despite his youth and inexperience, showed surprising levels of convention delegate support for that role. But the choice of a running mate was Stevenson's to make and, by chance, Eunice's husband, Sargent Shriver, found himself on a plane with Stevenson just weeks before the convention. Shriver no doubt knew Stevenson of Illinois from both his Merchandise Mart role as well as his Kennedy family membership. They talked. Stevenson expressed considerable misgivings concerning Jack's health and had, perhaps, heard rumors about Addison's disease, though he did not bring that particular ailment up. He asked Shriver about Jack's war injuries, his malaria, and his back surgery.

Jack was invited to narrate a film to be shown at the convention. Telling the history of the Democratic Party, it concluded with an excerpt from a Franklin Roosevelt speech with a Kennedyesque ring to it: "I propose to sail ahead. For to reach port we must sail, sail, not lie at anchor—sail, not drift!"[31]

At the convention Stevenson introduced drama to an otherwise undramatic convention by forfeiting his right to handpick a running mate. Instead, he let the delegates put it to a vote. When the first ballot was cast, votes were split among five candidates, with Jack coming in second to Estes Kefauver of Tennessee. Jack showed surprising support in states like Georgia and Texas, where conventional wisdom held a Catholic could not compete. Jack ultimately lost, but his near victory on a national level, and his graceful concession speech from the convention floor, positioned him for a future run nationwide. Ultimately, Stevenson-Kefauver was trounced by Eisenhower-Nixon.

Jack lost the nomination, but he won over the party. Showing such surprising strength in all regions of the nation, he now personified his party's future. He also avoided being half of a losing ticket and perhaps getting a share of the blame. Ironically, given Stevenson's concerns about Jack's health, in August 1963 Kefauver suffered a heart attack on the Senate floor and died three months before Jack's death by assassination.

~ In August after the 1956 convention, Jack wanted a vacation. Jackie, expecting in October, and having had one miscarriage already, stayed behind with her mother and stepfather at her childhood home, Hammer-smith Farm, in Newport, Rhode Island. Taking brother Ted and Harvard roommate Torby Macdonald along, Jack chartered a forty-foot sailboat and crew for a Mediterranean cruise, setting out from Cannes. Jack al-ways enjoyed sailing and male companionship, and there were reports of women aboard, not the first such evidence of infidelity, nor the last. Jack's choice of timing proved awful. On August 23, back at Hammersmith Farm, Jackie began hemorrhaging and was rushed to a hospital. After an emergency cesarean, their daughter was stillborn. Bobby Kennedy raced to be with Jackie, while Eunice went to work trying to get word to Jack. It took three days to finally reach him at sea.

It is well known, based on the tireless investigations of people who trade in such matters, that some Kennedy men have been less than good husbands at various times in their lives. Here Jack set a particularly low standard. Given that Jackie was out of danger, he thought he would con-tinue on with sailing. What difference would it make if he canceled the rest of the cruise? Ultimately, he was convinced that his wife needed him, and the *Boston Herald* headline, "Sen. Kennedy at Sea, Lacks News of Wife," gave him practical political reasons for exhibiting concern. Jack-ie's grief was profoundly deep and she needed support, particularly when women around her had so little trouble bearing children. Two days after the baby was lost, Patricia Lawford gave birth to their second child. A few days later Ethel and Robert had their fifth child. Both newborns were girls. Thousands of condolence letters poured in to Jack and Jackie, mak-ing Jack's initial insensitivity all the more apparent.[32]

Jack and Jackie were reunited and had time together, but it was not long before he was called to duty for the Stevenson campaign. Jack's new-found popularity with voters was not lost on the presidential candidate, and they were happy to have Jack on the road speaking for the top of the ticket. Jack was in high demand and receiving ovations everywhere. Bobby meanwhile traveled with the Stevenson campaign and used the experience to learn organizing strategies.

~ Jackie, who had busied herself readying Hickory Hill for a child, now could not stand the thought of living there. After only a year there they sold it to Bobby and Ethel. Jack and Jackie later renovated and moved into an early eighteenth-century three-story home in Georgetown. Also in 1956 they bought a house at Hyannis Port adjacent to the main house in which Jack and his siblings grew up. In the years that followed Bobby and Ethel bought another neighboring house there, thus establishing the "Kennedy Compound." Eunice and her husband bought another nearby house, and so did Ted. No matter how much the Kennedy universe expanded, it still revolved around Hyannis Port and continued to do so for decades to come.

As in-laws were added and families grew, there were more people to crew on sailboats and help out in races. In the years before Jack was commander in chief, he did not always command the respect he thought he deserved from the new crew. In one regatta off Martha's Vineyard, Ethel's colorful and independent-minded brother, George, worked the jib and main sheets while Jack steered. Jack's dictates as skipper were not well received.

"Look, Jack, are you going to keep screaming at me how to trim this sail when I know damned well better than you how it ought to be trimmed?" George said.

Jack, former navy commander and Olympic sailing aspirant, gave George a hard, hard look. "Shut the hell up and do as you're told!" he ordered. George, red-faced, raised his fist and gave Jack the finger. Then he stood, leaped into the water, and swam two miles to shore, leaving Kennedy infuriated and crewless.[33]

~ After two failed pregnancies, Jackie became pregnant a third time. It was 1957 and Jack was busy with travel, building grassroots support for an anticipated presidential campaign. Jackie's obstetrician recommended a cesarean section, and because they could schedule it in advance, Jack was at the hospital when their daughter, Caroline Bouvier Kennedy, was born on November 27, 1957. After all the insecurities of being unable to have a child, particularly in comparison to Bobby and Ethel, the event was an especially happy one for mother and father alike.

~ After Stevenson's loss the popular press became obsessed with the Kennedy story: first Jack, then Jack and Jackie, and then the Kennedy family as a whole, as it became apparent that they were all not only exceptionally accomplished individually but strongly committed to helping Jack's campaigns and one another.

The nature of fame and celebrity in American culture was transforming in those years as more media achieved national reach, fed off one another, and achieved self-perpetuating cycles, print feeding radio, feeding TV, introducing topics that went "viral" before that word took its current meaning in the Internet age. The *Saturday Evening Post* published "The Amazing Kennedys." *American Mercury, Catholic Digest, McCall's,* and *Redbook* published articles about Jack, the family, and Jackie. Jack was on the cover of *Time* and, once again, *Life*.[34] Patti Page's song "Old Cape Cod" shot to the top ten on radio and recording sales lists in the summer of 1957.

"I don't know how he does it," complained Senator Hubert Humphrey, a Democratic presidential aspirant. "I get into *Photoplay* and he gets into *Life*."[35]

Some were alarmed that a political leader was being marketed like a consumer product. *New York Post* columnist William V. Shannon wrote, "Month after month, from the glossy pages of *Life* to the multicolored cover of *Redbook*, Jack and Jackie Kennedy smile out at millions of readers; he with his tousled hair and winning smile, she with her dark eyes and beautiful face. We hear of her pregnancy, of his wartime heroism, of their fondness for sailing. But what has all this to do with statesmanship?"[36] As Kennedy biographer Michael O'Brien noted, it wasn't the Kennedys who emphasized charm and style over substance; it was the media.[37]

Jackie, image conscious as anyone, wanted to manage reputation too. Asked at a Georgetown gathering if Jack was becoming too much of a "glamour boy," she replied, "Nonsense, Jack has almost no time anymore for sailboats and silly things. He has this curious, inquiring mind that is always at work. If I were drawing him, I would draw a tiny body and an enormous head."[38] They kept on sailing, of course, and continued to invite photographers along. Jack and Jackie must have feared they were riding a media tiger, one that brought welcomed attention and even adulation, but one that could never be tamed. Celebrity was getting confused with leadership, glamour with governing.

The May 1957 announcement of Jack's Pulitzer Prize burnished his reputation for gravitas. But they kept feeding the tiger's hunger for lighter news, and in early 1958 allowed *Life* in for more photos, these of baby Caroline in the nursery. In just seven years' time, Andy Warhol began a series of paintings of Jackie that explored the workings of the media and popular culture on public perception of the Kennedys.

~ Throughout their younger years the Kennedys cultivated friendships by inviting classmates and others for weekends at Hyannis Port. As Jack looked toward running for president, he invited intellectuals and political figures to the compound. One was Arthur Schlesinger. A professor of history, Schlesinger for years was a pendulum swinging between the worlds of academia and politics, writing a speech for a candidate, then a book on American history, sometimes about a figure for whom he had worked. He had been active in both of Stevenson's presidential campaigns and would become a lifelong friend of Jack, Jackie, Bobby, and other Kennedys. In July 1959 he was just getting to know the Kennedys and was invited to dinner at the Cape with Jack and Jackie. Schlesinger's wife could not join them, so it was just the three of them. Schlesinger recalled,

> We all drank and talked from about eight to 12:30. I only brought two cigars, one of which Jack took, having (typically) no cigars in the house. . . . [Jackie] was lovely but seemed excessively flighty on politics, asking with wide-eyed naïveté questions like, "Jack, why don't you just tell them that you won't go into any of those old primaries?" Jack was in a benign frame of mind and did not blink; but clearly such remarks could, in another context, be irritating. This is all the more so since Jackie, on other subjects, is intelligent and articulate. She was reading Proust when I arrived; she talked very well about [composer/author] Nicolas Nabokov, [journalist] Joe Alsop and other personalities; and one feels that out of some perversity she pretends an ignorance about politics larger even than life.

Jack's opponents were spreading rumors about Jack's Addison's disease, which he always denied having. Schlesinger asked him about it, and the response was again less than honest. Referring again to his wartime malaria as the problem that was now beat, Jack claimed to have none of the symptoms of Addison's, adding, "no one who has Addison's disease ought to run for President; but I do not have it and have never had it."[39]

Whatever Jackie's political acumen, her love of literature was becoming distinctly visible in some of the most memorable passages of Jack's speeches. Just the month before the dinner with Schlesinger, at a speech in Yakima, Washington, Jack arrived with a prepared text in which he planned to quote, as he had so often before, from historical figures. His draft speech quoted three U.S. presidents, the historian Vernon Louis Parrington, Supreme Court justice Oliver Wendell Holmes, and British statesman David Lloyd George. His speeches were now drawing from literature too, and the prepared text also quoted Shakespeare's *King Lear* and the American playwright Robert Sherwood. Jack continued refining his Yakima speech right up until the final moments. He wanted a better ending than the one he held in his hands.

Sitting next to Jackie on the dais, Jack handed Jackie a note he wrote on the back of the speech draft. "Give me last lines from Ulysses beginning, 'Come my friends.'" On the surviving copy at the Kennedy Library you can see that after Jack's handwritten word "friends," Jackie's pen fills in the rest. "'tis not too late to seek a newer world . . ." Jack knew she had it memorized since childhood and Jackie did not disappoint, writing ten more lines, ending as the poem does with, "To strive, to seek, to find, and not to yield."

A year later, in July 1960, Jack arrived in Los Angeles for the Democratic National Convention. He had several rivals for the nomination, including two late entrants, Lyndon Johnson and Adlai Stevenson. Johnson, the powerful Senate majority leader, had a strong following, but not as strong as Jack's. Stevenson made a weak showing after having lost both previous presidential races to Eisenhower. Jack Kennedy won on the first ballot and Johnson accepted the second spot as running mate. The choice of Johnson came only after bitter behind-the-scenes maneuvering that left Bobby and Johnson with a dislike for each other so deep it never truly dissipated.

The Republican Party convention came just days afterward, diverting attention from Jack and allowing him another trip to Hyannis Port for a short rest and meetings before returning to the campaign trail as his party's presidential nominee. There he would rejoin Jackie, pregnant with John Jr. She did not attend the Democratic convention, staying back at Hyannis Port and watching the proceedings on a seventeen-inch rented television. She spent some of her time alone working on a painting to give to Jack upon his return.

Leaving the Hyannis airport for their home, Jack saw along the route scenes of increasing commotion the closer he got to his Cape house. Crowds of Cape Cod neighbors were along the streets, some with banners. At his house neighbors were at his lawn's edge and on a stone boundary wall. Getting out of the car, Jack looked out over to the beach and the Sound. "I'd like to take a swim, but I want to get in the house before Caroline gets to sleep," he said. To the onlookers he added, "I believe you know how you have made me feel by coming to see me tonight. You are my neighbors. I know you understand what is in my heart. I would like to talk to you all for a while, but I have to get inside before my daughter goes to sleep. Good night. May God bless you and thanks again."[40]

Inside, two-and-half-year-old Caroline presented her father with the homecoming present Jackie had made. It was a painting of Jack on *Victura*, wearing a tricorn hat, striking a pose like Washington crossing the Delaware, except that he was returning to a pier at Hyannis Port, filled with children, grandmothers, pets, and a marching band. On the hat were the words "El Senatore" and on a banner, "WELCOME BACK, MR. JACK." Jack picked up Caroline and returned to the front door with his daughter. Referring to the painting, he said, "I wonder where she ever got the idea I had a commander-in-chief complex."

Over the next two days, with Bobby and Ethel, they went sailing on *Victura* and picnicked on the *Marlin*, the family's motor cruiser. Over the few days that followed, time Jack might have preferred spending on *Victura* was instead given to a steady stream of important visitors. Adlai Stevenson needed his time—he could still command support from liberal activists and his state of Illinois would be important in the general election. Plus he wanted a role in a Kennedy administration if the campaign succeeded. They spent time with Lyndon and Lady Bird Johnson. President Eisenhower, acknowledging the possibility that his vice president, Richard Nixon, might not win, arranged for Jack to get national security briefings from CIA director Allen Dulles. On one occasion, however, press secretary Pierre Salinger cancelled a session with press photographers at the last minute. It was a beautiful day for sailing, and Jack set out on *Victura* instead.

Among his visitors was Norman Mailer, famous then for his novel, *The Naked and the Dead*. Like John Hersey, who had written in the *New Yorker* about PT-109, Mailer was experimenting with similar new forms of nonfiction writing, ones that applied a novelist's techniques to reporting news. Mailer was writing a piece for *Esquire* that would profile Jack and his victorious Democratic convention. Titled, "Superman Comes to the Supermarket," the article is still considered a groundbreaking work of New Journalism.

As the two sat down, "Kennedy smiled politely and said that he had read my books," wrote Mailer. Then Jack paused ever so briefly, not immediately recalling a title, before saying, "I've read *The Deer Park* and . . . the others."

This startled Mailer. "It was the first time in a hundred similar situations, talking to someone whose knowledge of my work was casual, that the sentence did not come out, 'I've read *The Naked and the Dead* . . . and the others.' If one is to take the worst and assume that Kennedy was briefed for this interview (which is most doubtful), it still speaks well for the striking instincts of his advisers."

Mailer continued,

What was retained later, is an impression of Kennedy's manners which were excellent, even artful, better than the formal good manners of Choate and Harvard, almost as if what was creative in the man had been given to the manners. . . . His personal quality had a subtle, not quite describable intensity, a suggestion of dry pent heat perhaps, his eyes large, the pupils grey, the whites prominent, almost shocking, his most forceful feature: he had the eyes of a mountaineer. His appearance changed with his mood, strikingly so, and this made him always more interesting than what he was saying. He would seem at one moment older than his age, forty-eight or fifty, a tall, slim, sunburned professor with a pleasant weathered face, not even particularly handsome; five minutes later, talking to a press conference on his lawn, three microphones before him, a television camera turning, his appearance would have gone through a metamorphosis, he would look again like a movie star, his coloring vivid, his manner rich, his gestures strong and quick, alive with that concentration of vitality a successful actor always seems to radiate. Kennedy had a dozen faces.

Mailer mused about Jack's past near-death experiences, all the illness he had survived, the heroism after the sinking of PT-109, and the fearlessness he exhibited on PT boat missions after that:

It is the wisdom of a man who senses death within him and gambles that he can cure it by risking his life. It is the therapy of the instinct, and who is so wise as to call it irrational? . . . His trials suggest the self-hatred of a man whose resentment and ambition are too large for his body. Not everyone can discharge their furies on an analyst's couch, for some angers can be relaxed only by winning power, some rages are sufficiently monumental to demand that one try to become a hero or else fall back into that death which is already within the cells. But if one succeeds, the energy aroused can be exceptional.

Mailer talked to a man who saw Kennedy at Hyannis Port and thought he showed "deep fatigue."

"Well, he didn't look tired at the convention." Mailer said.

"Oh, he had three days of rest. Three days of rest for him is like six months to us."[41]

Jackie made a strong impression on Mailer too. Mailer was invited to visit a second day and brought his wife. After Mailer interviewed Jack further, Jack and Jackie headed out toward the pier for a sail on *Victura* with Jack's brother Ted. Turning to Adele Mailer, Jackie said, "I wish that I didn't have to go on this corny sail, because I would like very much to talk to you."[42]

~ At around that time *Sports Illustrated* sent a photographer for a cover story that included a beautiful two-page color image of Jack at the helm of *Victura*. Asked about his sailing experience, Jack happily obliged. "I'll write it down for you," he said, and a photo shows him in the cabin of *Marlin* with pen and pad of paper recording his sailing resume as one might when applying to crew a serious race:

Victura (about to conquer)
31 years

---

raced on Nantucket
Sound 20 years

(Edgartown
Nantucket

Star Boats
Nantucket Sound
Champion
Competed in Atlantic
Coast Championship
With brother Joe
sailing other boat
won McMillan Trophy
(Eastern Intercollegiate Championship)
Sailed for Harvard[43]

Jack returned to the campaign trail for the final stretch, and Jackie was happy to have a good reason to stay home—her pregnancy. She did, however, accompany him to certain major events. Wisconsin was a key swing state in the November general election against Richard Nixon. Jack spoke in Milwaukee just days before election day and concluded by quoting Carl Schurz, a German immigrant who was active in Wisconsin politics and abolitionism, went on to represent Minnesota in the U.S. Senate, and then gave a historic speech at Faneuil Hall in Kennedy's city of Boston. Jack, straying slightly from the original quotation, said, "Ideals are like stars. You will not succeed in touching them with your hands. But the seafaring man who follows the waters follows the stars. And, if you choose them as your guides, you can reach your destiny."[44]

Another earlier Milwaukee campaign stop was at the Badger Home for the Blind, where residents planned to surprise him with a tribute to his World War II naval career. As he entered the door, a man at a piano started playing "Anchors Aweigh," and several stood to sing him the words:

Anchors Aweigh my boys.
Anchors Aweigh.
Farewell to college joys, we sail at break of day 'ay 'ay 'ay
Through our last night ashore, drink to the foam,
Until we meet once more:
Here's wishing you a happy voyage home!"[45]

As he watched and listened, Jack's eyes moistened and as he left, he tried not to let anyone see that he needed a handkerchief to wipe away tears.[46]

Speaking in his home state the day before the election, he said, "I am very sure if we do not continue to drift and lie at anchor, only seeing the beginning of our difficulties, but if this country goes back to work again, if it moves with purpose, if it moves with perseverance, there is nothing it cannot do, nothing."[47]

On election day, the Kennedy family converged from all points, reuniting at Hyannis Port to await results of what became the closest presidential race of the twentieth century. On the way from the airport to their home, Jack and Jackie passed the harbor where, "one sailboat flaunted its white canvas against the cold blue sky."[48] Jack had breakfast with his father and other members of the family, tossed a football with his brothers on the lawn, then visited Bobby and Ethel's house, which had been transformed into an election night command post. Tables were aligned in a T-formation and fourteen women monitored phones, collecting reports from the field. The pollster Lou Harris used a child's bedroom, painted pink, to analyze data as it streamed off teletypes, which Peter Lawford oversaw. Still more phones were in another child's bedroom, where Ted and Stephen Smith were on duty.

News media predictions of the election's outcome seesawed between the two, until the early morning hours when it looked near-certain that Jack was elected. Nixon went on camera and made a statement admitting it appeared that Kennedy won but not fully conceding, unnerving all those who wanted finality. Jack went to bed and urged others to do the same. When he awoke, he learned he had carried Nixon's home state of California. They had breakfast and Jack took Caroline for a walk along the beach, holding hands. He invited Ted to join. Then other members of the family joined, as did Ted Sorensen, and they made a processional across the dune grass above the beach. The secret service, whose presence had increased that morning, followed at a short distance.

Shortly after noon Minnesota's returns came in and gave Jack the necessary electoral college votes. Nixon, declining to personally make a statement, had his press secretary read a concession instead. Jack walked to Bobby's command center and opened the door. "When Jack came into the room he was no longer Jack," said one witness. "He was the President of the United States. We all stood up—even his brother Bobby. It was just an instinctive thing."[49]

There were plans for a family portrait to record the moment, so photographer Jacques Lowe tried to corral the Kennedys. Jackie was hardest to find; when no one was looking she grabbed her coat and left the house. "Through a window, I caught a glimpse of her rushing down to the sea" for a solitary walk, said Lowe. "That Wednesday morning when the rest of the family was jubilant and embracing each other and laughing it up, Jackie was deeply shaken. She was clearly in a state of shock. I felt sorry for her."[50]

"It's okay," Jack told Lowe. "I'll go get her." He caught up with her on the beach, put his arm around her, and they returned. She went upstairs and returned in a red scoop-neck dress and a triple strand of pearls. Jack moved to her side, took her arm, and faced the family. They all rose to their feet—the surviving brothers and sisters, Joe and Rose, the in-laws—and gave the couple a standing ovation.[51]

During his presidency, Jack and Jackie returned to Hyannis Port from time to time. They still sailed the *Victura*, cruised on the *Marlin*, and rented a nearby house that became known as the Summer White House. The Cape would never be the same while he was president. The crowds, the gawkers, the tour boats pointing out the Kennedy Compound, secret service in nearby boats, reporters in another boat—all confirmed that you can't go home again. What must they have thought that day, knowing their lives were transformed, gazing out over the waters where as children

The main house at Hyannis Port, first rented by Joe and Rose in 1925 and soon afterward expanded. Photo by James W. Graham, 2012

Probably the earliest surviving photo of the *Victura*, before its original white hull was painted navy blue. © John F. Kennedy Library Foundation, 1933

The *Daily Boston Globe*'s photo caption: "Bob advises his brother John how to bend the jib of the *Victura*." Photo courtesy of John F. Kennedy Library, July 1934

Best known for its catboats, the Crosby Yacht Yard designed and manufactured Wianno Seniors like *Victura* and their smaller sisters, Wianno Juniors. The first of about two hundred Seniors was built in 1914. Photo by James W. Graham, 2012

left: When they were a family of ten, they named a boat *Tenovus*. With Ted's birth, a new boat was christened *One More*, here with Eunice and a friend. © John F. Kennedy Library Foundation, Summer 1934

above: Teddy charming the London media, the same year Joseph P. Kennedy Sr. was named ambassador to Great Britain. Photo courtesy of John F. Kennedy Library, 1938

Photographer Alfred Eisenstaedt steadied himself on *Victura*'s bow to capture eight-year-old Ted (*forward*) and Jean, Rose, Joe, Bobby, Patricia, and Eunice (*left to right*). Photo by Alfred Eisenstaedt/Time & Life Pictures/Getty Images, 1940

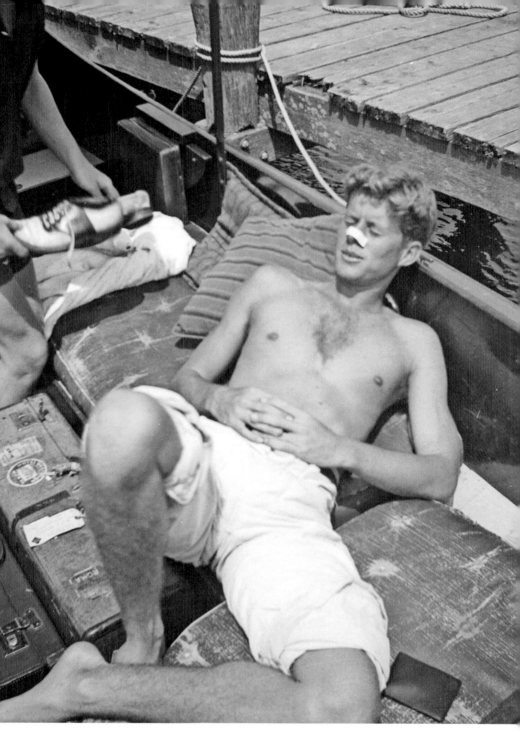

Shortly before he joined the navy, Jack rests at the Edgartown Regatta, Martha's Vineyard, which to this day is the annual racing highlight of the Cape Cod sailing season. © John F. Kennedy Library Foundation, July 1941

left: Ensign Joseph P. Kennedy Jr. (*right*) earned his navy wings, but Lt. John F. Kennedy outranked him. Photo courtesy of John F. Kennedy Library, May 1942
right: Crew of PT-109, Jack at right. Photo courtesy of John F. Kennedy Library, 1943

After the war, Ted and Jack on *Victura*. Jack is fifteen years older.
Photo courtesy of John F. Kennedy Library, 1946

Jack and Jackie, newly engaged, on the bow of *Victura* and on the cover of *Life* magazine, issue dated July 20, 1953. Hy Peskin's SL & WH, www.HyPeskin.com

Sailing became a frequent photo opportunity, as a young senator and his fiancée blended politics and celebrity. Photo courtesy of JFK Library, 1953

Jack, Democratic presidential nominee, and Jackie on *Victura*. AP Photo, August 7, 1960

The president sailing. Photos by Cecil Stoughton, White House/John F. Kennedy Presidential Library and Museum, Boston, July 28, 1962

The president sailing. Photo by Cecil Stoughton, White House/John F. Kennedy Presidential Library and Museum, Boston, July 28, 1962

A pleasant sail ended poorly with headlines that infuriated the president. "Kennedy Race Sloop Runs Aground in Mud," said the next morning's *Boston Globe*. Photo by Cecil Stoughton, White House/John F. Kennedy Presidential Library and Museum, Boston, July 29, 1962

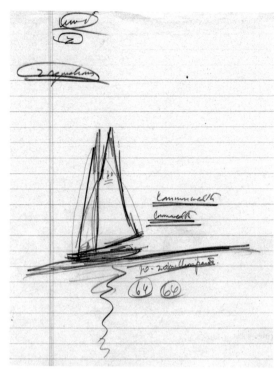

A presidential doodle during the days of the Cuban Missile Crisis. Photo courtesy of John F. Kennedy Library, ca. 1962

Anticipating Christmas, three Kennedy sisters collaborated to commission artist Henry Koehler to create three paintings of *Victura*, each featuring a different brother and his spouse. A sister was visiting Koehler's studio to inspect progress at the moment of Jack's assassination. This painting is of Robert and Ethel. Photo and painting © Henry Koehler, 1963, reprinted with permission

Robert F. Kennedy at the helm of *Victura*. *Left to right*: Maria Shriver, Courtney Kennedy, Bobby Shriver, Robert Kennedy Jr., Pat Prusyewski (a ward of the Shriver family), Robert F. Kennedy, David Kennedy, and Kathleen Kennedy. AP Photo/ Bob Schutz, July 30, 1961

left: Bob and Ethel's son Joseph P. Kennedy II, thirteen, tries out a set of sails made for his family's new sailboat, *Resolute,* hull and sail #132, on old *Victura,* #94. AP Photo, 1964

below: Ethel and children sail *Resolute.*
bottom: A mishap on *Resolute.* Photos by Ron Galella/Ron Galella Collection/WireImage/Getty Images, August 14, 1971

Ted Kennedy and Ted Jr., Thanksgiving Day, 1979.
AP Photo/Staples, November 22, 1979

U.S. Representative Joe Kennedy II, Senator Ted Kennedy, and President Bill Clinton astern of *Victura*, during the dedication of the museum at the JFK Presidential Library and Museum. Photo by Diana Walker/Time & Life Images/Getty Images, October 29, 1993

John F. Kennedy Jr. steers the Shriver family Wianno Senior *Headstart*, trailing cousin Joe Kennedy II at the wheel of a powerboat. Photo by John Tlumacki/ *Boston Globe*/Getty Images, August 23, 1997

Ted Crosby, a descendant of the founder of the Crosby Yacht Yard, makes repairs on the "new" *Victura*, one of the last of the wooden Wianno Seniors and in 2012 prone to leaking. Photo by James W. Graham, August 8, 2012

Captured by paparazzi, Taylor Swift and then boyfriend, Conor Kennedy, sail on *Ptarmigan*, striking a pose reminiscent of Jack and Jackie's from the 1950s and 1960s. A few months earlier, Conor recited *Ulysses* from memory for a class assignment. WENN.com, July 30, 2012

Mark Shriver, son of Eunice and Sargent, waves from his recently acquired *Dingle*, with a crew that includes brother Bobby Shriver and his wife, Malissa. Mark hopes his daughter will solo sail *Dingle* in a year or two. Photo by James W. Graham, August 2012

The author (*left*) aboard *Glide* with Ethel Kennedy, Ted Kennedy Jr., Max Kennedy, Sheila Kennedy (wife of Chris), Kiki Kennedy (wife of Ted Jr.), Chris Kennedy, and family friend David Nunes. Photo by crewman, August 6, 2012

the Kennedys raced their sailboats and then looking across the sea grass and dunes of Cape Cod? Some sense of normalcy would in time return for the rest of the family, but never for Jack and Jackie. Did they feel a sense of loss?

~ Thoreau described what the Cape dunes looked like at that time of year, late fall:

> I never saw an autumnal landscape so beautifully painted as this was. It was like the richest rug imaginable, spread over an uneven surface; no damask nor velvet, nor Tyrian dye or stuffs, nor the work of any loom, could ever match it. There was the incredibly bright red of the Huckle-berry, and the reddish brown of the Bayberry, mingled with the bright and living green of small Pitch-Pines, and also the duller green of the Bayberry, Boxberry and Plum, the yellowish green of the Shrub-Oaks, and the various golden and yellow and fawn-colored tins of the Birch and Maple and Aspen,—each making its own figure, and in the midst, the few yellow sandslides on the sides of the hills looked like the white floor seen through rents in the rug.[52]

Jackie expected her baby to arrive in mid-December. That would give her a month to recuperate before inauguration day. None of Jackie's preg-nancies went according to plan, however, and an ambulance was called to their Georgetown residence on November 27. John F. Kennedy Jr. was born premature, but healthy.

CHAPTER 7

The Presidency

≋≋≋ They turned the Oval Office into a shrine to American seafaring.

A few days after inauguration Jackie found a beautiful overlooked desk in a state of neglect in the broadcast room of the White House. Eisenhower had used it only for TV and radio broadcasts. It was made from the timbers of the HMS *Resolute*, a ship abandoned by its British crew in 1854 when it became locked in pack ice in the Canadian Arctic. She had it moved to the Oval Office.

The *Resolute*, first called *Ptarmigan* before it was renamed, was one of a number of ships sent to search for members of a missing Arctic expedition led by Sir John Franklin, not heard from since 1848 when it left Great Britain on a mission to find the Northwest Passage. After the *Resolute's* abandonment, the crewless barque-rigged ghost ship drifted with the pack ice until it was discovered by an American whaling ship's crew a full 1,200 miles from where it had been left behind. The *Resolute* was brought to New London, Connecticut, and refurbished. Shortly afterward, in a moment of tense relations with Great Britain, the repaired *Resolute* was sailed to England and returned to Queen Victoria as a gift from the Americans. Years later, in 1880, the Queen presented the desk to President Rutherford B. Hayes. A plaque on the desk reads in part, "This table was made from [*Resolute's*] timbers when she was broken up, and is presented by the QUEEN OF GREAT BRITAIN & IRELAND to the PRESIDENT OF THE UNITED STATES as a memorial of the courtesy and loving kindness which dictated the offer of the gift of the RESOLUTE."

One of the Kennedy presidency's most famous photographs is of little John F. Kennedy Jr. sticking his head out a front panel as his father worked on the desktop above his mop head.

In short order, they placed on the desk:

~ The original coconut from Jack's PT-109 adventure, with his SOS message carved in it, encased in plastic and wood.

~ Pieces from Jack's collection of scrimshaw, one carved with an image of a great frigate under full sail.

~ A Steuben glass etching of a PT boat with the presidential seal, presented by a group of PT boat veterans.

~ Bookend replicas of cannons from the USS *Constitution*, or "Old Ironsides," the last sail-powered ship in the U.S. Navy fleet. Jack's grandfather, John F. Fitzgerald, helped save the deteriorating ship from demolition and later took his grandson to see it. Jack wrote, "as a small boy I used to be taken to the USS *Constitution* in Charlestown, Massachusetts. The sight of that historic frigate with the tall spars and black guns stirred my imagination and made history come alive for me."[1]

~ Between the bookends copies of *As We Remember Joe* and *To Turn the Tide*, a collection of speeches and statements from the year following Jack's election to the presidency.

~ A small plaque with the Breton Fishermen's Prayer, presented to him by navy vice admiral Hyman G. Rickover. It said, "Oh God, Thy sea is so great and my boat is so small."

The collection of objects on display in the Oval Office grew with the help of presidential naval aide Tazewell Shepard, who would bring objects to the White House Map Room for presidential inspection and approval prior to installation. Over time, on side tables and along the Oval Office walls, there were a ship's clock and barometer and detailed models of great historical ships from the age of sail, including the *Constitution*, the *Wasp*, and the *Saratoga*. Another model, from Jack's personal collection, was of the three-masted clipper ship *Sea Witch*. In 1850 *Sea Witch* became the first vessel to travel from the East Coast around Cape Horn to California in less than one hundred days. The Oval Office walls were lined on three sides with paintings and photographs of other sailboats great and small, along with a pennant flown on the USS *Raleigh*, a colonial revolutionary warship that in 1778 ran aground south of Boston while being attacked by the British navy. One of the finest paintings was an oil of the *Constitution* engaged in a battle with the British ship *Guerriere* during the War of 1812. That was when the *Constitution* earned its nickname, "Old Ironsides," after cannon shot was seen bouncing off its sides. A large oil painting of John Paul Jones's flagship from the Revolutionary War, the *Bonhomme Richard*, hung above the marble mantle.[2]

In the sitting area of the office was a high cane-back rocking chair presented to him by Captain William F. Bringle and the crew of one of the navy's greatest aircraft carriers. It had cushions embroidered with a navy anchor symbol and the words, "U.S.S. Kitty Hawk, Commander-in-Chief." It had a mahogany contoured back that so effectively relieved Jack's back pain that over the years he acquired fourteen of the chairs, according to its manufacturer, the P&P Chair Company of Troutman, North Carolina.

Jack may have drawn some inspiration from a collection of naval artwork belonging to Franklin Roosevelt, on display in the summer of 1962 at a National Archives exhibit that the president himself chose to open. In his remarks he said, the prints "tell us more about a very important part of our lives—our lives at sea. We think of ourselves, I think, as land animals in a sense, but we really look to the sea—the Atlantic and the Pacific—which have defended us and have secured us and have enriched us. Our Naval history is one of the most exciting threads that runs throughout the long history of our country, and the combination of the Navy and the Maritime and the extraordinary men who served and who gave it life and thrust and thesis deserves to be recorded." So avid a collector was Jack that he turned to the curator of the exhibit, a noted naval historian, and asked him to autograph his exhibit program.[3]

One tiny object that helped Jack rekindle memories of his Cape boyhood was a gift from Jackie: a simple, hand-painted, wood-carved tern, a Cape Cod seabird abundant in Jack's youth but dwindling in population in the decades since.

~ By 1961 the imagery of the sea was evolving for the Kennedys into something that went beyond fond family memory. Jack used that imagery to describe the American story—its might, its global reach, its tenacity in the face of adversity, its destiny. The most powerful leader of the free world, a politician-writer-historian who understood metaphor and symbolism as much as anyone, used his office surroundings to tell the story of the great American voyage. Jackie's love of literature had been supplemented by her later studies of American history, taken up with earnestness when she married a politician. So together, through speechmaking and decorative arts, they drew from tales of the sea to lead Americans into the Space Age.

Speaking in a garden outside the White House to students and faculty of France's Institute of Higher National Defense Studies, Jack pointed to one of the ship models he had brought out from his office, a gift of the French minister of cultural affairs Andre Malraux, and said, "This ship that you see here was sent to me last week by M. Malraux. After his visit to us in January, when he was kind enough to accompany the Mona Lisa to the United States, and knowing of my interest in the sea, friends of the Naval Museum copied this ship, the *La Flore*, which was a French ship which fought for the Americans in our War of Independence. And this arrived in full sail and is in my office as a welcome reminder of our oldest alliance."[4]

His presidential speeches often contained the sea imagery heard during the campaign. At a Philadelphia Democratic Party gathering on October 30, 1963, and in other speeches, Jack repeated a favorite boast about the state of the economy: "We shall be sailing this country next year on the longest and strongest peacetime expansion of our economy in the history of the United States. It is well within our reach."[5]

Jack closed one of his State of the Union addresses to Congress by saying,

We are not lulled by the momentary calm of the sea or the somewhat clearer skies above. We know the turbulence that lies below, and the storms that are beyond the horizon this year. But now the winds of change appear to be blowing more strongly than ever, in the world of communism as well as our own. For 175 years we have sailed with those winds at our back, and with the tides of human freedom in our favor. We steer our ship with hope, as Thomas Jefferson said, "leaving Fear astern." Today we still welcome those winds of change—and we have every reason to believe that our tide is running strong. With thanks to Almighty God for seeing us through a perilous passage, we ask His help anew in guiding the "Good Ship Union."

Jack's reference to "Good Ship Union" was an allusion to a Civil War–era poem by Oliver Wendell Holmes Sr., the Boston poet-physician who used a great ship as a metaphor for the then-young union threatened by dissolution over slavery. As a young man, in 1830, Holmes also wrote a poem about the USS *Constitution*, a poem credited afterward with generating the popular support needed to save the great frigate from demolition. Jack's grandfather "Honey Fitz," as a member of Congress, sponsored an 1897 bill to make Massachusetts the historic ship's permanent residence. As president, Jack sought to have the ship sail to New York Harbor for the 1964 World's Fair but was dissuaded when the navy said it was not then sufficiently seaworthy. "If anything happened, an Act of God for instance, the President would certainly bear the responsibility and Massachusetts citizens would have another Tea Party," warned a navy adviser.[6]

Jack's frequent use of metaphor was not limited to seascapes, of course. As a presidential candidate, he called for Americans to establish a "New Frontier," an image that conjured covered wagons more than boats. But "frontier" is a word that shares with seafaring a sense of the venturous and unexplored, of voyages of discovery. Jack understood the power of great speechwriting and of the well-chosen metaphor. Space was a "new ocean." We "sail this country." "Tides of human freedom."

Thirty years before he spoke at President Kennedy's inauguration, the New England poet Robert Frost spoke of the awesome power and potential hazards of metaphor, for both good and ill.

> I do not think anybody ever knows the discreet use of metaphor, his own and other people's . . . unless he has been properly educated in poetry. Poetry begins in trivial metaphors, pretty metaphors, "grace" metaphors, and goes on to the profoundest thinking that we have. Poetry provides the one permissible way of saying one thing and meaning another. . . . I have wanted in late years to go further and further in making metaphor the whole of thinking. . . . Unless you are at home in the

metaphor, unless you have had your proper poetical education in the metaphor, you are not safe anywhere. Because you are not at ease with figurative values: you don't know the metaphor in its strength and its weakness. You don't know how far you may expect it to ride and when it may break down with you.[7]

The power of metaphor has lately caught the attention of neuroscientists and psychologists. James Geary, in his 2011 book, *I Is an Other*, wrote,

Metaphor is not just confined to art and literature but is at work in all fields of human endeavor, from economics and advertising, to politics and business, to science and psychology.

Metaphor conditions our interpretations of the stock market and, through advertising, it surreptitiously infiltrates our purchasing decisions. In the mouths of politicians, metaphor subtly nudges public opinion; in the minds of businesspeople, it spurs creativity and innovation. In science, metaphor is the preferred nomenclature for new theories and new discoveries; in psychology it is the natural language of human relationships and emotions.[8]

Stock markets are "up" and "down," a meaningless metaphor when applied, as it often is, to one's own investment decisions about individual companies. Geary describes the ways that psychologists pick apart their patients' metaphors, how healing from physical ailments advances faster when the patient visualizes healthy outcomes. A runner in a marathon is coached to imagine a big rubber band pulling him closer to the runner ahead.

Ted Kennedy's son Patrick was asked about his father's late-in-life observation that sailing, for him, had always been a metaphor for life. Had the experience of sailing influenced the public life and political rhetoric of his father, uncles, and aunts?

"Yes," said Patrick, "in very transcendent ways. So, you know, 'a rising tide lifts all boats.' The very philosophy of the Democratic Party, that through increasing the number of people who benefit from the rising economy everybody benefits at all ends of the income scale. Well, this was internalized by my uncles and my father and my family's work. . . .

'A rising tide lifts all boats,' it was a way by which everybody can benefit. ... The philosophy of everybody being part of the crew." He and other younger Kennedys recalled the lessons learned as youngsters that they could contribute importantly to the sailing of a complicated boat, using their light weight, for example, to adjust a line without unbalancing the boat. He likened it to Kennedy family support over the decades of civil rights for people of color or people with disabilities.[9]

~ Did Jack's love of the sea influence public policy? Certainly, as an outdoorsman, Jack's interest was more in the nation's seashores than inland wildernesses, a fact that disappointed his own interior secretary, who found him lacking compared to great conservationists like Franklin or Teddy Roosevelt. "I long for a flicker of emotion, a response to the out of doors and overwhelming majesty of the land," wrote Stuart Udall of Jack. Unlike the Roosevelts, he was not indignant over "despoilers" and showed no "excited interest" in natural landscapes.[10]

Jack's conservation legacy concerned the topography he loved most. As he approached the end of his years in the Senate, Jack sponsored legislation creating the Cape Cod National Seashore. It passed and was signed during Jack's first year as president. He later signed a bill to protect the seashores of Point Reyes, California, and Padre Island, Texas.

~ Nowhere did the metaphor of the sea influence American thought more than in its perception of humankind's first trips into space, the "new ocean," as Jack called it. The comparisons of astronauts to Columbus and Magellan were a constant in the media. Once Jack decided to embrace "spacefaring" and called for landing a man on the moon, he could barely speak of the subject without making the comparison to sea explorers. It was visionary rhetoric when he and others used it in those years, at a time when lunar colonies and a trip to Mars seemed like the logical next steps. In retrospect it had little in common with sixteenth-century ocean exploration and world circumnavigation. Once a lunar landing was done, colonizing space and harvesting its riches proved a lot harder than most had thought.

Jack's presidential campaign made great use of what he called a "missile gap," the numeric and strength advantage that Soviets supposedly had over Americans. The Soviets had launched the first satellite, *Sputnik*, in 1957, and as a candidate Jack exploited the perception that Republicans let the United States fall behind. In a campaign speech in an Idaho high school auditorium, Jack said the nations of the world "have seen the Soviet Union first in space. They have seen it first around the moon and first around the sun. . . . They come to the conclusion that the Soviet tide is rising and ours is ebbing. I think it is up to us to reverse that point."[11] After Jack became the party nominee, Eisenhower's CIA director traveled to Hyannis Port to give him a confidential national security briefing, where he was told the numeric "gap" was largely illusory. Photo reconnaissance by satellite and spy planes found no evidence the Soviets had either the rocket launch facilities or numeric missile advantage many believed. Fear remained real, however, and though the Soviets lacked strength in numbers of intercontinental ballistic missiles, they did have an edge when it came to rocket lift capacity. They had fewer but bigger rockets. Three months after Jack's inauguration, on April 12, 1961, the first Russian cosmonaut, Yuri Gagarin, orbited the earth.

Funding to develop a new American heavy-lift Saturn rocket had been withheld under Eisenhower, and the previous month the Kennedy administration, with Vice President Lyndon Johnson's support, had begun considering spending the money. Two days after Gagarin's flight, Jack assembled in the Cabinet Room key advisers and NASA experts. Once again, *Life* magazine was present at the meeting. Reporter Hugh Sidey was given extraordinary access in exchange for constraints on what could be published. After hearing various discouraging assessments, Sidey watched Jack run his hand nervously through his hair and mutter, "We may never catch up."

"Now let's look at this," Jack told the men. "Is there any place where we can catch them? What can we do? Can we go around the moon before them? Can we put a man on the moon before them? . . . Can we leapfrog?" After listening to advisers weigh the enormous costs and odds of success, Jack looked around the room and said, "When we know more, I can decide if it's worth it or not. If somebody can just tell me how to catch up. Let's find somebody—anybody. I don't care if it's the janitor over there, if he knows how." He paused, looked at the faces in the room, and said, "There's nothing more important."[12]

Adding to the crisis atmosphere of that time was the Bay of Pigs disaster, which occurred the week following Gagarin's flight. The United States had provided CIA training to a small army of 1,400 Cuban exiles who were to invade Fidel Castro's Cuba, but the plan the president approved was poorly executed and did not provide American support sufficient to ensure victory. In two days Castro's forces squashed the invasion, a disastrously embarrassing military failure for which Jack publicly accepted responsibility. Jackie later recalled that he privately wept over the fiasco.

As the Bay of Pigs failure ramified, Jack met again with his vice president to discuss the space program, asking him to lead a hasty assessment of options for an American response to Russian achievements. Jack had Ted Sorensen provide Johnson with a letter listing questions that needed answering: "Do we have a chance of beating the Soviets by putting a laboratory in space, or by a trip around the moon, or by a rocket to land on the moon, or by a rocket to go to the moon and back with a man. Is there any other space program which promises dramatic results in which we could win?" One presidential scholar called the memo, "redolent of presidential panic."[13]

"Dramatic" and "win" were the operative words. Jack wanted a feat that could capture humankind's imagination. Until this time the Soviets had proven their space superiority with a series of one-off feats — *Sputnik*, then a dog, then striking the moon with *Luna 2*. Shortly after Jack took office the Soviets put an actual man in orbit, returning a hero. Jack instinctively knew, and made clear in his questions about a trip to the moon, that the focus of the competition with the Russians had to change from stunts of the month to a feat for the ages. Jack eventually decided to redefine the competition as a great and epic race to the moon. This was a race Americans could win.

In the short term, however, until Americans developed heavier-lift missiles that could compete, they would continue to be embarrassed by the Soviets. Making matters worse would be repeated failures of unmanned American test launches in full public view. Missiles exploded in midair, went astray, or barely left the ground.

~ With Jack's letter in hand, Johnson, in his role as Space Council chair, put key advisers to work. Wernher von Braun responded with an April 29 letter explaining that the Soviets probably already had the rocket power necessary to create a modest "laboratory" in space with multiple astronauts in a single launch. They were much closer than we were to soft-landing an unmanned payload on the moon, though he believed we had a "sporting chance" of beating them to it. We also had a "sporting chance" of first sending a three-man crew around the moon, though the Soviets might beat that with a one-man trip if they were willing to accept significant risk to his safe return.

"We have an excellent chance of beating the Soviets to the first landing of a crew on the moon (including return capability, of course)," wrote von Braun. "The reason is that a performance jump by a factor of 10 over their present rockets is necessary to accomplish this feat. While today we do not have such a rocket, it is unlikely that the Soviets have it. Therefore, we would not have to enter the race toward this obvious new goal in space exploration against hopeless odds favoring the Soviets. With an all-out crash program I think we could accomplish this objective in 1967/68."[14] Put another way, in 1961 both side's space missions were mostly just puttering offshore in day-sailer rocketry. America needed to build the greatest schooner ever and aim for the moon.

~ Still playing catch-up, still risking a publicly embarrassing failure on the heels of the Bay of Pigs, the United States succeeded in launching the first American into space on May 5. Alan Shepard's trip was up and back, with no plan to orbit as the Soviets did on their first try. Just six weeks after Gargarin's orbit, three weeks after Shepard's flight, Kennedy summoned Congress into session for a special message on "urgent national needs." In it was his famous challenge: "For while we cannot guarantee that we shall one day be first, we can guarantee that any failure to make this effort will make us last. . . . I believe that this nation should commit itself to achieving the goal, before this decade is out, of landing a man on the moon and returning him safely to earth."[15]

~ He did not think of it as a scientific endeavor worth the effort, and privately said so. What mattered to him was winning the race and showing the world American technological superiority. "No single space project in this period will be more impressive to mankind," he told Congress. For a man who had grown up with a thirst for competition and a hunger to win, who had pointed *Victura* at distant race markers and worked so intently to round them first, a race to the moon was a challenge that came more naturally to him than most. It would be an oversimplification to attribute Jack's decision to his love of sailboat racing, but it must have added subconscious allure. Historian Michael Beschloss cites three motivations: Jack's need for a "quick theatrical reversal of his administration's flagging position," vis-à-vis the Soviets; Lyndon Johnson's grab for larger "turf"; and secretary of defense Robert McNamara's desire to find a use for aerospace industrial overcapacity.[16] Surely Jack had geopolitical motivations, for other nations were choosing sides in the Cold War. He had domestic political motivations too, as voters wanted Americans to score some wins against the communists at a time of so many defeats.

Jack saw the achievement of the boldest of human endeavors as an end in itself. The decision to so audaciously redefine the competition as a race to the moon was not one others would have made. Eisenhower wrote a friend that he thought Jack's decision "almost hysterical" and "a bit immature." Ike publicly called it a "stunt" and even "nuts." When astronaut Frank Borman asked the former president to support the space program, Ike replied with a letter complaining that the moon program "was drastically revised and expanded just after the Bay of Pigs fiasco. . . . [It] immediately took one single project or experiment out of a thoroughly planned and continuing program involving communication, meteorology, reconnaissance, and future military and scientific benefits and gave the highest priority—unfortunate in my opinion—to a race, in other words, a stunt."[17]

~ The race was the point, not the science. In November 1962 Jack summoned NASA administrator James Webb to another Cabinet Room meeting that also included other NASA leaders and his own anxious budget chiefs. After reviewing the space agency's budgetary priorities, the president said to Webb, "Do you think this [moon mission] is the top-priority program of the agency?"

"No sir, I do not," said Webb. "I think it is *one* of the top-priority programs, but I think it's very important to recognize here . . ." and he listed other scientific and technical objectives.

That was not the answer Jack wanted, and in his words that followed are heard echoes of his father when the children put insufficient effort into a regatta:

> Jim, I think it is the top priority. I think we ought to have that very clear. Some of these other programs can slip six months, or nine months. . . . But this is important for political reasons, international political reasons. This is, whether we like it or not, in a sense a race. If we get second to the Moon, it's nice, but it's like being second any time. So that if we're second by six months, because we didn't give it the kind of priority, then of course that would be very serious. So I think we have to take the view that this is the top priority with us.

In that meeting, whenever Webb alluded to other scientific objectives, Jack returned his focus to the task of winning the race:

> Look, I know all these other things and the satellite and the communications and weather and all, they're all desirable, but they can wait. . . . Why are we spending seven million dollars on getting fresh water from saltwater, when we're spending seven billion dollars to find out about space? Obviously, you wouldn't put it on that priority except for the defense implications. And the second point is the fact that the Soviet Union has made this a test of the [political] system. So that's why we're doing it. So I think we've got to take the view that this is the key program. The rest of this . . . we can find out all about it, but there's a lot of things we can find out about; we need to find out about cancer and everything else.
>
> Everything that we do ought to really be tied into getting onto the Moon ahead of the Russians. . . . I do think we ought get it, you know, really clear that the policy ought to be that this is *the* top-priority program of the Agency, and one of the two things, except for defense, the top priority of the United States government. I think that that is the position we ought to take. Now, this may not change anything about that schedule, but at least we ought to be clear, otherwise we shouldn't

be spending this kind of money because I'm not that interested in space.

Then, still vividly channeling his father, Jack told Webb, "But we're talking about these *fantastic* expenditures which wreck our budget and all these other domestic programs and the only justification for it, in my opinion, to do it in this time or fashion, is because we hope to beat them and demonstrate that starting behind, as we did by a couple years, by God, we passed them."[18]

~ Shooting for the moon increasingly gained detractors who shared Ike's view. Public support waned. Roger Launius, NASA chief historian, later wrote, "While there may be many myths about Apollo and spaceflight, the principal one is the story of a resolute nation moving outward into the unknown beyond Earth."[19]

In September 1962, speaking at Rice University, Jack relied once again on the metaphor of the journeying mariner:

Those who came before us made certain that this country rode the first waves of the industrial revolutions, the first waves of modern invention, and the first wave of nuclear power, and this generation does not intend to founder in the backwash of the coming age of space.... The vows of this nation can only be fulfilled if we in this nation are first, and, therefore, we intend to be first. . . . Our obligations to ourselves as well as others all require us . . . to become the world's leading spacefaring nation. We set sail on this new sea because there is new knowledge to be gained, and new rights to be won, and they must be won and used for the progress of all people.... Only if the United States occupies a position of pre-eminence can we help decide whether this new ocean will be a sea of peace or a new terrifying theater of war. . . . As we set sail we ask God's blessing on the most hazardous and dangerous and greatest adventure on which man has ever embarked.[20]

Kennedy was far from alone in comparing the great sea ventures to space exploration, but it proved a misleading analogy. Compared to space travel, it took only a few short years for Columbus's voyage to the Americas to reap financial rewards and introduce Europe to unknown food crops that had world-changing dietary impact, particularly corn and potatoes. Popular dreams of colonizing and mining the moon and Mars never materialized. On the other hand, the gains from those objectives that Jack treated as secondary—weather satellites, GPS navigational aides, communications—in years that followed profoundly affected the day-to-day lives of humankind. The moon race enchanted and inspired billions of people, particularly young people, and it changed forever how we view our own planet. It is probably true that winning the race gave our country a lasting geopolitical edge against the Soviets. It certainly altered global perception of the two superpowers.

~ By all accounts, Jack enjoyed the personal company and conversation of his great new mariners. He invited them to the White House and to Cape Cod, peppering them with questions. John Glenn became a family friend and a frequent visitor to Hyannis Port and Hickory Hill years after Jack was gone.

Even before Glenn's famous first orbit, while he was preparing for his flight, Jack invited him to the White House and asked detailed questions about the upcoming mission. Glenn recalled,

> It was just a very cordial get-together. He just wanted to talk about what was planned on the flight, and I went into some details of what we expected to experience. In fact, later on after the flight when I came back, he recalled quite a number of these things I had said in this preflight meeting. . . . He evidently had remembered all the things we talked about that [preflight] day.
>
> He was interested very much in the anticipated G level during launch, what kind of sensations we expected during the launch, what kind of control we had over the booster during launch, were we actually going to drive it like we did an airplane or were we pretty much at the mercy of the guidance systems until we were in orbit. Problems of that nature—what pressures we would be operating under; what we would do if the pressure in the spacecraft failed. He was interested in real detail.[21]

After Glenn returned, Kennedy peppered him again. "He wanted to know about things that occurred on a space flight—what I saw, what things looked like, how I felt during reentry, was it hot or wasn't it hot, how did I feel when it banged down on the water, how did it feel when I got out. He seemed to be more interested in what had occurred on a personal experience basis rather than the scientific details of the event. What did it feel like to me as a man."[22]

Alan Shepard, whose suborbital flight preceded Glenn's, had the same experience. "I never have been able to analyze completely why he reacted this way to us, why he provided the time to be with us on these occasions and essentially on a very informal basis—access which I suppose not too many people had."

Shepard said his wife had a theory. She said he wanted to be "associated with you as a group and as individuals because of what you've done, not because of any great abilities but I suppose because of the one ability to recognize a challenge and to be willing to meet the challenge."[23]

Glenn did not think Jack's questions were rooted in concern about the feasibility of the mission. "I took it, and I think he meant it, as an interest in one human being to another—as one 'guy' to another, if you will, if you can put the president in that context."

At a ceremony, bestowing a medal on Glenn, Jack said, "Some months ago I said that I hoped every American would serve his country. Today Col. Glenn served his. . . . We have a long way to go in this space race. This is the new ocean and I believe that the United States must sail on it and be in a position second to none."[24]

Before long Glenn was sailing the old-fashioned way too. When he was a guest of the family at Hyannis Port, Ethel Kennedy invited him out on *Victura*. The president and first lady were not present at the Cape, or so Glenn thought. "I didn't feel qualified to take [it] out in the twenty-five- or thirty-knot wind blowing this particular day," said Glenn, a Korean War jet fighter pilot who only months earlier orbited the planet. "Ethel said, 'No, no, that's all right. We'll go sailing; we can take care of it all right.'"

"It was a blustery, blowing day," Glenn recalled. "Well, when my family walked from the house down toward the dock with Ethel, we could see someone working on the *Victura*. They were wearing leather jackets and old clothes, and as we got out toward the end of the dock it became a little more apparent who these people were. It was the president and Mrs. Kennedy, rigging the sails. Any doubts I had had about sailing in that weather were somewhat alleviated."

The weather was extreme enough that Jack chose not to strain his back working the tiller. Helmsman's duty went to Glenn's son, Dave. "Dave had to brace his feet and really pull on the tiller to keep things under control this particular day, and the president would give him instructions as to what direction he wanted to go and exactly how to handle things." Back and forth they went across the same harbor—the president, the astronaut and their young families—where Jack himself learned to sail, same boat, same waters, Jack's father's house ashore.[25]

~ In early 1963 the famed rocket scientist Wernher von Braun found himself at the annual Presidential Prayer Breakfast seated next to Jack's brother Ted, then the junior senator from Massachusetts. "It seemed from the way Senator Ted Kennedy spoke that the Kennedy brothers had one favorite topic when they were among themselves and that topic was spaceflight!" von Braun said shortly after Jack's death. "He was very well informed about our program and asked several questions that were amazingly similar to the questions the president himself had asked. So I can only conclude that there must have been quite a bit of discussion among the brothers on the subject."[26]

A few months later, when Jack toured Cape Canaveral and, with von Braun, saw models of rockets, he picked up one of the smaller ones and said, "So this is the Redstone." It was an early rocket, the one that got the first Americans into space but not high or fast enough to achieve orbit. To the right of the twelve-inch Redstone model was another: the Saturn V moon rocket then under development, standing nearly six feet tall. "Are these models to the same scale?" Jack asked, as von Braun and the others there nodded.

"Gee looks like we've come a long way!" said Jack.

"There was something like a boyish enthusiasm about him," said von Braun, "at the same time deeply sincere and very charming."[27]

~ Neil Armstrong, the man who set foot on the moon just six years later, died about fifty years after Jack held the little Redstone model in his hands. Eugene Cernan, the last man to walk on the moon in 1972, said Armstrong was never prouder than when he received his wings of gold, the pin he and Cernan both earned—as did Jack's brother Joe— upon first becoming naval aviators. Armstrong was buried at sea in 2012. "Maybe the sea had always made him think of endings, of the final acts of great Odysseys," wrote Ross Anderson in the *Atlantic*. "You can picture him, those 43 years ago, watching the Earth shrink in the window of the lunar module, seeing it hang, a strange moon in the abyss, a goddess robed in life-giving oceans, as blue as any seen before or since. Imagine his relief upon returning to Earth three days later, his landing cushioned by the Pacific Ocean. How good it must have felt to bob and sway in the waves that day, not even a week removed from touchdown in the Sea of Tranquility. It's hard to imagine a sweeter way to go home."[28]

~ Jack and Jackie's son, John, was born just a few days after the 1960 presidential election. About a year later Jack's father suffered a stroke. Joe lived another eight years, badly debilitated, unable to speak. "Old age is a shipwreck," Jack said then of his father.[29] Short vacation breaks at the Cape in the summers of 1962 and 1963 became occasions for the president and first lady to spend time together with both their own young children and the ailing patriarch. Rose's health remained good, and she could still enjoy the rapidly growing family of grandchildren, dominated above all by the ever-fertile Bobby and Ethel, whose children would, by 1968, number eleven in all.

As much as they loved returning to the Cape, Hyannis was never to be the same thanks to the crush of tourists, the invasive press corps, and the hovering of Secret Service agents and their security measures. Half a mile down shore from the big house, Jack and Jackie rented a house with hilltop view of the sea and more seclusion from visitors and security risk. It became the summer White House.

The summer of 1962 had several memorable Cape days in it. On one July afternoon, after a family party off Great Island, a short distance east of the compound, Jack returned on their powered yacht *Marlin* with his father and brother Ted to the harbor at Hyannis Port. The wind was blowing thirty knots, waves three feet.

"There, straining at her hawser and dipping her bow invitingly was the *Victura*, the twenty-two-foot [*sic*] sloop that the Kennedy boys used to race," reported the *New York Times*. "As soon as the President had seen his ailing father ashore, he and his brother Edward—together with other members of the family unidentifiable through binoculars from the press boat half a mile away—dropped into the *Victura*, set mainsail and jib and cast off."

"With the President at the tiller, the boat scudded out beyond the breakwater on the starboard reach. As soon as she cleared the jetty, she heeled over sharply with her port gunwales awash." After a while Jack turned the tiller over to an unidentified young boy. They returned to the harbor, dropped off the rest of the crew, then Jack and Ted headed seaward once more.

"The President has been favoring his back for some time. Today's turn at the tiller indicated that it was considerably improved," said the *Times*.[30]

A few days later Jack took Caroline out on *Victura*, then returned to board *Marlin* with Joe Sr. They anchored off Egg Island, no more than a sandbar connected to Great Island along the east side of Lewis Bay, which connects Hyannis's harbor to the Sound. The small party swam and picnicked on the sand and were eventually joined by a larger contingent of Kennedys, arriving in a flotilla consisting of *Victura* and *The Rest Of Us*.[31] Egg Island would for years come to be an almost daily summertime destination for Ethel Kennedy and a crew of children and friends, often arriving in another Wianno Senior, *Resolute*, the sister boat to *Victura*.

As news accounts of those days suggest, carloads and boatloads of reporters commonly trailed Kennedys wherever they went on Cape Cod and the islands. The coverage was friendly enough, with the occasional exception, but their constant presence was robbing the family of the refuge the place had always offered. Instead of courting *Life* photographers, the Kennedys took to dodging them and their professional brethren. The disparaging term "paparazzi" first came into usage in 1960. The family could scarcely have imagined then how Jackie, young John, and other Kennedys would spend the rest of their lives stalked by them.

~ In mid-July 1962 Jack and Jackie invited the writer William Styron and his wife for a boat ride around Martha's Vineyard, where the Styrons had a home. Styron described the voyage to his father in a letter:

> We were sitting around a big table in the open cockpit and occasionally [Jackie] would put her feet up in JFK's lap and wiggle her toes, just like you'd imagine the wife of the President to do. . . . We picked up Caroline (who had been taken ashore swimming with her little cousin while we ate) and she came aboard shivering her teeth out, a cute kid, as they say, with Irish written all over her. By this time, word had gotten around and the harbor was jammed with boats filled with people trying to get a look at their Excellencies. . . . We were about to pull into the Edgartown Yacht Club (membership composed of the blackest of black Wall Street Republicans) when all of a sudden JFK called to the Captain: "Better not put in there. Go to the town dock." And he said in an aside to me: "There's not a Democrat within three miles of heah. They'd resent it for weeks." Thus I saw, even in such a minor matter as docking a boat, the constant politicking that goes on in the Presidential mind.[32]

~ In the same month was an incident where a private sail became publicly vexing for the president. After a Sunday sail in *Victura*, Jack awoke the following day, boarded *Air Force One* for the return to Washington and opened the morning papers. Members of the press corps were aboard, as usual. Shortly after take off, the portly presidential press secretary Pierre Salinger, round faced with a Frenchman's nose, came rushing up the aisle, distressed, eyes darting around for United Press International reporter Al Spivak. The president was in a rage, Salinger told Spivak, and pointed to the UPI story only he could have written appearing on page 1 in that morning's *Washington Post* and in other papers.

"President and Family Run Aground in Sloop," was the headline the *New York Times* used for Spivak's story. "President Kennedy and other experienced sailors in his family ran aground today in a twenty-two-foot [*sic*] racing sloop while docking at a pier. To add to their embarrassment, the mainsail of the sloop *Victura* collapsed and fell overboard after the boat had been pushed free of the mud."[33]

The *Boston Globe* was even harder:

President Kennedy, who in schooldays used to race his sloop *Victura* in summer regattas, found his seamanship a little rusty yesterday.
Heading back in the *Victura* towards his father's pier here, the President missed the dock and grounded the yacht in a mud bank.
The mainsail collapsed and fell into the water as the boat was being pushed free by a secret service jet boat.[34]

The president was furious, Salinger said. The captain of America's ship of state well understood imagery and knew critics couldn't resist snarky comparisons to his presidential leadership. The president denies it ever happened, insisted Salinger, and he demands a retraction. "Spivak, are you trying to cost me my job?" The reporter saw both fear and anger in Salinger's face.

Spivak would not retract an accurate account, but he did offer a solution to Salinger's problem. He reached into a bag and pulled out a glossy photo of Jack and his crew, standing waist deep or deeper in water, trying to push *Victura* off a shoal. Salinger brought the picture back to the chief executive. Nothing further was heard about it.[35]

~ As that summer of 1962 came to an end, Jack and Jackie traveled to Newport, Rhode Island, to dine with Australian and American diplomats and sailors gathered for the America's Cup race. It was one of the few places where Jack's soul searchings about the sea could be openly expressed to an understanding audience. He was both picture painter and philosopher:

I really don't know why it is that all of us are so committed to the sea, except I think it is because in addition to the fact that the sea changes and the light changes, and ships change, it is because we all came from the sea. And it is an interesting biological fact that all of us have, in our veins the exact same percentage of salt in our blood that exists in the ocean, and, therefore, we have salt in our blood, in our sweat, in our tears. We are tied to the ocean. And when we go back to the sea, whether it is to sail or to watch it, we are going back from whence we came. Therefore, it is quite natural that the United States and Australia, separated by an ocean, but particularly those of us who regard the ocean as a friend, bound by an ocean, should be meeting today in Newport to begin this great sea competition.

He then offered a toast to the competing crews, the Australians sailing *Gretel*, and the Americans aboard *Weatherly*. "As the Ambassador said so well, they race against each other, but they also race *with* each other against the wind and the sea."[36] The *Weatherly* was skippered by Bus Mosbacher who, nineteen years earlier, sailed for Dartmouth to win the 1943 MacMillan Cup, the prize Joe and Jack won for Harvard in 1938.

On that September day in 1962, though Jack might have preferred to sail the *Weatherly*, he instead joined the first lady and boarded the USS *Joseph P. Kennedy, Jr.* to watch Mosbacher secure the cup for America. The following month the *Kennedy* sailed for Cuba.

~ The Cuban Missile Crisis of October 1962, the Kennedy presidency's greatest challenge and, in the opinion of many, the closest the world ever came to nuclear war, was on a personal level for Jack an event during which childhood memories strangely intermingled with some of the most momentous decisions any human adult ever made. One handwritten page of notes attributed to him shows the words "Blockade Cuba!" and "Castro" scribbled in pencil above a sketch of a gaff-rigged sailboat. Better-rendered and authenticated Kennedy sailboat sketches, also gaff rigged, appear on another page from a yellow legal pad of those days. From those meetings came the decision to establish a naval "quarantine," thought a less militarily provocative word than "blockade." Though the conflict was over airborne nuclear-armed missiles, it was militarily played out at sea. When the time came for a U.S. warship to physically board and inspect a ship bound for Cuba, the Lebanese merchant freighter *Marucla* was chosen. The task of executing the "first quarantine interdiction" was given to navy destroyer *Joseph P. Kennedy, Jr.*[37] This is a ship that, when launched in 1945, was "sponsored" by Jean Kennedy, Joe and Jack's youngest sister, sponsorship being a kind of feminine blessing that all male-crewed vessels received. Aboard the *Kennedy* for its 1946 shakedown cruise was apprentice seaman Robert Kennedy, who in October 1962, despite domestic duty as attorney general, was also his brother's closest and most valued White House adviser, one who could be completely trusted during the crisis.

~ In the summer of 1963, for reasons of security as well as to favor his back, Jack did little or no racing in *Victura*. Instead, he watched his youngest brother, Ted, the junior senator, compete. On several occasions they anchored or drifted aboard his father's *Marlin* or the presidential motor yacht *Honey Fitz*, just to watch Ted race *Victura*. On July 19 they cheered Ted on to second place in the Edgartown Regatta, an impressive feat according to a local journalist, who said *Victura* was "not one of the better Wianno Seniors and she may be one of the worst."[38]

On Labor Day weekend, Jack and Jackie took Caroline, five, and John Jr., two, on *Honey Fitz* for the thirty-five mile crossing to Nantucket from Hyannis Port. Jack and Jackie lunched on the boat while their two children and five other youngsters, accompanied by four Secret Service agents went ashore to tour the Brant Point coast guard station and tower. They all then motored back in time to watch Ted race *Victura*, this time finishing "a strong first in his class." That evening, easing back into the realities of official responsibility, the president entertained Vice President Lyndon Johnson at the summer White House.[39]

~ At the end of the 1963 sailing season, *Victura* made its annual sail back to Crosby Yacht Yard, where it was kept in winter. But before going into storage, it was brought out onto Nantucket Sound one more time at the request of three Kennedy sisters—Eunice, Patricia, and Jean. They had an idea. They had seen a painting of sailboats that Jackie had given to Jack as a gift in 1960. The painting had appeared in *Sports Illustrated*, where Jackie first saw it. Jackie tracked down the artist, Henry Koehler, bought the original, and shortly afterward wrote the artist, "It's by far the prettiest picture in our house and by far the only one I have given him that he actually likes."

Wanting to duplicate Jackie's success, the sisters contacted the same artist and commissioned him to create three paintings, one each of Jack, Bob, and Ted and their wives, each sailing *Victura*. The three sisters would give the paintings of *Victura* to their three brothers—the president, the attorney general, and the senator—at Christmas.

In early November the young artist, Henry Koehler, traveled from his New York City studio to Hyannis Port. *Victura* was brought out from the Crosby boat shed and two boatyard workers sailed it out into the Sound, where it met the *Marlin*. Aboard the latter were Koehler and Joe Sr. Despite the ambassador's incapacitation from his stroke, the family knew Joe would enjoy a boat ride and the opportunity to watch Koehler make sketches as *Victura* sailed back and forth for the benefit of the artist.[40]

~ On November 4, in the Oval Office, Jack picked up a Dictaphone to record for the historical record his thoughts about a coup in South Vietnam leading to the overthrow and death of President Ngo Dinh Diem and his brother. In the middle of his recording he was suddenly interrupted by his son, John, almost three. The audio betrays no difficulty transitioning from beleaguered leader to patient father.

"Do you want to say anything?" Jack asks, holding up the Dictaphone. "Say hello."

"Hello."

"Say it again."

"Naughty, naughty Daddy."

"Why do the leaves fall?"

"Because it's autumn," John answers.

"Why does the snow come on the ground?"

"Because it's winter."

"Why do the leaves turn green?"

"Because it's spring."

"When do we go to the Cape? Hyannis Port?"

"Because it's summer."

"It's summer."

John Jr. started laughing and then said, inexplicably, "your horses."[41]

~ Henry Koehler returned to his New York studio and began work on his three paintings, classical music playing on the radio as he worked. Later in November a Kennedy sister came by his East Forty-Ninth Street studio to check on his progress. Recalling the story fifty years later, Koehler could remember only that it was either Pat or Jean. "Not Eunice," he said. Preparing for the appointment, Henry turned off the radio so the conversation would be undistracted. The sister arrived, inspected his work, approved, and encouraged him to keep on. Christmas was a little more than a month away.

The Kennedy sister left and moments afterward, Koehler's phone rang. It was his fiancée.

"Do you have the radio on?" she asked.

The Kennedy sister had walked too far from the studio for Koehler to rush out and find her. What direction had she walked? He learned later that as she continued down the sidewalk someone recognized her and told her the news Koehler's fiancée had just relayed. The president had been shot in Dallas.

Fifty years later when Koehler was in his mid-eighties, he still recalls with regret that he let the Kennedy sister leave his studio. Perhaps he could have helped her, kept her safe, alerted the Secret Service to her whereabouts.[42]

That was the same morning that another sketch of *Victura*, by a less skilled artist, was being discovered by the housekeeping staff at the Rice Hotel in Houston where Jack stayed the previous day.

~ At that hour Ted was fulfilling a freshman senator's obligation by presiding over a dull session of the Senate. A press aide rushed to him and guided him from the podium to a nearby Associated Press teletype machine that was clacking out the news. Bobby was at Hickory Hill at lunch with Ethel when FBI director J. Edgar Hoover called.

Jack was the third of the nine children of Joe and Rose to die young. Ted called his mother at Hyannis Port. Rose already knew. Joe was asleep, so, by helicopter and jet, Ted hurried home to tell his father to his face. At Hyannis Port Ted found the house filling with relatives and close friends late into the night. He still hadn't talked to his father when he went to bed for an awful night's effort at sleep. He told Joe in the morning. Ted said decades later that still "the memory of that conversation brings me to tears."[43]

~ With the enormity of that tragedy, Koehler figured that was the end of his commission. They wouldn't want his paintings now, he thought. But in a few days the phone rang. How were the paintings coming along, the caller wanted to know. "Just fine," Koehler said.

"I painted with both hands" to get them finished in time, he said.

The Kennedys had their Christmas of 1963, and the paintings were presented. Later, Koehler received a letter from Jackie about the painting of Jack, which depicted her by his side: "Dear Henry, you will never know how much the painting of the *Victura* means to me, and I shall treasure it forever. You are right in saying it will serve as a constant reminder of happier days."

The letter was typewritten. Some time later Koehler received another note from Jackie, handwritten and oddly betraying a different state of mind. It rambled a bit. Jackie's secretary, Nancy Tuckerman, told Koehler the grieving widow had taken to staying up late and writing things she would normally not write. "Just don't even acknowledge the letter," Tuckerman said. Jackie's letter asked Koehler if he would repaint the picture, take her out of it entirely, and recast Jack as "vague and far away."

Koehler did not respond.[44]

~ A week after the president's death the *New Yorker* magazine appeared on newsstands. Less than 20 years earlier the *New Yorker* was first to publish John Hersey's tale of PT-109. Now its cover was a painting of simple sailboats at dusk docked in front of a boatyard dock house, beneath a bridge carrying New York commuter trains over a river. The boat sketches had the simplicity of one of Jack's doodles. Inside the magazine, E. B. White's reflection on Jack stated, "When we think of him, he is without a hat, standing in the wind and the weather. He was impatient of topcoats and hats, preferring to be exposed, and he was young enough and tough enough to confront and to enjoy the cold and the wind of these times, whether the winds of nature or the winds of political circumstance and national danger. He died of exposure, but in a way that he would have settled for—in the line of duty, and with his friends and enemies all around, supporting him and shooting at him. It can be said of him, as of few men in a like position, that he did not fear the weather, and did not trim his sails, but instead challenged the wind itself, to improve its direction and cause it to blow more softly and more kindly over the world and its people."[45]

~ Jack once said, "I always come back to the Cape and walk on the beach when I have a tough decision to make. The Cape is the one place I can think and be alone."[46]

In the days that followed Jack's death, Ted took many long walks there. "I was out of sight of anyone else," he said, "just the sea on one side of me and the sand on the other, that I would let go of my self-control." As for his brother, Bobby's grief was so deep it frightened Ted.[47]

CHAPTER 8

Bobby and Ethel

The casket was placed in the East Room of the White House. After midnight Bobby and Jackie approached it together, raised the lid, and placed personal objects to be buried with Jack. There were letters by Jackie, Caroline, and John; a pair of Jack's cuff links that had been her gift to him; and a piece of scrimshaw. Bobby added an engraved silver rosary that Ethel had given him for their wedding. Bobby, wearing a PT-109 tiepin, a popular accoutrement since the campaign, unclipped it and placed it with the other items. Jackie cut a lock of Jack's hair.[1]

"The whole family was like a bunch of shipwreck survivors," said Lem Billings. "I don't think they could have made it at all without Bobby. He seemed to be everywhere. He always had an arm around a friend or family member and was telling them it was okay, that it was time to move ahead."[2]

After the funeral Jackie spent several months at Hyannis Port. She poured effort into a memorial issue of *Look* magazine, choosing quotations from favorite authors, including Tennyson's "Ulysses." Less than a year after Jack's death, Bobby appeared before the 1964 Democratic National Convention and read from Shakespeare's *Romeo and Juliet*, a literary flourish Jackie supplied, just as she had so often done for Jack.

> . . . when he shall die
> Take him and cut him out into stars,
> And he will make the face of heaven so fine
> That all the world will be in love with night
> And pay no worship to the garish sun.[3]

At the Cape Jackie enjoyed watching her children by the sea, and Bobby and Ted took Caroline and John sailing with the other children. But no place reminded Jackie of Jack more than Hyannis Port, and that made it hard. She moved her children to New York City in 1964 and took up summer residence at Martha's Vineyard, close but not too close to the Kennedy Compound, a short sail or ferry ride away.

~ Bobby shared the family love of sailing and, as an adult, acquired some beautiful sailboats, including the fifty-foot yawl *Glide* that his widow Ethel, his children, and extended family sail to this day. But he was never in his youth the sailing competitor his brothers were.

Eight years and four sisters separated Jack's birth from Bob's when he arrived in 1925. The familiar images of Jack and Bobby are of brothers side by side in the White House, but in the 1930s their age difference caused teen Jack to pay little attention to the youngster Bobby. Said Jack, "The first time I remember meeting Bobby was when he was three and a half, one summer at the Cape."[4]

From a young age Robert felt a need to please; "the nicest little boy I ever met," said a lifelong friend of Jack's. Awkward and shy, he was accident prone and fearful of being anything less than perfectly punctual.[5] As a boy he had an earnestness and altar boy's sense of moral responsibility that as an adult transformed into passionate and righteous feelings about social justice. Perhaps he lacked a passion for sailing because it was hard to see the point of competitiveness for its own sake. What was the purpose, since the outcome was merely first across a finish line? Competition for a purpose was something Bob better understood.

In the summer of 1940 Rose wrote her husband that Jack was enjoying "the most astounding success" with his book *Why England Slept*, but she said his fourteen-year-old younger brother was another matter. "Bobby is a different mold. He does not seem to be interested in reading or sailing or his stamps. He does a little work in all three but no special enthusiasm." Later that summer she told Joe, "I am trying to get Bob to do some reading. He doesn't seem to care for sailing as much as the other boys. Of course he doesn't want to go to any dances."[6]

In 1942 Bobby's letter from boarding school again showed something of his parents' priorities: "My sailing so far has been awful, and I lost a race yesterday in which I sailed poorly." For sport, he sought firmer footing by trying track, "to see if I can't run faster."[7]

That summer Jack visited Hyannis Port on leave from the navy. He raced *Victura* to third place in a Senior-class race in June. A few weeks later it was Bobby's turn to skipper *Victura*. He came in thirteenth out of fifteen.

Back at school in the fall, Bobby wrote his mother, "We got our marks on Wed. and I'm afraid I flunked math, but it's getting better all the time." In a letter to his father, though, things were looking up: "On our last day of school the math teacher made a small speech to the class in which he said that two great things had happened to him, one that Rommel was surrounded in Egypt and 2nd that Kennedy had passed a math test."[8]

Bobby turned seventeen on November 20, and though the Kennedy children had eight siblings, they all wrote one another on birthdays. Bobby heard from them all, and selected three to quote directly in a letter to his parents, suggesting his mother add them to the round-robin summaries of correspondence she circulated within the family. "Here are quotes from your two older sons and smart daughter in Washington," he wrote. His two big brothers took special note that Bobby was a year from eligibility for military service:

Joe: "The army and I wish you a very happy birthday [and] are eagerly awaiting your next one. Brother Joe." (Joe Jr. was in the navy, so perhaps Bobby's quote is inaccurate.)

Jack: "Both Uncle Sam and I express our hardiest congratulations to you on the occasion of your birthday as does General Hershey. Jack." Hershey was the recently appointed director of the Selective Service.

Kathleen: "Just because you're ugly and only seventeen, don't think we don't love you and think you're rather keen. Kick"[9]

The terrible events of the two years that followed pressured Bob to grow up faster than he might otherwise. That was the time when Jack's PT-109 sank, followed by four awful months of 1944, during which Kick married over her mother's strenuous objections, brother Joe's plane exploded near France, and Kick's new husband was shot dead in battle. Just week's after Joe's loss, Bob entered Harvard.

Joe Sr. and Rose, so in control of their children's prior lives, now saw events careening out of control. It might help explain Joe's emotional reaction not long afterward when Robert brought his new Harvard friend,

Kenny O'Donnell, home to Hyannis Port. At dinner Bobby and Kenny joked and kidded each other about finishing last in a sailing race. Joseph Kennedy was outraged. "What kind of guys are you to think that's funny?" he fumed, then stood and left the table.[10]

~ Joe's disapproval was hard on Bob, who had adopted his parents' habits of structure, punctuality, and discipline. But Bob eventually came to meet a woman so rebellious and undisciplined that he found the contrast with himself positively delightful. Skiing in Quebec in 1945, Bob's sister Jean introduced him to her college roommate, Ethel. She was of the Skakel family of Chicago, one that often did not know if dinner would be at five or ten. Her father's self-made millions came from turning a small business into the Great Lakes Carbon Corporation. There Ethel rode horses and learned to sail at Larchmont Yacht Club from Cory Shields, a boat designer and sailing enthusiast of such renown his image was on the cover of *Time* Magazine in 1953.[11] She was a yacht club race champ at eleven. A yearbook said of her, "An excited hoarse voice, a shriek, a peal of screaming laughter, the flash of shirttails, a tousled brown head—Ethel! Her face is at one moment a picture of utter guilelessness and at the next alive with mischief."[12]

~ Bobby's short romance was interrupted when he found an opportunity to uniquely but briefly serve in the navy. He had been in the Naval Reserve Officers' Training Corps at Harvard. When the navy destroyer *Joseph P. Kennedy, Jr.* was readied for its maiden voyage, Bobby, without his family's knowledge, appealed directly to the secretary of the navy, James V. Forrestal, to be allowed to serve as seaman. He and the *Kennedy* set sail for Guantánamo Bay, Cuba, on February 1, 1946. His duties, he wrote, began among the "the lowest grade of chippers, painters & scrubbers," but he showed resilience to seasickness—in contrast to some shipmates—and a facility for celestial navigation.[13]

Honorably discharged after four months' service, he returned home just in time for the final days of his brother Jack's first campaign for a congressional primary nomination, which, in the overwhelmingly Democratic district, was as good as winning the seat. Jack's sister Jean had recruited her friend Ethel to join the campaign, which facilitated Bobby's rekindling of the relationship he had begun with Ethel before his sea duty. Jack won his election, of course, and Ethel in those months secured from Jack help with her college thesis, which she based on his book, *Why England Slept.*

Bob returned to finish at Harvard. His academic performance was unremarkable, but for his size he had notable success on a football team that also had war veterans on the GI Bill. As a senior he scored a touchdown in the first game. He broke his leg in practice shortly afterward, but kept playing until he collapsed.

Just as older brothers passed their sailing skills on to Bob, so too was the habit of losing crew in mid-sail. The Kennedy DNA must have an amphibian chromosome or two, for they move from boat to water with careless ease, thinking nothing of abandoning the security of cockpit for the embrace of the sea. Bob surprised acquaintances with this quality. With an inexperienced visitor crewing for him and lunchtime approaching, the wind failed, making it impossible to get ashore in time to live up to Joe Sr.'s expectations of punctuality.

"Bobby stood up and dove into the water. He yelled back that mooring the boat was up to me," recalled James Noonan, who knew nothing of sailing. "I foundered around the harbor for what seemed to be endless hours. After a few near collisions in my futile attempt to reach the mooring, I decided it was best to stay in the outer harbor, away from traffic." Finally, a passing boat helped get him ashore. When he saw Bob that evening, he told him of the ordeal he had caused. "To him my story was comedy at its best. His reaction—'terrific, kid, but we've got to do something about your sailing!'" This was not, by the way, adolescent self-centeredness. Bob was twenty-two.[14]

~ The first time Ethel sailed with Bob in *Victura* was in a hurricane. It might have been the year they were married, because in early September 1950, a hurricane came within two hundred miles of Cape Cod, a weather event of particular menace in a vessel as small as *Victura*. Ethel loved every minute of that sail. The boat showed all its resilience in the highest winds and waves. They made the long crossing to Nantucket and along for the adventure were Bob's sister Jean and Bob's Harvard roommate George Terrien, who a few years later married Ethel's sister, Georgeanne. "A lot of connections were made on those boats in that generation," remarked Bob's son Chris.[15]

Bob was the seventh born of the Kennedy children but the first of the surviving children to marry. They were wed June 17, 1950, when Bob was twenty-four and Ethel twenty-two, giving Joe and Rose their first grand-child in 1951. Honoring Kick, who died three years before, and Kick's late husband, they named the baby Kathleen Hartington Kennedy. Their second child, born a year later, was christened Joseph Patrick Kennedy II, named for Bob's late big brother rather than his father. Nine more children would be born to Bob and Ethel, the youngest still in the womb when Bob died.

Bob saw in Ethel a personality that counterbalanced his own. She was funny, tireless, extroverted, competitive, a thrower of parties. Her face always burst with hilarity and playfulness. Where Bob was introverted and serious, she was neither. Life dealt her blows, but she didn't change much; fifty years later when her daughter Rory tried to interview her for a documentary, she burst out, "All this introspection—I hate it!"[16] She lived for the moment, and it was a good perspective, given those in her family who died young, robbed of such moments.

~ In September 1951 Bob set off with his congressman brother Jack on their twenty-five-thousand-mile tour of Israel and Asia, a voyage that cemented the bonds between the much younger brother and the older. A year later Bob was thriving as a Justice Department investigator when he reluctantly agreed to put his career on hold to help his older brother, whose campaign for the U.S. Senate against incumbent Henry Cabot Lodge was floundering. Bob became campaign manager. Bob's performance in the role impressed all but the old-school Boston Democrats for whom the twenty-six-year-old had little patience and no trouble offending. The dynamic chemistry of Jack's and Bob's contrasting personalities is much written about, and, to be sure, Bob had one of the most complicated and interesting personalities of the entire family. Bob was less cerebral, more intense, less tolerant of injustice, more loyal to family, less capable of emotional detachment, more enraptured by his life with wife and children. Bob and Jack proved to be unalike in useful and complimentary ways, much as Bob and Ethel were.

As Jack entered the Senate and his fiancée, Jackie, entered the family, the Bouvier from East Hampton was so dissimilar from the Skakel of Chicago that neither was much interested in the approval of the other. The family dynamic soon grew even more complex as marriages introduced other new in-laws: Sargent Shriver in 1953, Peter Lawford and Stephen Edward Smith in 1954, and Joan Bennett Kennedy in 1958. It was a time of marriages and pregnancies, especially for Ethel. Having eleven children was made slightly easier if you so firmly believed as she did in letting them off on their own, little supervised, to make their own mistakes. Some faulted Ethel for that, but none of them had eleven children.

Airplanes figure prominently in the fate of Kennedys and Skakels both. In 1955 both Ethel's parents were killed in a plane that crashed near Union City, Oklahoma. Bob, who already had experience with the grief that accompanies sudden losses and who came to show unusual sensitivity to the suffering of others, was a great comfort to her. Also of comfort to Ethel was her deep Catholic faith, a trait shared with Rose, one that clearly helped them both at many difficult times, before and after that crash.

~ The Kennedy family had been famous since the New Deal, and Jack's rise to national prominence was appropriately regarded by the media as both an individual and a family achievement. Bob's fame grew too as he and Jack had greater accomplishments, individually and together. When Jack lost the vice presidential nomination at the Democratic Convention in 1956, and then sought the presidential nomination four years later, Bob was tactician in the convention floor battles, which in those years actually decided outcomes.

In those thousand days between 1961 and 1963, when the possibility of global nuclear annihilation was as real as at any time in history and when domestic racial conflict was so ugly, deadly, and tense, it is hard to imagine any family with more power than the Kennedys. For a family with a global reach of influence at a time of such turbulence, Hyannis Port provided rootedness, connection to family, and simple pleasures. From the summer of Jack's first year as president, there survives a photo of a shirtless Bob steering *Victura*, children gunwale to gunwale. Three kids from the Shriver household are aboard—little Maria, Bobby, and Pat Prusyewski, who was in the family's care. Also in the crew were Bob's own children, Courtney, Bobby Jr., David, and Kathleen. This was a typical sail for Bob and Ethel: when anyone wanted aboard there was always room to squeeze one more.

Bob was Jack's controversial choice for attorney general; Sargent Shriver was Jack's director of the new Peace Corps; Ted was Jack's replacement in the U.S. Senate; and Stephen Smith was slated to be campaign manager for Jack's planned reelection campaign of 1964. Every branch of the Kennedy family had two lives, the public life on a global arena centered in Washington DC and life at Hyannis Port, where they and their families lived next door to one another, sailed together, and raised children. Sister Patricia and her husband, Peter Lawford, were a bit of an exception, but they visited often and provided an important entertainment industry connection of considerable political value.

For Bob and Ethel there were many family cruises on *Victura*, but not so much racing. The club races were held on both Saturday and Sunday, with crews of no more than four, exceptions sometimes allowed for an extra child. This would take Bob away from his ever-growing family, a sacrifice that held no interest for him when he could cruise with as many as possible. Bob's male siblings raced more because they married later and had children later in life. Son Chris has observed among sailor friends a strong correlation between the births of children and the selling of beloved sailboats.

Even inside the Washington Beltway, removed from their Cape home, the Robert Kennedys manifested fondness for water in particularly infamous ways. Ethel, with a bemused but no-doubt alarmed Bob's acquiescence, presided over raucous pool parties with the most influential figures of the day. There was the 1961 party to celebrate their eleventh anniversary, recorded by guest and historian Arthur Schlesinger in his journal:

In the later stages of the evening, Teddy Kennedy emerged as the dominant figure, singing, plunging fully dressed into the swimming pool and demonstrating in general that the Kennedy vitality is far from extinct in the lower reaches of the family. Judy Garland, Kay Thompson and Ethel sang; there was wild dancing, in which I took an enthusiastic but inexpert part; and around four in the morning, as things began to grow increasingly uninhibited, with more and more people being pushed into the pool, I decided that the better part of valor would be to go home. As Teddy emerged from the pool, a huge dripping mass in a now hopelessly rumpled dinner jacket, Ben Bradlee said, "It's just like a horror movie."[17]

Bejeweled-guest-in-the-pool parties were repeated. At a 1962 party for Peter and Patricia Lawford, the dunking started with Ethel—"evening dress, shoes and all," said the *Washington Star*—when her chair leg, perched precariously on a plank extended across the water, slipped. Others followed her into the pool, involuntarily or otherwise, at that and subsequent parties. Among the baptized were Schlesinger, defense secretary Robert McNamara, Jack's press secretary Pierre Salinger, Ethel's friend Sarah Davis and various celebrities and members of the cabinet. Characterized by a news magazine as "near misses" were astronaut John Glenn and Supreme Court justice Byron White. After a few such press accounts, Jack is said to have called Ethel and suggested that it would be fine if she and Bob weren't in the newspapers for a few months.[18]

Jack and Bobby and their wives had different social styles, but together Jack and Bob were two parts of a whole. "It was very funny, so often people said they couldn't understand their dialogue," recalled Ethel. "And it was because one of them would start a sentence and the other would finish it. He knew exactly where the other one was going."[19] John Seigenthaler saw that too: "One would start a sentence; the other would finish it. . . . It was as close to one heartbeat, one pulse beat, as you could get."[20]

~ The gaiety of those days made the nightmare of Jack's death all the more unbearable. And all the world watched them. Fame became martyrdom, forever altering the world's emotional reaction to the name "Kennedy."

Jack was buried on the Monday before Thanksgiving, a holiday until then invariably spent at Hyannis Port. Bob could not bear to go back. Decades later Ethel told her daughter Rory, "it was like Daddy had lost both arms."[21] In the days leading to and after the funeral Bob was strong and attentive to family and friends, writing letters to each of his children on the day of the burial. But in the winter that followed the assassination, he was crippled by his grief and turned darkly inward. One biographer said, "He literally shrank, until he appeared wasted and gaunt. His clothes no longer fit . . . [including] a leather bomber jacket with the presidential seal—which he insisted on wearing and which hung on his narrowing frame. . . . [His grief] seemed too overwhelming, so all consuming."[22]

Ethel again found solace in her faith, including her conviction that those who die watch over, and wait for us, in heaven. Bobby drew little solace from that. Having lived tragedies of Greek or Shakespearian dimension, he sought to make sense of it through the classics—Aeschylus and Shakespeare, Emerson and Camus.

In the spring of 1964 Jackie gave him a copy of Edith Hamilton's *The Greek Way*. Of Aeschylus, Hamilton wrote, "Life for him was an adventure, perilous indeed, but men are not made for safe havens. The fullness of life is in the hazards of life. And, at the worst, there is that in us which can turn defeat into victory."[23]

One passage from Aeschylus's *Agamemnon* Bob committed to memory. It meant a lot for a grieving brother, and he paraphrased it in one of the most moving impromptu speeches in modern history, in Indianapolis, telling a crowd not all aware that Martin Luther King had just died, "In our sleep, pain which cannot forget falls drop by drop upon the heart until in our own despair, against our will, comes wisdom through the awful grace of God."[24]

~ The presence of his growing number of children, Ethel said, helped pull Bob out of his despair.[25] In the summer of 1964 their oldest son, Joe, was approaching his twelfth birthday and showing a growing enthusiasm for sailing. It was time for Bob and Ethel's family to have a boat of their own to race against *Victura* and the south Cape fleet of Wianno Seniors. Hull #132 was christened *Resolute*. It was the name of the British ship from whose timbers Jack's Oval Office desk was made, and it was perhaps the legend of the original ship and its lessons of tenacity and survival that made the name *Resolute* resonate with Robert and Ethel.

From that summer there is an Associated Press photo of young Joe sailing *Victura*, hull #94, with sails displaying *Resolute*'s #132, giving a new set of sails a try on the older boat. For years another photo, taken on the day the family took delivery of their boat, hung on the second floor of Ethel's Cape house wall, showing young Joe on *Resolute*, riding in the cockpit as it was lowered into the water. New Seniors were still made of wood then, all built at the Crosby Yacht Yard, about three miles across Centerville Harbor from the Kennedys' Hyannis Port seaside homes. With Joe, as the boat entered water, was Jack Fallon, a now legendary Senior sailor who took to mentoring younger Kennedys in those years.[26]

Resolute became *Victura*'s sister boat, with various family members out in one or the other, in big races or one-on-one match races or cruising, every day no matter the weather. Jackie's children, John Jr. and Caroline, joined for a sail from time to time. Ted and Joan's first two children were born in 1960 and 1961 and would soon be sailing. The children of Joe Sr. and Rose, now having children of their own, were replicating that decade of the 1930s as best they could, albeit with the ever-present eye of reporters and Kennedy gawkers gazing from the shoreline.

Bobby lasted less than a year more as President Lyndon Johnson's attorney general, resigning to run for a U.S. Senate seat in New York, which he won by 719,693 votes in November 1964. To the election night campaign workers celebrating his victory, he turned to Tennyson's "Ulysses" as had his brother: "Come, my friends, / 'Tis not too late to seek a newer world."[27]

Jackie's influence lingered. She once wrote to Rose recalling how she had shown that poem to her husband, and then, "Later I showed Bobby the poem and he fell in love with it. He often used in his speeches the lines, 'Come my friends / 'tis never [*sic*] too late to seek a newer world.' That is really what Bobby's message and dream was, wasn't it?"[28] In 1967, as he positioned himself to run for president, Bob published a collection of his views on the major issues facing the nation. His book, *To Seek a Newer World*, opened with the familiar lines from Tennyson.

~ In those summers, in the larger sailboats of friends, Bob and Ethel took cruises up to the coast of Maine, overcrowded with children and guests, haphazard in their stowing of gear, food, and belongings. One whose coastal home they visited along the way said they navigated with highway maps, even though the rocky coast defeated many another boat.[29]

Whether sailing off the Maine Coast or kayaking down rapids, Bob alarmed not a few by his propensity to leap for a swim into roiling surf. Once, when Jack was president and cruising at a good clip in the *Honey Fitz*, Bobby was cruising alongside in the *Marlin* with other members of the clan, too numerous to fit on one boat. Jack called to his dog in the opposite boat, "How's it going with you, Charlie," prompting the dog to leap into waves between them. The dog looked at risk of being caught in the propellers, so Bobby impulsively leapt in after him, disappearing beneath the surf to fetch him back.

Ted was once overheard telling his niece Caroline, Jack's daughter, how extraordinarily powerful his brothers were as swimmers. "I remember how as teenagers in Florida, your father and Bobby, on even the roughest of days, would swim miles out into the ocean," Ted told Caroline, shortly after her brother, John F. Kennedy Jr., died piloting his own plane. "They had an insatiable appetite for adventure. The storm-warning flags would be flapping furiously in the wind and rain, and they'd be frolicking in the surf like a couple of polar bears. Your brother was cut from the same cloth. He loved a challenge. He'd kayak in the most turbulent seas and fly under conditions that grounded even the most experienced pilots. Like Bobby and your father, he had the desire to live life to the fullest."[30]

On one sailing cruise in 1965 in rough seas, with Bobby, Ethel, and most of the children aboard, the coast guard was sent on an hours-long search for the Kennedy vessel. Finding it, the cutter pulled close as it could in the waves and, with a bullhorn, informed them that fourteen-year-old daughter Kathleen had been injured when her horse, Attorney General, tripped trying to clear a hurdle. Her head injury left her unconscious. Insisting he be at her side, Bob leapt into waves of at least ten feet and swam the fifty-yard distance separating him from the coast guard cutter, which pulled him in and powered him ashore.[31]

Bob's passion for adventure, always extraordinary, remained so despite the responsibilities that come with the death of siblings and the abundance of dependent children. In the Canadian Yukon was a peak the government renamed "Mount Kennedy" in honor of the late president, roughly 370 miles east of Anchorage, Alaska. At fourteen thousand feet, it was the highest in North America never to have been climbed by any human, at least not in recorded history. Bob joined an expedition to be the first to scale it. It was led by Jim Whittaker, the first American to climb Mount Everest, an achievement that earned him the National Geographic Society's Hubbard Award, presented by President Kennedy in the White House Rose Garden in 1963. It was an extraordinary physical challenge for a man not accustomed to mountain climbing, but Whittaker let Bobby push ahead and be first at the peak. There, so far from sea level, Bob left three gold PT-109 tie clasps like the one he left in his brother's casket and an encased copy of his brother's inaugural address. Bob's picture at the summit was on the cover of *Life* and chronicled in *Sports Illustrated*.

"He hated every minute of it," Ethel said.[32]

"I'd never go back up there again," Bob said, once down from the mountain. "I understand why climbers like it. They are a special breed of men. I'm mindful of the story General Maxwell Taylor tells of reviewing paratroopers during World War II. Each man in turn said that he had become a paratrooper because he liked to jump. Finally Taylor told them, 'I don't like to jump, but I like to be with people who like to jump.' Well, I like to be with people who like to climb. But I don't want to climb again. It's not exactly a pleasant experience. I kept thinking, 'How did I get myself into this?'" Then he got on a plane for Seattle and pulled over his head a worn old cashmere sweater. Like a sweater from boarding school, the original owner's name was inked onto the neck label: John F. Kennedy.[33]

~ Bob did like to be with Jim Whittaker, and he became a family friend. Whittaker visited Hickory Hill and went on adventurous vacations with the family and their widening circle of friends, people like Andy Williams and his wife, Claudine; George Plimpton; Henry Mancini; and Art Buchwald. Jackie, Caroline, and John Jr. were sometimes along. At one dinner John Glenn arose to propose a toast: "To Jim Whittaker," said the astronaut. "The first American to summit Everest. And a chimp didn't do it before him!"[34]

Three years after their climb Whittaker was put in charge of Bob's presidential campaign in the states of Washington and Oregon. In April 1968 Bob appeared at the Ramada Inn at a professional journalists' conference in Tualatin, Oregon, where Whittaker would surely have been, and in his speech quoted "Ulysses" again:

> The lights begin to twinkle from the rocks;
> The long day wanes: the slow moon climbs; the deep
> Moans round with many voices. Come, my friends,
> 'Tis not too late to seek a newer world.

Two months later Bob's campaign gained momentum with a pivotal win in California. Whittaker gathered his volunteers to watch as the results came in and confirmed the victory. Bob called and spoke to Whittaker's volunteers over a speakerphone, concluding by saying, "Thanks, Jim, for helping to pull me up." Then Bob gave his victory speech at the hotel and was guided to a shortcut through a hotel kitchen, where he encountered a Palestinian militant who fired a .22 caliber handgun, hitting Bob twice in the back and once in the head.

It took a day for him to die. Whittaker got the call and immediately left to be with his fellow adventurer and Ethel.

"Alone with Ethel and Teddy in the hospital room that night, I held Bobby's hand and wept," said Whittaker. "At 1:44 a.m., as Ethel and I held him, he turned gray and cold. Ethel fainted. I gathered her up and, while Teddy held the door, carried her to a room they had reserved for her. I held her until she regained consciousness."[35]

~ Kennedys sometimes write letters to one another to document important moments, and this was Ted's to the children of Bob and Ethel, written a few months later:

> When I think of Bobby, I shall always see Cape Cod on a sunny day. The wind will be from the southwest and the whitecaps will be showing and the full tide will be sweeping through the gaps in the breakwater. It will be after lunch, and Bob will be stripped to the waist and he'll say, "Come on, Joe, Kathleen, Bobby and David, Courtney, Kerry, come on Michael, and even you Chris and Max—call your mother and come for a sail." One of the children would say, "What about the

baby?" and the father would reply, "Douglas can come next year." They push off from the landing. The sails of the *Resolute* catch the wind, and the boat tips and there are squeals of laughter from the crew. And Bob says, "I think today is the day we'll tip over" and there are more squeals and the *Resolute* reaches toward the end of the breakwater. . . . He will dive overboard and catch hold of the line that trails behind, inviting the children to join him. Child after child jumps into the water, grabbing for the line, and those who appear to miss it are pulled toward it by his strong and suntanned arms.[36]

Ted's letter was included in a privately published book of remembrances of Bob, edited by Patricia Lawford. Jackie contributed a quote from Lawrence Durrell's *Reflections on a Marine Venus*, which she said were written about a statue but expressed how she felt without Bobby:

Ahead of us the night gathers, a different night, and Rhodes begins to fall into the unresponding sea from which only memory can rescue it. The clouds hang high over Anatolia. Other islands? Other futures?

Not, I think, after one has lived with the Marine Venus. The wound she gives one must carry to the world's end.[37]

~ For decades afterward Ethel and Eunice sailed every day in their Wianno Seniors *Resolute* and *Headstart*, respectively. The Kennedys will be the first to say they are privileged and that among the privileges is sailing as frequently as they do in such a beautiful setting. Offshore from their cluster of handsome Cape homes, even when keeping warm requires many bulky layers of sea garb, when the winds are good, which is every day, they sail. Every day. Of course there are exceptions, but they are not the rule. Kennedys travel and reside far from the Cape, spread out to adopted new homes in New York, Baltimore, Chicago, and California, and they enthusiastically obligate themselves and their time to important social, political, and philanthropic causes, but they are fortunate enough, and know it, to have more time than most to sail. A few of them are always around Hyannis Port to skipper or crew a boat.

Bob was forty-two when he died. About a month after his death, Arthur Schlesinger wrote, "I went on to Hyannis Port, where I have gone so many times in the last nine years and had such happy times. Now John Kennedy is gone, and Robert Kennedy is gone, and the effort to keep things going as they always were breaks one's heart." Ethel was playing tennis when he arrived. "Then we went into the bay for the usual picnic. Ethel wanted to go on the sailboat."[38]

Ethel's picnic sails continue to this day, the ritual of gathering children and packing coolers becoming rote as the years passed. In the summers after Bob died, their son Chris said, the kids were all summoned to the dock to head out, each day, "twelve-thirty, no screwing around. Unless it was raining. But it didn't matter what the weather. If there was no wind or howling, howling wind . . . and in the afternoons there it will blow 25 almost every day, almost guaranteed. It'll start light and then by three, four o'clock it will build and then it dissipates by six-thirty, seven o'clock."[39]

"Every day without fail," said Chris's sister Kerry. "It didn't matter how many people were at the house. Everybody was invited, everybody knew they were invited at all times. I never once heard my mother say, 'oh no we're too crowded, why don't you go on another boat.' She loved having as many people as possible. We would sail to Great Island or Egg Island, a sandbar, or sometimes to Stinkpot Cove."[40]

Interviewed in 2012, a childhood friend of some of Bob and Ethel's children remembered joining the crowded picnic sails, amply provisioned, that usually included a bottle of Pouilly-Fuissé for the adults. "Picnics on the *Resolute* were legendary," wrote Chris, "and most of our cousins would follow us to whatever our destination to get fed. Great Gramma Rose, watching from the window, not sure she approved of the lavishness, referred to them as 'The Moveable Feast.'"[41]

"We would have two or three coolers," Chris continued. "There were dozens of Cokes, root beer, ginger ale, Orange Crush and Concord grape drinks. Plus bottles of Pouilly-Fuissé, Heinekens and a separate cooler of daiquiris . . . [and] the best iced tea I have ever had," from a recipe of the Royal Hawaiian Hotel on Oahu, where Ethel and Bob honeymooned. There was a thermos of clam chowder and Tupperware filled with tuna salad, "served by whoever chose the wrong seat, which meant that they had to sit next to the cooler and spoon the tuna salad onto Cars table water crackers, for the whole crowd. There were usually 15 sandwiches of all varieties from steak (cooked just for the sandwiches) to peanut butter and jelly, some with and some without the crust. A couple of days each week we would also have fried chicken."[42]

More than forty years later, in 2012, on a sail aboard *Glide* with Ethel and members of the family, out came fried chicken, cupcakes, and, sure enough, a nice bottle of Pouilly-Fuissé.[43]

Their destination was often Egg Island, the same sandy beach to which Jack took Caroline, a short two-mile sail east from Hyannis Port, across the mouth of Lewis Bay. "Island" was a misnomer; it was only a sand bar that rose above the water's surface as the tide ran out, then was re-submerged at high tide. It was a popular place to sun and rest and toss a ball while Ethel stayed on the boat and finished a crossword puzzle. In the early days Grandpa Joe's *Marlin* would be there and *Resolute* could tie to it. But without the *Marlin*, the approach to the shore and anchoring could be tricky. They found there a friend willing to help with the heavy anchor.

They called him "Putt," because of the noise made by the old outboard motor on his fishing boat. A World War I veteran, he lived in a harbor-side shack and was rumored to have lost the ability to speak after a gas attack in the trenches. "He'd watch us land at Great Island and just shake his head," said Ethel, recalling he always wore the same old baggy pants. "He was really skinny, like an island lookout," said Chris, who perhaps as a child on the beach daydreamed of his Uncle Jack's wartime Pacific survival story and his native rescuers.[44] Putt "was not much bigger than we were as kids . . . and he was missing most of his teeth." So day after day Putt helped with the anchor, too heavy for the children. "He kept an eye on the currents lapping at the Resolute, cleating a loose line or hauling in a trailing life vest, probably wondering how we made it over without him and how in the world we would make it back on our own. Putt's twinkling eyes peering out of a grizzled face made it clear he relished the company of the high-spirited children and the pride he took in looking out after us," wrote Chris.[45]

"His IQ must have been off the charts," marveled Ethel, noting how well he communicated despite his speech impediment.[46] She regretted never seeing the scraps of paper on which he would frequently scribble notes. Before setting out for Egg Island, Ethel made sure to include a couple of beers and sandwiches for Putt.[47]

~ Sailing the *Resolute*, loaded with children and adult guests and coolers, in those waters required a constant outfoxing of the shoals, the underwater sand dunes, always shifting to someplace unexpected. Seniors are shallow keeled for this reason, but not shallow enough for Ethel. She was always running aground. "I lost more pairs of shoes getting out to push that boat off," recalled Tim Fulham, a friend of the children.[48]

Ethel blamed some of the groundings on her sister-in-law, who sailed the Shriver Wianno Senior, *Headstart*, making a game of pestering Ethel. "I'd race Eunice. Eunice would try to put me aground every day, she kept heading up and heading up!"[49] Eunice's son Mark, hearing Ethel's version of events, said, "That's a ridiculous exaggeration," and laughed. "No, I don't think mummy or Ethel had problems running aground, they did it by themselves regularly. They'd cut across sandbars and either forget or not pay close attention to the tide."

On return, when the boat was sharply heeling under a steady strong wind, and if there were no gusts, the sail practically touching the water, Ethel let the children scamper, "up the outstretched sail and try to touch the top of the mast before sliding back to the bottom of the sail and resting again on the boom. . . . The only time sitting on the boom ever caused a problem was when Rory took her dog Spanky up there," recalled Chris of his sister. The pet's paw nails scratched through the sail and Spanky fell right through the hole, requiring a quick jibe by Ethel and a rescue. Promptly written was a new rule about dogs on the boom.[50]

One particular sail involved a hasty and more-chaotic-than-usual boarding and launching of *Resolute*. No one took time to pump water from the bilge, so it was carrying weight before anyone even boarded. In the telling of the story the children apparently enjoy exaggerating details for the fun of hearing Ethel's vehement denials. The water in the bilge was "over the bunk racks!" Chris said. Never ones to concern themselves much with a Senior's weight capacity, they were entertaining fifteen to twenty visitors from Ireland that day, a hard-to-imagine crew size, given the boat's dimensions. Three oversized coolers were so overpacked that sandwiches in baggies were left unstowed around the cuddy cabin and cockpit.

They made it to Egg Island safely enough, enjoyed a visit, then, running behind schedule, pointed *Resolute* homeward toward the channel crossing. As skipper, Ethel thought she'd try a shortcut across a sandbar. The boat, well-heeled by a strong wind, cut through the waves. Suddenly the keel hit bottom. *Resolute* pivoted. The wind caught. Water started pouring into the cockpit. Designed to take on a certain amount of water, the boat's scuppers normally drain it out. This time, plastic sandwich bags clogged the scuppers, and the water soon was knee-deep in the cockpit.

In her retelling of that tale, Kerry emphasized, "you can't tip over a Wianno Senior when it's sailing. You can heel a lot, you can heel so much that the sail will touch the water, but you cannot flip it. Unless you're on land." In this instance, the problem was the land just beneath the water's surface.

The boat began to sink. At about that moment, the Irish guests aboard disclosed that two of them, one age twenty-five, could not swim. "It was all kind of jolly and not very scary at all," claims Kerry. "It wasn't scary at all," she repeated for emphasis. "But we had maybe fifteen, twenty people on the boat; two of them could not swim. They were sitting on the edge of the boat and bobbing all around were sandwich bags floating around with sandwiches in them, and Coca-Colas floating."

A cooler was emptied, latched closed, and tied with a halyard, so non-swimmers and a few others had something to grasp. "We were rescued, I would say, in about two minutes because we were right next to the [heavily trafficked] channel. My mother never lost her cool; she always had this incredible sense of joy and laughter and fun about her. I have to say if I were skippering that day another soul might find that a terrifying situation. The people on the boat unable to swim weren't planning on sitting on the side of the boat unable to get off. . . . She had none of that," said Kerry of her mother's tolerance for fear of the water. "She was just as cheerful as ever. She sized up the entire situation, which is infectious because it made everybody feel great."

Chris wryly noted that Ethel's oldest son, Joe, was "one of the few people in Hyannisport who had not been on board." So Joe was summoned to the scene. "There was no explaining to a champion sailor [like Joe] how it could have happened." Joe dove down to rescue the sails and the next day Crosby's Yacht Yard sent a barge to rescue the *Resolute*. "We were sailing again by Labor Day, though the boat was in sorry-looking shape," wrote Chris.[51]

~ The channel into Hyannis Harbor was the scene of not a few navigational confrontations. It is and was heavily trafficked by pleasure boats, tourist boats, and tired-looking large ferries running cars, trucks, people, and cargo between Cape Cod, Nantucket Sound, and Martha's Vineyard. As a rule, boats under sail have the right-of-way over powered boats, but practical exceptions are made if, for example, the channel is too narrow for a large powered vessel to maneuver out of the way. Thus, approaching the channel at Hyannis, questions of right-of-way fall into gray areas.

Ethel was not known for subtle parsing of rules of navigation. If you were under power, you were to yield to the *Resolute*. Thus emerged years of animosity between the Kennedys and one particular boat, the ferry *Uncatena*. Originally built in 1965 to be smaller and faster than the other lumbering ships that crisscrossed Nantucket Sound, *Uncatena's* owners had it retrofitted in 1971 with the addition of a middle section that lengthened it. For those who admire ship design, this operation "didn't do much to improve the boat's dowdy lines, with the vessel's windows slightly out of true after reassembly," recalled a local.[52]

From sea level looking up, *Uncatena* seemed enormous. That was the perspective one had on *Resolute* as the two drew near. Nonetheless, on more than one occasion the captain of the *Uncatena*, upon encountering the skipper of the *Resolute*, had to adjust course in the latter's favor. Thus thrown off schedule as well as inconvenienced, the larger vessel's captain's frustration grew at each subsequent encounter. To give voice to that frustration, he once dashed out to the flying bridge, high in the air above the *Resolute*, and made clear to Ethel his views concerning right-of-way. Meanwhile, the *Uncatena's* helmsman, seeking permission to alter course, could not be heard over the red-faced captain's protestations. The *Uncatena* hit a sand bar, bent its prop, and left hundreds of passengers stranded within sight of their destination. Afterward, local navigational rules were amended to favor large ferries in such situations.[53] Asked about the *Un-catena* affair long afterward, when she was eighty-four, Ethel fixed her eyes squarely on the questioner. Lips firm, barely moving, she said, "when people are big, sometimes it goes to their head."[54]

"Mummy is a Skakel," said Chris in another context but apropos here, "and as a Skakel she inherited a healthy disregard for authority in all its forms."[55]

~ Hyannis has an outdoor music performance venue, Melody Tent, that attracts big-name talent. When Sammy Davis Jr. came to town one year, Ethel invited him for a sail. The story is remembered with some relish, and Ethel and Chris took turns recounting portions of it during a recent sail together, filling in details the other missed. A note taker had trouble recording who remembered what. "Sammy was so pleased to be going out on the Kennedy 'yacht,'" said Chris. They set out from the dock on a club tender that delivered sailors to their boat moorings. Heading in the direction of an impressive sailing yacht, they saw Sammy admiring it with anticipation. The tender then made a wide arc around it, and the waves and wind grew more intense as they passed the yacht by. *Resolute* drew nearer and it became clear this little vessel was to be their "yacht." Sammy's face fell. "Surely this is the boat taking us to the bigger boat," Sammy must have been thinking, according to Ethel.

Sammy watched, "as we all got in, kids and dogs, his wife, a hanger-on of his," said Chris. Out to sea they went and before long, Sammy wasn't feeling very well. He tried going down into the tiny cuddy cabin, which is never a good place to be when you're feeling seasick. Better to fix your eyes on the horizon. From the family's point of view, the bigger issue was the avoidance of vomit in the always-damp bilge, all but impossible to clean. It would smell all summer long. Eventually Sammy expressed an interest in returning to port. "We told him he had to sing if he wanted to go back," said Chris.

Bracing himself in the companionway, Ethel said, "Sammy was singing every great song" he was known for. Presumably that included, "I've Gotta Be Me" and "What Kind of Fool Am I?" surely sung with a sense of irony. As they entered the harbor the wind all but died, forcing him to continue singing even longer, now within hearing of other people relaxing on their boats, his deep wonderful voice booming across the harbor toward the Kennedy Compound and the neighbors' homes and boats.

At his Melody Tent concert that night, the weather and perhaps the seasickness did not favor his throat. He struggled to keep from losing his voice altogether, and the audience heard a much less impressive performance than the one aboard *Resolute*.[56]

By the early 1970s, Sammy became a supporter of President Richard Nixon, and the relationship with the Kennedys soured a bit.

~ "She taught all of us to sail," said Kerry of her mother. They took lessons in sailing school too, but "the real learning was on *Resolute*":

> It's a wonderful way to spend times with kids because there was always something for kids to do. If you're in charge of the jib . . . or the mainsheet or the tiller, or if you're the one who is in charge of picking up the mooring or tossing it off, that's a real job and if you do it wrong there are going to be real consequences. So it is a very empowering experience for kids to feel that even at a young age they are making a contribution to the community, to the whole. That was a wonderful thing and a real bonding thing.[57]

Sailing on his Wianno Senior *Ptarmigan*, Ethel and Bob's son Max squinted his eyes at the bow and cocked his head to adjust his line of sight so he could watch the tip of the boat against the backdrop of the approaching water. "Mom taught me how to steer," he said, pointing forward. "The tip of the bow should be making small circles." If the tip is making lines back and forth or at angles, it isn't pointed just as it should be. Make little circles.[58]

~ One November day, when Ethel was in Washington and the short, cold, gray days made clear that the year's sailing season was past, she received a phone call from a Hyannis Port barkeep. Putt, the little man on Egg Island, had died. Ethel called a family friend, William Barry, a former FBI agent and the man who was there to help wrestle Bob's assassin to the floor after the shots were fired. She and Bill flew up from Washington for Putt's funeral. Afterward they went to the one-room shack where he lived. "You know I never photographed well," said Ethel. "But there was a picture of me on his wall. The rest of the wall was filled with pornography!"[59]

CHAPTER 9

Eunice

≋ You might say Eunice was the best sailor among the daughters of Joe and Rose Kennedy. Say it to her, however, and you would have been scolded.

"I don't think she'd like it if you said just 'the daughters,'" her son Mark cautioned with a chuckle. "She'd say she was the most gifted, period. Not segregated by sex."[1]

"Joe set the standard for Jack's and Kathleen's sailing," wrote the younger Joe's biographer. "Eunice needed no example: she was as aggressive at the tiller as he."[2]

"Of all the daughters," added another chronicler of the family, "none of them sailed with the fierce intensity of Eunice, with wild daring recklessness, shooting ahead at the starting flag, rashly turning at the windward buoy, carrying full sails when the less daring reefed, and with her brother Joe Jr., the last to seek the shelter of the harbor in a summer's squall."[3]

"Mother and Dad put us through rigorous training in athletics," said Eunice. "Dad wanted his children to win the sailing and swimming races. I remember racing fourteen times a week when I was 12 years old! We attended two swimming classes every week all summer long for eight consecutive summers. We did well—but I hesitate to think about the consequences if we had lost them all!"[4]

Despite the athleticism that implies, Eunice, born four years after Jack in 1921, had in common with him nearly identical health problems—back pain, stomach disorders, and Addison's disease.[5] She gained the nickname "Puny Eunie."

Especially thin in those years, Eunice lacked the charm and clever repartee that made her older sister Kick so magnetic to men. She was always restless and her words "spurted" in "nervous staccato," delivered so fast, with so much earnestness and intensity, that it took a listener extra effort simply to keep up. When Jack and Kathleen were the popular attractions dancing at the yacht club, she stayed home.[6]

She looked frail into adulthood, but she was anything but. Her stubbornness and indefatigability, her Catholic piety and moral indignation, her willingness to challenge convention, all were foreshadowed in her teen years.

When Eunice was fifteen, she and Joe were the only Kennedy children to earn mention in a *Boston Globe* account of a 1936 Hyannis Port Yacht Club race, "in a strong southwest breeze and rough sea which caused the withdrawal of five of the small yachts." Joe took third racing *Victura*; Eunice took fourth in *Tenovus*, the family's Wianno Junior, nine feet shorter than the twenty-five-foot Senior.

She could be tenacious and demanding in one instant, patient and sensitive in the next. This showed itself in the 1930s in what was among the most historically consequential Kennedy sibling relationships of all—the one between Eunice and Rosemary. As Rosemary's intellectual disability became more apparent in those years, Eunice more than anyone took the time to play with her sister and include her in the overactive life of the family. "[Eunice's] heroes were the Virgin Mary, Mother Teresa, Dorothy Day, her own mother, her sister Rosemary," said daughter, Maria, many years later. Eunice's love for her sister grew into a lifelong mission to help people similarly disabled.

Ted remembered that during childhood games like dodge ball or in sailing races, whenever he saw Rosemary, Eunice was nearby, making her sister feel included. In adolescence, Jack and Joe escorted Rosemary to dances.[7]

Said Eunice, "I would take her as crew in our boat races, and I remember that she usually could do what she was told. She was especially helpful with the jib, and she loved to be in the winning boat. Winning at anything always brought a marvelous smile to her face."[8]

Rosemary, an attractive twenty-three-year-old woman in 1941, was frustratingly surrounded by overachievers and grew emotionally more disturbed as she grew older. She began exhibiting aggressive behavior and angered easily. The Kennedys had the money and connections to get advice from the best neurological experts in the world, and they did. On advice it might make her better, Rosemary received a lobotomy that yielded a result opposite its intent. Her remaining sixty-three years were spent in the institutional care of Catholic nuns in Wisconsin. From time to time and on holidays she was brought to visit the family at the Cape, but the family was devastated by the mistake. Eunice grieved over the shortcomings of medical science and the unfulfilled promise of people like her sister.

Eunice's grief was compounded by the loss of her brother Joe and then the loss of a Stanford University friend in a car accident. Her sister Kathleen's unsanctioned marriage had been a strain on the family too. Eunice's respite was unceasing activity—work, sports, games, sailing. Her intensity was hard to bear. A pregnant female acquaintance, inexperienced at sailing and recruited by Eunice to crew in a Labor Day race, later complained of Eunice as "cruel," "barking" orders and intolerant of error.[9]

After the war Eunice was still unmarried, which worried the family. Jack was at least feigning worry when she was just eighteen and studying at a convent. Tongue in cheek, writing to his skinny sibling, Jack said, "It always seemed to me that if you worried less about your chances of getting to heaven and more about your chances of getting a man, which are getting slimmer and slimmer as you get fatter and fatter—it would take a great load off your brother's mind."[10]

In her early twenties her ambitions were apparently still not for marriage but for a meaningful contribution to public service. In this regard, Eunice stood apart from her sisters, sharing with her brothers an inheritance of their father's ambition. "Of the Kennedy daughters, only Eunice shared this sense of herself as an active player in the world beyond her family."[11]

In 1947, at twenty-four, she moved to Washington, DC, the same year Jack started in Congress. She was working for the Justice Department in Washington and put in charge of a committee of the National Conference on Prevention and Control of Juvenile Delinquency. Jack was in Congress, but his younger sister was getting the headlines. "Eunice Kennedy Tackles Job to Cut Delinquency" was the headline of an International News Service article that ran in newspapers. "Eunice Kennedy

Praised for Fight on Delinquency" was another headline less than a year into the job.[12] Any member of Congress would be jealous.

Stated one newspaper, "At the moment, Miss Kennedy, who thinks and talks with speed and assurance, is hard at work selling states and communities on the idea of holding conferences to attack the problem" of delinquency. Eunice's "speed and assurance" rarely waned in the fifty years that followed.[13]

Not until she was thirty-one, an "old maid" by the standards of the 1950s, did she marry. And she strung that poor fellow along for years. In 1946 Eunice was in New York City and met a young war vet who, like Jack had done, was trying a stint in journalism before deciding that doing things was better than writing about people doing things. He was Sargent Shriver, a junior editor at *Newsweek*. After dating Eunice just once he was startled to soon afterward get a call from her father. Hearing the voice of the famous and powerful Joe Kennedy on the phone was surely intimidating, but Sarge made a good enough impression to earn an invitation to breakfast, where he learned the patriarch was looking for an editor who could turn a collection of papers about his late son, Joe, into a book. It turned out this was why Eunice had given her father Sarge's name. Shriver's later honest assessment for Joe was that it would not make a particularly good book, stories of war heroes then being in abundance. Joe quickly acknowledged that was likely true. The conversation afterward went so well that Joe came to offer Sarge a change of careers: a job, reporting to him, at his newly acquired Merchandise Mart in Chicago, which at that time was in square feet the largest building in the world.

Sarge's courtship of his boss's daughter was long and had odd qualities to it. While dating, there was an oedipal moment or two, such as when Sarge wrote Eunice love letters on his boss's stationary, crossing out Joe's name and inserting his own.[14] Courting the boss's daughter might have seemed opportunistic, but years later theirs was by all accounts among the healthiest Kennedy marriages of that generation.

At her Justice Department job, Eunice's drive was not enough to make up for inexperience. Joe sent his Chicago man to Washington to help Eunice out. Sarge, still romantically interested in Eunice, was thus now her employee. Years later, after Sarge's illustrious career in public service—

from his high-profile roles in the Kennedy presidential administration to his own run for his party's presidential nomination—he found himself in a state of diminishing political relevance. Again he went to work for his wife. Eunice was by then in an opposite state of professional ascendance with the Special Olympics and related causes. A man of an uncommon happy disposition, he always seemed delighted by the work they did together.

~ Beginning around 1948 Sarge tried to convince Eunice to marry him. She declined but kept on seeing him. For years. He dated other women, but Eunice never strayed far out of his romantic sight. He had all but given up on her when, in 1953, Eunice asked Sarge to accompany her to Mass. At the service's conclusion, she asked Sarge to join her in kneeling at a side altar dedicated to the Virgin Mary. She said a prayer. Then she turned to him and said, "Sargent Shriver, I think I'd like to marry you." On May 23, at St. Patrick's Cathedral in New York City, Cardinal Francis Spellman officiating and three bishops, four monsignors, and nine priests assisting, they married in what a Kennedy family press release said was "one of the most important and colorful weddings ever held in America."[15] It's doubtful anyone present quarreled with the characterization. Within a year of their wedding, Eunice's brother Jack and their sisters Jean and Patricia were all married too.

~ When young Kennedys are old enough to leave the nest, they do not go far. Since 1925 Hyannis Port had been the place to which Joe and Rose brought their children back from their boarding schools and colleges and early careers. As spouses and grandchildren entered the picture, it didn't matter that the big house became not big enough. In the 1950s the character of the Kennedy presence began changing from a single household to something like a Kennedy village. Such was the Kennedy attraction to that seaside place that the sons and daughters of Joe and Rose convinced spouses to join them in buying surrounding and nearby houses. That these young married couples all had the immediate means and amenable spouses to do such a thing meant this extended family never extended far geographically.

First were Jack and Jackie, who in 1956 bought a smaller white-frame clapboard home at 111 Irving Avenue, behind his parents. Ted bought another adjacent house in 1959, the year after he married Joan. Two years later, in the first of the White House years, Ted sold his house to Bob and Ethel and their multiplying brood. Ted and Joan moved to a house on nearby Squaw Island, a misnomer since it was connected by land and was only a short walk from the compound. Jack and Jackie spent two seasons at two different houses on Squaw Island. Their last summer White House was at Brambletyde, a less publicly accessible rented house on the waterfront, near Ted and Joan.

Men who married into the Kennedy family followed suit. They joined their spouses in establishing additional Hyannis Port homes for their own new families. When Jack and Jackie relocated to Squaw Island, Eunice and Sarge moved in for at least one season at Jack and Jackie's Irving Avenue home. Before long Eunice and Sarge had a home of their own, steps from the big house, one where years later daughter Maria married Arnold Schwarzenegger and where their children and grandchildren still summer today.

The youngest daughter of Joe and Rose had probably the strongest ties to Kennedy sisters-in-law Ethel and Joan, since both were her friends at college and met their husbands, Bob and Ted, through her. So, for Jean, it was siblings and college buddies all brought together for long summers of fun by the sea. Before long, she and husband, Stephen Edward Smith, had a home there and watched the outcomes of her matchmaking multiply.

By the early sixties, the Kennedy real estate footprint on Hyannis Port was big by any family standard. It has grown bigger since. Robert F. Kennedy Jr. owns a home adjacent to the compound. Chris and Sheila Kennedy in 2011 acquired Brambletyde. Ethel lives full-time in that family's Cape home, having sold Hickory Hill in Virginia. Ted Jr. and his wife, Kiki, now summer in Jack and Jackie's Irving Avenue home. Max and countless other cousins are regular visitors and keep sailboats there. Across Nantucket Sound on Martha's Vineyard, Caroline Kennedy and her husband are turning Jackie's Red Gate Farm property into a place for them and their children to stay.

It was not without exception that marrying a Kennedy meant summering with Kennedys. Eunice introduced sister Patricia to Hollywood actor Peter Lawford, and California had its allure too. Santa Monica was an easy place to live. Though they bought no Cape house, Patricia visited Hyannis Port regularly and was active in Kennedy campaigns.

~ Eunice was unwaveringly loyal to and defensive of the Kennedy family. Her marriage to Sarge was, if not engineered by her father, at least very strongly a result of Joe's extraordinary influence on his daughter. Sarge's loyalty mirrored that of his wife. His lifelong career before and after their marriage was built on his Kennedy relationships, initially as Joe's employee, then as a member of Jack's administration, where he became founder of the Peace Corps and went on to help lead President Johnson's War on Poverty.

Jack's arrival in the White House was seen by Eunice as license to be army general in the battle for people with disabilities, whether or not she had sufficient formal authority. The tirelessness and intensity of her political campaign work for Jack and of her work for the cause of those with intellectual disabilities engendered fear, exasperation, awe, and grudging respect by all who encountered her. "If that girl had been born with balls, she would have been a hell of a politician," her father said.[16]

"Mummy wore men's pants, she smoked Cuban cigars, and she played tackle football," said daughter Maria, who idolized her.[17] Speaking of her husband, Arnold Schwarzenegger, and his extraordinary ambition and drive, Maria more than once said, "I married my mother."[18]

Eunice was unrelenting and, of course, how could the president say no to her or to the interests of people like Rosemary, his younger sister by one year? Her cause was his, but he soon was losing patience. "Let's give Eunice whatever she wants so I can get her off the phone and get on with the business of the government," Jack once said to Bob.[19]

The president and first lady were one evening enjoying a delightful private dinner with Leonard and Felicia Bernstein and journalist Tom Braden and his wife Joan, a popular Washington socialite. In the midst of it, Eunice telephoned and bent Jack's ear for so long that the exasperated president handed the receiver to a surprised Bernstein, who had never met Eunice. "You talk to her," Jack said. "I can't talk to her anymore."

"Oh, come on, what are you all doing?" Eunice asked Bernstein and then went on for twenty minutes more. "You have all the fun, and I'm never asked when it's fun. What did you have for dinner?"[20]

An early victory was the president's formation of a national panel for the study of mental retardation. Eunice was a consultant to the panel, but lack of formal title did not keep her from controlling it. Using White House intermediaries, she was quickly giving orders to any federal authority who could aid the cause.

"Hello, Wilbur," president Kennedy said, welcoming his secretary of health education, and welfare, Wilbur Cohen, into the Oval Office. "Has my sister been giving you trouble again?"

"How did you know?" asked Cohn.

"I know my sister," Jack said.[21]

Maria said, "I think my mother does put the fear of God in most people. She's a perfectionist. She's very demanding of herself and therefore, I think, demanding of the people around her."[22]

~ In 1962 Eunice made use of her brother's bully pulpit to raise awareness about what was then more commonly known as mental retardation. With Jack's blessing she authored an eye-opening article on the topic for the *Saturday Evening Post*, beginning with a frank description of Rosemary's childhood, the family's handling of her disability, and Rosemary's institutionalization, the kind of information other families secreted away.

"We are just coming out of the dark ages in our handling of this serious national problem," she wrote. "Even within the last several years, there have been known instances where families have committed retarded infants to institutions before they were a month old and ran obituaries in the local papers to spread the belief that they were dead."[23]

In addition to accelerating federal effort and awakening public awareness, Eunice also used her influence over her father to repurpose the family's Joseph P. Kennedy, Jr. Foundation so it became almost entirely focused on her new life cause. The foundation funded various research programs and, in 1968, received a grant application from Anne Burke, a twenty-four-year-old instructor with the Chicago Parks District who years later became an Illinois Supreme Court justice. Research funded by the Ken-

nedy Foundation showed that people with disabilities benefited from rec-
reation and competitive sport, so Burke proposed what became the first
Special Olympics at the famed Soldier Field in Chicago. Eunice—who
knew something about competitive sport—not only approved the grant
but spent the rest of her life expanding the concept around the globe,
with Sarge helping to lead the effort in the later years.

Eunice's son-in-law, Arnold Schwarzenegger, said of her, "What she'd
accomplished, to my mind, was larger than the work of most mayors, gov-
ernors, senators and even presidents. Not only did she expand the Special
Olympics to encompass more than 175 countries, but she also changed
people's thinking around the world. Many nations viewed the mentally
challenged as a drag on society or a danger to themselves, to be treated as
outcasts or warehoused in mental institutions. Eunice used her name and
her influence to free those people to have regular lives and the same social
benefits as other citizens."[24]

~ At the Cape she had a Medusa-like appearance that seemed to fit her
character, the sea winds taking rule of her hair, wildly framing her face
and her wide, round blue eyes and expressive mouth with bright white
teeth. With a hummingbird metabolism that could be tiring to be near,
she pinned reminder notes to the sweaters she wore, adding to the impression of undisciplined purposefulness. Despite the force-of-nature impression she made on those in her way, she turned completely opposite in
the presence of a person in need of attention. If someone at a gathering
looked withdrawn and alone, Eunice sought them out, listened intently
to them, and helped include them in conversation. At Special Olympics
events, among athletes with disabilities, she abandoned any authoritative
posturing in favor of good-natured, unpretentious fun, jumping in the
pool, running along the track, or showing how to swing a tennis racket.
She was tough around tough people, soft around those who needed a
helping hand or word.

~ Sarge and Eunice had five children, born between 1955 and 1965, adding
to the growing number of cousins to play with during the White House
years and afterward. Family outings could be complicated. Preparing for

one presidential family cruise on the *Marlin*, the other mothers brought elaborate luncheon fare for children and adults. Ethel enlisted her cook, and, like Jean and Pat, arrived with a rich variety of elaborate picnic foods. Jackie brought "dainty tea sandwiches and French desserts."

Eunice was "last to arrive, her shirt hanging out, sneakers untied, hair uncombed, rushing up the dock holding a paper bag full of Wonder bread and big jars of peanut butter and jelly." While the others spread their elegant dishes out on a tablecloth, Eunice assembled PB&Js. Reportedly, the children of Jackie, Ethel, Jean, and Pat were more interested in good old peanut butter and jelly than the gourmet stuff.[25]

A typical sailing adventure was on the Kennedy and Shriver Wianno Seniors, with Sarge preferring to tag along separately in a twenty-foot powerboat. The Shriver children grew up in, on, and by the water just as the other Kennedy children, often sailing side by side, *Resolute* passing the slower *Headstart*, on the way to Egg Island and elsewhere. Mark Shriver recalls,

> As a kid we'd go out seven days a week. [Sarge] would often take the motor boat and meet us out there. . . . You could jump back and forth between the boats. In the ocean you jump in and swim to the Senior, or the Senior would luff into the wind and could pick you up that way, or you'd jump overboard and swim over to the motorboat. Every day we'd meet at the end of the pier at 12:15 or 12:30, go sailing for a couple of hours, come in at, you know, 3:00. We went every day and rarely missed it. I mean even if it was howling we were out there.[26]

When daughter Maria was in her twenties and tried to coax a new boyfriend to visit Hyannis Port for the first time, she told him, "We go out sailing and taking turns getting dragged behind the sailboat, and we go out to the Egg Island. And we have a great time! All we do is water stuff." Schwarzenegger recalls the night he arrived at the main house, when Maria took him out across the famous lawn for a night swim: "We swam to a boat quite a long way out. She was a regular water rat, climbing on board to catch our breath, then swam back in."[27]

Mark remembers,

learning how to sail and having mother on a little motorboat—a Boston Whaler—going alongside of us, giving us pointers, and shouting directions as we were practicing . . . I remember sailing and there being coolers of food, and dogs, and then when the wind really blew and the boat would tip . . . on more than one occasion, the food going overboard and dogs going out of the boat . . . and people would fall down to the leeward side and—boom-boom—they'd go over or over the dog would go, over the food would go.

Mark still loves small Seniors more than yachts. Every family member has a job to do:

You kind of knew, if . . . [Eunice] said, "ready about," you know you're either letting the jib out or you're pulling it in. If she said "give me some mainsheet," you knew that that meant let it out . . . She was laughing and loved it, and she went out every day for as long as I knew her, in the summertime. . . . She loved telling stories, hearing stories, gossiping a little bit, exchanging ideas.

Mark bought a Wianno Senior in 2012 and now sails *Dingle* with his children. He hopes the oldest of them, at fourteen, will be ready to solo sail *Dingle* in a year or two.[28]

~ In the years after Jack and Bob died, about once a year Eunice skippered *Victura* in a race. Her brother Ted crewed for her and she was competitive with the other sailors. It would have been good to hear two opinionated sailors, Ted and Eunice, debating race tactics.

In one such race, Ted Kennedy Jr. remembered, "We were in first place, we had the spinnaker up coming back from Southwest Rock heading back to the break wall and Eunice was sitting in the back of the boat and she leaned too far back and flipped over and fell into the water." Ted Jr. and his father worried not just about her but about the cost of dropping the spinnaker and turning around. Eunice shouted, "You'll lose the race if you turn around . . . round the mark and come back and pick me up." Treading water for twenty minutes, she met them on the upwind course of the race. They picked her up and went on to win the race.[29]

As she did for her brothers, she started doing for her son-in-law. Schwarzenegger was interested in politics, and Eunice advised him to pick an issue around which he could build a reputation. This is how Jack did it, she said. So Arnold sought to chair President George H. W. Bush's Council on Physical Fitness and Sports. Physical fitness was a logical choice, but Arnold's reputation was tainted by steroid use, movie violence, and cigar smoking.

"Eunice engaged in an aggressive lobbying campaign on behalf of her son-in-law, with repeated letters and calls to Bush and top aides," reported Joe Matthews, a journalist who covered Schwarzenegger's political career. "Finally, Bush overruled some of his own aides and gave Schwarzenegger the job. In a handwritten note, the president made clear whose recommendation had carried the day: 'Eunice, a guy really must be good if his mother-in-law says great things about him!'"[30] Until 1990 Schwarzenegger was best known for his movie role as *The Terminator*. Now he would have public service credentials.

As the decades passed Eunice and Sarge kept an aggressive pace promoting the expansion of the Special Olympics around the world. Aging, encountering serious health problems, Eunice showed an amazing capacity for full recovery.

In 1991 Eunice crashed a car in an accident so serious that the phone call to Sarge left him thinking she was dead or dying. Extracted with "jaws of life," she had broken both arms, shattered her elbow, and damaged a hip socket; she was also lacerated in multiple places. The severity of the accident and her age of sixty-nine notwithstanding, in a matter of days she was on the phone, dispensing with niceties and talking business.[31]

Six years later there she was on the lawn of the big house, running a relay race of Kennedy grandchildren, she anchoring one team, Ted the other. For the final lap Ted, several years younger, had a good lead. Eunice sprinted past him, yelling, "Hurry up Fatso!"[32]

In 2000 she suffered complications from pancreas surgery and fell into a coma. The coma lasted for days and doctors told Sarge to prepare for the end. Last rites were administered. She had been in the same state for weeks when Sarge swore he saw an eye open. The doctors doubted it, but over the next several days her eyes fluttered open again and more frequently, and for weeks she returned slowly to consciousness and was eventually up and about, back and fully engaged at her work. Then in 2001, a day before a party for her eightieth birthday, a car accident shattered a leg and she was bedridden for weeks once again. She recovered yet again.[33]

One would think she was fit for retirement. Not so. Schwarzenegger began a run for governor of California by supporting the recall of the incumbent officeholder, Gray Davis. "During Schwarzenegger's first big public appearance of that campaign in the Orange County community of Huntington Beach, Eunice appeared—without prior notice to the star's disbelieving team of advance men—and began working a rather raucous crowd of wetsuit-wearing surfers and bikini-clad sunbathers on the beach. A few weeks later, she assembled the campaign's team of education advisers, convincing several Democrats to help her son-in-law, even though he was seeking the recall of a governor of their own party."[34]

~ Through it all, when her health allowed, she was out sailing every day she could until her mid-eighties. If there wasn't a member of the family available to crew, she sometimes brought her reluctant nurse along to help with the jib sheets and mooring line.

Chris Kennedy, returning from a long day's sail with his family, walking up the dock back toward shore, came upon Eunice and her nurse heading out to the launch. He saw in the nurse's eyes a look of great trepidation. "Very frightened," was Chris's impression.

"What are you guys doing?" he asked.

"We're going sailing."

"Alone?

"What do you mean by that?" asked Eunice.

"I'd like to come," said Chris, not at all actually wanting to sail again but worried about Eunice.

"You're not coming just because you think we can't do this?" The nurse of course, with her eyes, supported Chris's every word.

Eunice said, "You're with your wife and children, and they're dying to go back in."

Chris *was* dying to go back in but did not say so. Though he let Eunice pass on toward her sailboat, he immediately alerted Eunice's children.[35] Her son Mark said,

> You know mother died at eighty-eight years of age, but she was out sailing on a Herreshoff, a twelve-and-half-foot boat, which is really low to the water, two years before she died, definitely out there racing that boat, which is quite similar to a Senior but is smaller, obviously, about half the size. She raced that thing into her mid-eighties. She'd race against Vicki Kennedy and a couple of other people in the community that were there. And yeah, her crew was her nurse. If she couldn't find one of her children or grandchildren, she'd grab her nurse. Sometimes it was her nurse's son. Her nurse's son was a pretty good sailor, and he'd go out and crew for Mother.[36]

Eunice and Sarge spent the summer of 2008 together at Hyannis Port, she battling recurring small strokes, he Alzheimer's. Ted was being treated for a brain tumor. Despite their ailments, the three set sail for what they surely knew was a last time together, this time on Ted's beautiful fifty-foot schooner *Mya*. Eunice had to be wheeled down the pier. Sarge walked it painfully slow. Ted's wife, Vicki, joined the crew. Out of the harbor, wind was light and Sarge complained about the boat's meandering speed. A powerboat was the better option, he said. Eunice told him to just enjoy the sail, and Ted, sitting between them, goaded them on with an occasional verbal provocation.

Mark was on the beach watching them beat slowly out as the sails rounded out. "It was the image of the four of them together in the back of the boat, heads bobbing and arms moving, that I will never forget. At first I tried to imagine what they were talking about, but I forced my brain to shut off—there are things in life we will never know. I just sat there and took in the scene of the four of them, out for a sail on the Nantucket Sound, enjoying God's grandeur, together, one last time."[37]

CHAPTER 10

Ted

〰〰〰 "Teddy had his usual line of stories and seemed as fat as ever, having now reached the 120 lbs. mark," wrote Bob, eighteen, of his eleven-year-old brother in 1943.[1] The family saluted the 1932 birth of the youngest of the nine children—arriving a full four years after the next-to-youngest, Jean—by naming the family's new Wianno Junior *One More*. Their other Junior, *Tenovus*, had been named before Ted made them a family of eleven.

When Ted was eleven, Joe Jr. was twenty-eight, a naval aviator and more like a father figure than big brother. Ted was a constant source of amusement, always laughing. After Joe died and Jack returned from the war, Ted's baby fat vanished and he became at Harvard such a football standout that he was offered, but turned down, an opportunity to play professional football.

The fullback on that Harvard team emerged as a lifelong friend and a man for whom the family would all gain particular affection, in part because of his distinct but amusing *lack* of seamanship. In the spring of 1951, Ted invited a fellow Harvard freshman, John Culver, for one of the first of many visits to Hyannis Port. Tossing a football on the lawn with other members of the Harvard football team, Culver saw a limousine pull up and deposit Jack Kennedy. Jack walked into the house without stopping. A few minutes later, from a window above them, came Jack's voice: "Culver's a bum!" Culver had never met Jack.[2] But he soon was in the circle of Kennedy friends growing ever wider as young Kennedys entered colleges and began professional careers. Culver went on to work in Kennedy campaigns and served in Congress for sixteen years, including a term as the U.S. senator from Iowa.

Culver's story of another visit was one of the best remembered of the tributes at a memorial service for Ted given at the JFK Library in 2009. To fully appreciate Culver's folksy, deftly timed delivery, replete with exaggeration for effect, you must watch it on video. Standing over Ted's flag-draped coffin, Culver took his audience back to the summer of 1953, when he and Ted were in summer school at Harvard. Ted invited Culver to come down to the Cape to crew for him in the Nantucket Yacht Club Regatta.

"Ted, I'm sure that's an honor to be invited . . . but I've never been on a sailboat," Culver said. "I think I've seen a picture of a sailboat. I come from Iowa and the only boats I ever saw were barges on the Mississippi River."

"There's nothing to it," said Ted.

"At that time we were both young," recalled Culver. "I didn't quite understand that comment but I grew to understand it later."

They drove down to the Cape, listening to music on the radio, when the broadcast was suddenly interrupted: "Serious storm warnings! Danger at sea! Don't anyone go out in the ocean!"

"Well, Ted, I guess the sailboat trip is off," said Culver.

"Ugh, there's nothing to it."

"Well the fellow on the radio thought there was something to it."

"There's nothing to it," Ted said, shaking his head and jutting out his lower lip.

Culver figured, "he must know what he's doing. He lives down there and I've never been on the ocean."

They arrived at the big Kennedy house where "there were dark black storm clouds gathering."

"Ted, doesn't it look kind of scary?"

"Nothing to it," said Ted.

It was mid-afternoon and they had missed lunch, so they went to the kitchen where the cook offered to make sandwiches with leftover salmon salad.

"We both thought that was a good idea," said Culver. "We didn't have a whole lot of time so I only had two salmon salad sandwiches, and I had a quart of milk with it." Ted hurried him along as the clock approached four.

Culver was taken aback by the *Victura*'s small size against a backdrop of such big seas. "It's 26 [*sic*] feet long. Ted and I both at the time weighed over 200 pounds. We were both over 6 feet tall."

They maneuvered the boat from shore. "There were huge waves now. There was thunder. There was lightning. The sky was black. I could hardly get in the boat, it was bouncing so much and he's at the tiller. Suddenly, I realized this 'friend' of mine I thought I knew quite well started screaming at me. Shouting at me. I was terrified. After a while I was more terrified of him than the storm. I didn't know this man. He kept screaming at me—'the spinnaker, the jib, portside, secure that.' As you know, Ted's not always easy to understand even when you know what he's talking about."

"And now . . . this little, tiny boat bouncing all over like a cork—it's my fault!"

"I'm just hanging on for dear life. We'd gotten about 200 miraculous yards out, and I lost the sandwiches. I thought I was going to die. I've never been so miserable—hanging over the side of the boat and he's screaming at me."

The weather kept on and they sailed for hours before finally making Nantucket around eleven o'clock.

"Which hotel do we stay in?" Culver asked, wet, cold, exhausted.

"We're not staying in a hotel," Ted informed him. "We're staying on the boat."

"I realized then that I was with something out of Captain Ahab. Moby Dick."

The tiny cabin's berths had two damp cushions each and "there were three inches of cold seawater, seaweed, everything."

The next morning they wandered around Nantucket. To race they would need another man to crew. Eventually they found an acquaintance from Cambridge.

"We shanghaied him. We took him, just like I was taken," said Culver.

". . . and off we go for the races. The races started and from that point on all I remember is Ted yelling, yelling to me to get up on the right side, the front of the boat, or the left side. He always claims that when I was to rotate with the other guy, I said, 'You heard him, get up there!' Of course it was really my turn to go up."

"Finally, this thing was mercifully over, and Ted seemed satisfied. I had no idea, but probably I was satisfied too—I lived through it."

They headed back toward Nantucket and, "like a mirage, here's this great, big yacht," the *Marlin*.

"He hadn't told me, but Ambassador Kennedy had come out to watch the race. . . . I never saw anything that looked so good to me as that boat."

Ted then explained that they would board the *Marlin* and that *Victura* would be towed behind for the return to Hyannis Port. Culver, wet, cold, in a miserable state for longer than he could have imagined, was filled with relief.

Then the ambassador picked up a megaphone. "Good race, good race, Teddy. But I got some bad news for you. The captain says the sea is far too rough to tow you boys back on that boat. So you'll have to sail back."

"I wanted to jump out of the boat and take my chances they'd pick me up," said Culver. The yacht crew used a rope to lower down a thermos filled with clam chowder. Culver claims Ted always exaggerated when he said Culver ripped open and drank it all down straight from the container. "The only thing I missed was what went down my t-shirt," Culver said. Ted's share vanished.

The return trip took hours but the sea was calm and eventually the lights of the big house came into view. "I'm 24 hours on this boat. . . . I'm thinking, 'Boy, we'll be in a hot shower in no time.'"

Half a mile from shore, the wind grew faint and then was gone. They were dead in the water, the house close enough to see, too far to swim. The only solution, Ted said, was for both to get in the water, one to push, the other to pull the boat by a rope. They made it ashore as midnight approached, then back to school the next day, but "it was a whole week before I could get the seaweed taste out of my mouth."[3]

Ted took Culver on many more sailboat voyages in the decades that followed, but Culver never did learn how to sail.

~ Ted's college academic achievements were not up to the standards set by his brothers. He was suspended for a year for cheating on a Spanish exam. But he earned a law degree and experienced political apprenticeships as good as any by working on Jack's Senate and presidential campaigns. In 1962, with one brother in the White House and his other brother as attorney general, Ted ran for the U.S. Senate seat Jack had held. Thus, all three simultaneously held positions of power.

For years to come, no matter his accomplishment, Ted's status as a presidential younger brother made him seem even less self-made than the other sons of Joe Kennedy. The exceptions were accomplishments racing the *Victura*, where nepotism gave no aid. One thing his oldest brother the president did do on the water, however, was ensure Ted's racing received public notice. The president often traveled to the Cape, taking the *Honey Fitz* or *Marlin* out with cabinet members or others of high rank, just to watch Ted compete.

"The nation's number one sailboat came out to race Friday and all over Nantucket Sound young yachtsmen could be heard exclaiming: 'I saw him,'" reported the *Boston Globe* in the summer of 1963. "It wasn't the President of the United States they saw. It was his youngest brother who did a remarkable job in the opening day of Edgartown Yacht Club's 40th annual regatta." Always the highlight of the season, that year's Edgartown Regatta attracted 149 boats, including 22 Wianno Seniors, all but one of which Ted beat in the race offshore from Martha's Vineyard.[4]

"What's so good about second place in a family where only first place matters?" asked the *Globe* reporter. "Just this. *Victura*, famous as she is, is not one of the better Wianno Seniors and she may be one of the worst. Her sails are old and if there is a spinnaker in the sail locker it saw no action Friday." Yet Ted stayed close to the winning boat, *Venture*, and held off *Marna*, sailed by family sailing nemesis Jack Fallon, soon to be a life-long family friend.[5]

Ted might have enjoyed the attention, but not the following month when Jack watched from the presidential yacht *Honey Fitz* as Ted jumped the starting gun in a race at Stone Horse Yacht Club. Required to circle *Victura* back to the start, he finished seventeenth out of twenty-six Seniors. Watching with the president were Jack's World War II pal Paul Fay, who Jack appointed undersecretary of the navy, and John Kenneth Galbraith, the former ambassador to India and noted economist. "Ted Loses Boat Race" was the next morning's *Boston Globe* headline, above the subhead, "Kennedys Watch Him Jump the Gun." Any freshman senator would cringe at such a headline in his state's biggest newspaper.[6]

By Labor Day weekend that year, Ted redeemed himself with a first-place finish on *Victura*, with the president and first lady personally cheering him on from the *Honey Fitz*. The *Globe*, however, buried that news deep in the story and omitted it from the headline, acknowledging at least that "The Senator finished a strong first in his class."[7]

~ When Jack was assassinated, Ted had the awful duty of rushing to Hyannis Port to tell their father. Bob became the oldest son and—as Jack's attorney general and closest adviser—heir to his brother's political dynasty. As grief faded and political realities set in, eyes focused on Bob's future. Ted's was secure enough, his immediate path defined. He had taken his brother's Senate seat in a special election, requiring him to run again in 1964. In June he and four others boarded a small private plane for West Springfield, Massachusetts, where the state Democratic Party convention was to nominate him by acclamation. On his plane's approach to landing, it began a suddenly steeper descent and, three miles short of the runway, slammed into a tree. The pilot and Ted's legislative aide were killed. Ted's friend, U.S. senator Birch Bayh and his wife, Marvella, were not seriously hurt, but Bayh had to drag Ted from the wreckage. Ted broke three vertebrae and two ribs and had a collapsed lung. It was just seven months since the assassination.

Ted spent more than five months hospitalized and couldn't campaign, though he stayed on the ballot. In the meantime Bob resigned as President Lyndon Johnson's attorney general and in August announced his run for a senate seat in New York. Thus, in November 1964, two Kennedys won elections to the U.S. Senate.

Ted wore a back brace for months afterward, and the pain never left him. He spent months at the Cape recovering and, with two brothers' and a sister's lives lost, and his nearly lost too, confronted the fleeting nature of the opportunities his life and circumstance presented. He took up painting—he and Jack had tried it before—with the sea, sailboats, and Cape Cod as favorite subjects. Ted had become owner of Jack's *Victura*, and after the crash sailing became an even larger part of his life. He better appreciated time with family and friends, sharing the exhilaration of a race and conversation on a cruise. His son Ted Jr. said that as he regained back strength and the ability to walk, he decided that most forms of exercise would be more challenging than before, but sailing was a sport he could still pursue.

~ Ted wanted advice on racing, so he looked around for the best local authority. He scanned the race results from recent Wianno Senior regattas and saw one winner's name repeated again and again. "There was John T. Fallon . . . John T. Fallon . . . John T. Fallon," said Ted Jr. "Dad decided he had to meet him. So Dad picked up the phone and called him. After that they became great friends." Would a sailor as competitive as Jack Fallon share his secrets? "Jack was not threatened by Dad," said Ted Jr., "Dad had a back brace."[8]

Fallon, a Boston real estate executive, took up Wianno Senior racing in the 1950s. He had never sailed before then, so he read books on sailing, bought a boat, and on race days just showed up at the starting line. Before long he was winning race after race.[9]

Ted and Fallon shared an obsession for the sport. The Kennedys still speak with wonder of Fallon's magical ability to squeeze speed out of a Senior. Over seventeen years he was nine times the winner of the Scudder Cup, awarded to the best racer in each year's series of interclub Wianno Senior races. The year of Ted's plane crash was also the start of Fallon's glory years; he won the Scudder in 1964, 1965, 1967, 1968, and 1970.

"Jack put Eastern Airlines paint on the bottom of his boat," said Ethel of Fallon. "He was also a pilot. He had more secrets. He knew the wind; he knew where every wave was coming from."[10]

Fallon's exhaustive rituals for preparing *Marna* for the season started with the meticulous nurturing of the moisture content of the wood forming the hull. In winter he stored *Marna* on a damp dirt floor. In spring he set it in the water at its mooring, waiting one week before adding lead ballast or its rig. He then carefully loaded six hundred pounds of lead ingots, or "pigs," in forward bays and under the cockpit, so the boat was optimally and perfectly balanced for speed. He let it sit at its mooring for another week before stepping the mast and adding the boom, gaff, and other rigging. He then waited another week. "This allows the boat to come together slowly, before she's stressed in any way," he said. "The reason she's so light and dry is that I've gone through this process every single year."

He calculated the perfect rake for his mast, using numbered and marked wedges, soaked for a week before being tapped into place. He said his shrouds and headstays—the steel wires holding the mast up—compress slightly every year, so "I've learned that a half-turn in each turnbuckle will take up one thread—the equivalent of a year's stretch in the wire."[11]

On top of his infinitely precise boat maintenance habits, there was his encyclopedic knowledge of how to actually sail a Senior. He once summarized his best advice in a 1989 article for *Wooden Boat* magazine, weighing his text down with technical details such as "Take your foot [bottom of the sail] tension out to the max. . . . The downhaul is where you accommodate halyard stretch. . . . Over tightening the standing rigging is the biggest sin committed on Wiannos. . . . If I really wanted to give it to them I'd drop the peak and trim the main and just power out." Fallon continued, "There's no end to what you can do with a Wianno, and when you think you've got her perfect after almost 40 years, you still find there's more to try."[12]

Fallon gave Ted sailing tips and helped coach many of the Kennedy children too. Bob's son Chris remembers an old family photo of his father in *Victura*, in a match race side by side against Bob's oldest son, Joe, in *Resolute*. "They are overtaking *Victura*, and my father is yelling at Joe, trying to distract him, and he's pointing at the sail, trying to get Joe to look. And Jack Fallon, you can see him talking to Joe—'don't look, don't pay any attention to that.'"[13]

A local journalist remembers being among a group of Boston news reporters covering a tech company's office opening in the early eighties, and there was Fallon, who had a business stake in the real estate, talking to Ted. The promising company was called Symbolics. The reporter was himself a Wianno Senior sailor. So, as Ted and Fallon chatted, the reporter approached and raised the subject of their shared interest. At that point, "the discussion gets very animated, to the exclusion of the other reporters and Symbolics staff, none of whom have the faintest idea of what we are talking about when we get into a discussion about that year's new jib from the Hood sail loft."[14]

Fallon's life was so tied to the sailing of Wianno Seniors that when he died in 2001, his service was held at Our Lady of the Assumption Church in Osterville, a half mile stroll from Crosby Yacht Yard, birthplace of all Wianno Seniors. Make that walk today and you'll pass the Osterville public library with a weathervane modeled after a Senior. Mourners were told that in lieu of flowers, donations could be made to the Wianno Senior Class Association. A Wianno Senior race trophy is named in Fallon's honor, and a pier named for Fallon juts from shore a few steps from the JFK Library and Museum in Boston.

~ Ted never sailed as expertly as Jack Fallon—few did—but Kennedy children were almost equally in awe of Ted's skills at a Senior's tiller. He could win often enough during Jack's White House years, and he only got better as more Kennedy children were born to crew for him.

"He had amassed so much knowledge, especially in those waters," said son Patrick. "When the tide came in, which direction it was heading two hours after low tide or two hours after high tide could make the difference in whether we tacked. . . . If we tacked and it was a certain wind direction and we were able to hold to twenty degrees off the wind, we could get a lift from the tide if we were at a certain mark. . . . He knew the tide runs in an east-west direction most powerfully at this mark."[15]

From Ted and the other Senior racers, Ted's nephew Chris learned to be a student of tides too, making sure always to study before a race the little yellow-covered *Eldridge Tide and Pilot Book*, published annually since 1875, filled with tables and charts for locations up and down the Atlantic coast. "You have to study that book before a race," said Chris. "That's like half the race."[16] Year after year, the book has had precisely 272 pages. An *Eldridge* has sun and moon phase tables, navigational guides, and short articles with titles like "Bluefish, a Grudging Appreciation."

"On account of the disturbing effect of strong winds, it is not possible to predict at all times the exact time of high or low tide or *the turning of the current*," reads a typical Eldridge passage, adding dramatic effect through liberal use of italics and bold face. "When the winds blow strong from the **southward** or **eastward**, the effect is to increase the tides and make them **later**."[17]

~ In the immediate years after Jack Kennedy's death, the families of his brother and sisters found on the waters of Nantucket Sound the comfort, diversion, and togetherness that they had so long found in previous times of trouble or joy. The death of a sibling they had experienced, but never after reaching such heights of achievement and fame. After the extraordinary White House years came the ascent of Bob's political profile, also halted by gunfire.

Ted was just thirty-six when Bob was killed in 1968. Ted, the youngest of the children of Joe and Rose, became the eldest male and patriarch of the family, his father by then frail and disabled, months from his own death. He had by then lost brothers Joe, Jack, and Bob and sister Kathleen. Counting the lobotomized and institutionalized Rosemary as living but lost, siblings originally nine in number were now four. On top of that was the intense public attention. Ted was a U.S. senator but ill-prepared for the new level of scrutiny to which he was now subjected. Ted and his then wife, Joan, had three children. Kara and Ted Jr. were born just before and just after Jack's inauguration, respectively. The third, Patrick, arrived in 1967. With Bob's death Ted was the soul surviving Kennedy uncle to Bob's and Jack's thirteen children combined.

Ted had a lot left in his family, though it might not have seemed so after so much loss. He had his sister, Eunice, and her husband, Sarge, both by then formidable figures in their own rights. Sisters Patricia and Jean had married men powerful in their own ways, even though the women themselves were constrained by gender roles of their era. Just four months after Bob's death, Jackie married Aristotle Onassis. Ted was still surrounded by a strong and connected family, but Ted would be its most public face.

After Bob's death, Ted secluded himself with family at Hyannis Port. Once he tried to return, driving from Hyannis Port to Washington, but as Capitol Hill came into view he could not bear the thought of climbing the steps toward those faces around the Senate. He turned around and returned home, never getting out of the car.[18]

The burden was awful in its suddenness and enormity. Ted said he knew it begged the question, was he next? It was shock and terror. Richard N. Goodwin said, "He was really terribly shaken up by Bobby's death. He used to sail all night long by himself in the days and weeks after that happened, just sailing."[19]

His son Patrick, too young when Bob died to remember, had heard of

Ted's nighttime sails in those days, often on *Victura*. "There's something majestic and absolutely other worldly when you are out in the midnight sky and you see all the stars and you know that for millennia people have used those stars to navigate their way around the world. It's just this sense of mystery of life. And I think what absolutely *captivated* my father was the sense that as inexplicable as life was, you know the mystery of it was captured in the sea, in the stars in the sea, in the nighttime."[20]

In his memoir, *True Compass*, Ted said much the same of those sails in those sad days when his grief was put into another perspective by "a sense of oneness with the sky and the sea. The darkness helped me to feel the movement of the boat, and the movement of the sea, and it helped displace the emptiness inside me with an awareness of *direction*." He sailed farther out from Hyannis, away from shore lights. "And that is the truly magical time of sailing, because the North Star appears . . . the guiding star for all seamen through time . . . the guide to home."[21]

Asked about his father's observation that sailing is a metaphor for life, Patrick said,

> I'm telling you when you are out at sea and you're feeling the rise and fall of the boat and the wind and know that everything could blow up, that things are changing all the time . . . that gave my father direction when he was seemingly without direction. It gave him a sense that nothing in life is that certain and that you've got to steer through the storms as they come and you'll do the best you can to make it to the other side. Some days you win, some days it will be sunny, others will be raining, it is just a terrific metaphor for life.[22]

After his long period of silent removal, Ted went on television to announce his return:

> In the last ten weeks I've not been active in public life. I have concerned myself with my family. I have spent much time by the sea, clearing my mind and my spirit of the event of last June. Some of you have suggested that for safety's sake and for my family's sake, I retire from public life. But there is no safety in hiding for me nor for any of us here today. Like my three brothers before me I pick up a fallen standard. Sustained by their memory of our priceless years together, I shall try

to carry forward that special commitment to justice, to excellence, to courage that distinguished their lives.[23]

~ With the following spring of 1969 came a new sailing season, one with Ted in a new role as an uncle with responsibility like few uncles ever. His memories were filled with Bobby and his children swimming and sailing together. Children, resilient, would quickly want that again. So, he said, he became "counselor, skipper and mentor to the sailors among them" and found with them on the shore of Nantucket Sound that which Kennedys by growing tradition found replenishing. They set out together on sea and on land too. Over a period of about fifteen years, Ted led ventures in a Winnebago, out on the road, stopping to hike, camp, and tour civil war battlefields and other historic sites.[24]

Through the 1970s and 1980s they fell into a rhythm of family life by the sea that one after another of the children would remember with great fondness. But before they could establish that rhythm, there came one more tragedy of a new kind, one not of random victimization or accident, but one of a Kennedy's own making. The previous tragedies all seemed partly the product of the heroic trajectory of the Kennedys. This one was a product of—and suggesting of—a Kennedy human weakness.

~ Since the days before World War II, when his brothers Joe and Jack competed so fiercely under sail, a highlight of the season was one Martha's Vineyard race in particular. By the summer of 1969 Ted was dealing with grief, he later said, by pouring his thoughts and energy into his work and, on occasion, pouring a drink or two too many for himself. Though his June and July calendar of speeches and professional obligations was "frenzied," he said, one date he wanted to keep for himself. The Edgartown Regatta was July 18, 1969.[25]

Ted raced *Victura* with old friend and crewmate Joey Gargan, the cousin adopted into the family in the 1930s after his mother, Rose's sister, died in a car crash. Joey was there when the family learned that oldest brother, Joe, died in World War II. And he and Ted sailed with Jack in an Edgartown Regatta in the early 1950s, when Jack flew in to join the crew at the last minute.

Ted, Joey, and their crew did not have their best showing that year, coming in ninth by one account; "the top half of the fleet" was Ted's recollection.²⁶ As fun as the race itself was, the postrace social life on the Vineyard was a highlight too. Many traveled by means other than racing sailboats to join the parties, and on this evening one gathering was a reunion of young women from Robert Kennedy's presidential campaign staff. After the race Ted celebrated with the crew of the winning Wianno Senior, as was tradition. Later they made their way to the reunion that had gathered on a tiny island, separated from Martha's Vineyard by a narrow channel of water.

At the party Ted said he remembered stepping outside for a breath of fresh air, where he was accompanied by one of the campaign staff workers, Mary Jo Kopechne. Out beneath that night sky they surely looked up at the moon because at that moment the Apollo 11 crew was two days into its mission and a day away from going into orbit around the moon, in preparation for the landing of Armstrong and Aldrin, the product of Jack's extraordinary 1961 gamble that the United States could win that race.

Ted and Mary Jo left in a borrowed car, saying they were ready to end the evening. Ted lost his way in the pitch-dark night and, squinting, distracted by any number of much-debated causes, came to a narrow bridge without guardrails, out of alignment with the direction of the road. His car went off the bridge, flipping and trapping them both underwater. He somehow escaped, but it was several nighttime hours before he reported the accident. The mystery of his behavior forever stained his reputation. The word "Chappaquiddick," the name for a tiny island, was ever after associated with Ted Kennedy, shorthand for questions about his judgment and character. "A horrible tragedy that haunts me every day of my life," wrote Ted forty years later.²⁷

~ The nature writer Henry Beston, writing when Ted's brothers Joe and Jack were still children, described nights over Nantucket Sound. "With lights and ever more lights, we drive the holiness and beauty of night back to the forest and the sea; the little villages, the crossroads even, will have none of it. Are modern folk, perhaps, afraid of night? Do they fear that vast serenity, the mystery of infinite space, the austerity of stars? Having made themselves at home in a civilization obsessed with power, which explains its whole world in terms of energy, do they fear at night for their dull acquiescence and the patter of their beliefs?"[28]

~ The year before, the Democratic presidential nominee, Hubert H. Humphrey, tried to recruit Ted to run as vice president. Now he wondered if he should resign his Senate seat. Fortunately for Ted, poll numbers held and he was easily reelected in 1970. But the Kennedys moved for a few years off center of the national political stage. The Shakespearean quality of their lives, the triumphs, assassinations, and scandals, kept the family ever present in headlines, every move chronicled. The shared experience of all that must have strengthened the collective family bond even as it also strained and weakened adult relationships.

In the decade of the 1970s that followed, they as a family made ample time to be together by and on the sea. Ted spent endless hours with those children out under sail. The boys enjoyed sailing with Ted, and he sought to bend the race rules to allow an extra crew member if he or she was under twelve. Typically he would arrive from Washington late on a Friday afternoon and head straight out on *Victura* with whatever children or friends he could corral. They needed practice if they were to win the weekend's races.

"We'd be out late," recalled Teddy Jr. "The sun would be setting, and the family dinner would be getting cold. We'd be out there practicing our jibes and our spinnaker sets, long after everyone else had gone ashore."

"One night, not another boat was in sight on the summer sea. I asked him, 'why are we always the last ones on the water?'"

"Teddy," his father said. "You see, most of the other sailors that we race against are smarter and more talented than we are. But the reason why we're going to win is that we will work harder than them, and we will be better prepared."

"He wasn't just talking about boating," recalled Ted. "My father admired perseverance."[29]

The children's stories from those years of *Victura* and *Resolute* are filled with moments of misery or terror or exhaustion or comic situations, experiences they would invariably never trade. Once during the 1970s, Ted took his son and daughter, Teddy Jr. and Kara, and his nephew John F. Kennedy Jr. out on the *Victura*. Sailing from Falmouth, where the wind was blowing twenty-five knots, they heeled the boat over, an exhausting sail for a helmsman struggling with the tiller. To sail an old wooden Senior for any length of time was to also battle water leaking in.

"Time to pump the boat!" said Ted. That meant the three would need to crawl into the little cuddy cabin and put one end of a hand pump in the bilge water, with a hose on the other end tossed over the gunwale. They took turns pumping, pulling the handle to suck water into the plastic tube, then pushing the handle to expel the water over the side, endlessly repeated. In the cramped quarters it was hard to obtain good leverage. The three youngsters were getting tired and mutinous. "Why doesn't *he* pump for awhile," they asked one another, gesturing up to Ted in the cockpit.

Noticing a slowing of the flow of pumped water, Ted called down, "How's that pump coming?"

Brief silence. Then, from a high-pitched voice down in the cuddy: "We think it's *your* turn to come down and pump."

A pause.

"Ok, I'll pump," said Ted with that booming baritone, the boat pounding through surf and straining in the wind. "But which of you is going to drive the boat?"

The three were quiet for a bit. "We hadn't thought about that," recalled Ted Jr. They looked at one another, and "we kept on pumping" and said no more.

Retelling that story in 2012 Ted Jr., a cancer survivor himself, was the only surviving member of that day's four-person crew on *Victura*. Ted, Kara, and John—all gone.[30]

~ With Jackie marrying Aristotle Onassis, the rich Greek shipping magnate, her children, Caroline and John, were pulled in more directions than the other youngsters. In 1973 Onassis's twenty-four-year-old son, Alexander, died in a plane crash, and Onassis himself died two years later. Caroline and John, still just children, were able to visit Cape Cod and Martha's Vineyard from time to time, stayed connected to the Hyannis

Port Kennedys, and sailed with Ted in *Victura*, the boat so closely associated with their father and their own slight memories of him. "It all fell to Ted—he picked up where his brothers left off," said a neighbor. "You could see him with Caroline, and they'd be walking along the beach skipping stones on the water. It was really very touching."[31]

In 1973 Teddy Jr. was diagnosed with osteosarcoma in his right leg—bone cancer. That leg was amputated in November. "You know, at age 12, losing your leg pretty much seems like the end of the world," he said.[32]

Teddy long remembered a day in the winter that followed when there was a heavy snow at their Washington, DC, home. The senator asked his son if he wanted to sled down the hill in front of their house. Though Teddy was still unaccustomed to his artificial leg, the father fetched the Flexible Flyer.

"The hill was covered with ice and snow," said Teddy. "And it wasn't easy for me to walk. And the hill was very slick. And as I struggled to walk, I slipped and I fell on the ice. And I started to cry and I said, 'I can't do this.' I said, 'I'll never be able to climb up that hill.'

"And he lifted me up in his strong, gentle arms and said something I will never forget. He said, 'I know you can do it. There is nothing that you can't do. We're going to climb that hill together, even if it takes us all day.'

"Sure enough, he held me around my waist and we slowly made it to the top. . . . But as I climbed on to his back and we flew down the hill that day, I knew he was right. I knew I was going to be OK."[33]

~ There is one area of Nantucket Sound with shoals so treacherous that Ted's sons Teddy Jr. and Patrick had separate tales of them to tell, which they both brought up in separate interviews. Ted took his sons out on father-son sailing and camping trips, just the father and one child at a time for four days, give or take. The point on the map imprinted on the boys' memories was in the vicinity of the little islands of Tuckernuck and Muskeget, between Nantucket and Martha's Vineyard.

Teddy was about ten on one such sail. They were battling wind and wave and found themselves trapped amid shoals near the islands, in a too-familiar battle to keep from grounding their boat. "Dad was riding the waves, trying to time it so when a wave lifted the boat he could surf on the wave over the sandbar. But all of a sudden we'd lose a wave" and have to try again and again, shoal after shoal. "I was so terrified." They finally got through the shallows and made it up to Nantucket, but not until after dark.[34]

In the same area Patrick said he and his father had to get out of their boat to push *Victura* off a sandbar. He remembered "running aground but having the sails up so you could push off. But if you push off and then it goes you could be left behind because the wind would take the boat. Sometimes in those situations Patrick would be in the boat, and his father would be in the water pushing it off a shoal.

"I can't tell you the number of times I'm on the tiller, I've got the mainsail out, the wind's blowing thirty-five knots, my dad's holding on, white-knuckling on the back of the rails. He's holding on because he had been pushing to get the boat off the sand bar, and if I head up into the wind I might run into another sandbar; at the same time I may lose my dad over the back, and there's no engine to get back there."

Fearful as they might have seemed at the time, they loved the memories. On Patrick's father-son sails with Ted, he recalled it would not be until after they left shore for the start of their journey that they would consider their destination. Their plan was sail out, find one of the islands they knew, camp, then move on to someplace else.

"We would totally be at the mercy of the winds and the tide and used to try to go to either Martha's Vineyard or Nantucket, depending on where the prevailing winds were taking us when we set off from Hyannis. It was just magical. We would run into pilot whales, we would get caught in cross currents and rip tides in between Nantucket and Tuckernuck and Muskeget," islands he said once were a land mass connected to Martha's Vineyard.

"We'd dig a pit and make a grill; we'd try to catch a bluefish or a striper on the way over, and we'd sit at night looking at the stars and in our sleeping bags. But invariably every trip was filled with adventure. And that was the beauty of it because it was always an adventure when you went out, because you never knew where the tide was going to take you, where the sea was going to take you, and we were always precariously close to being demolished."

Anchoring *Victura* by a beach was especially challenging, said Patrick:

That rip current would take you out and if you didn't anchor in enough time and secure the anchor with the wind coming in one direction and the tide taking you in another, when you tried to go into the wind you couldn't because the tide would sweep you out, so you had to anchor while under sail. It was all very perplexing . . . especially when you have to secure for the night and you don't have an engine, so it leaves you at the whim of how well you succeed the first try, because the second try is going to put you in a more dangerous circumstance.

All of these stories . . . you know catching a fish but not being able to pull it in because if we didn't get it in on time we would run into the shallow end, and the rocks . . . All I'm painting for you is a picture of how it was an adventure, and whenever we went sailing it was more than a prescribed set of events. It was always up to the unknown. And that's what gave my father such exhilaration and why he loved sailing so much.[35]

~ Bobby's daughter Kerry remembers voyages to Martha's Vineyard with her uncle skippering larger boats like *Mya* or *Glide.* "Every summer my Uncle Teddy used to take us to visit my Aunt Jackie on Martha's Vineyard, and we'd all sail over in the morning, and we had a wonderful picnic on her beach. And then we'd always dock near the Styrons—Bill and Rose Styron."[36]

Alexandra Styron, daughter of novelist William Styron, remembered those Kennedy invasions well. "Our house was Teddy's home base on the Vineyard. He would sail his boat, the *Mya,* over from the Cape often, have dinner with my parents, and spend the night. Once a summer his whole extended family sailed over with him, a veritable Hyannis Port boatlift, to camp out on the lawn. . . . Rosy Grier came once and did his knitting on the beach. And Maria's boyfriend, Arnold Schwarzenegger, showed up in alarmingly small shorts and smoked a cigar while playing touch football. Anything that amused him, which was a lot, was 'too mucking fuch!'"[37]

"We often would then come back on his boat at night . . . underneath the stars," Kerry said. "And it is an incredibly peaceful experience, beautiful and crystal clear and cold and you're huddled up next to one another and singing songs or Teddy was always telling stories, wonderful stories about politics or family or American history. And then I always loved to lie out on the deck, near the bow of the boat, away from everyone, and look up at the stars, at the sky that seemed so heavy. So many stars because you're not near any lights to compete with them. You know, there is a very profound understanding that we are a speck in the vast universe. And also of being in touch with water and nature and the outdoors . . . and all the wonders that that brings." She paused a moment and said, "you know it always made me feel close to God and his extraordinary creation. So that's a beautiful lifelong gift that our parents passed on to me."[38]

~ The children of Ted and Bob, as adults, look back on those years of crewing on *Victura* and *Resolute* as a time they learned self-confidence and self-worth. "As a little kid, I didn't look much like a sailor. But my father thought otherwise," said Patrick, who as a child struggled with asthma:

> In sailing there are rules as well, much like government. Tireless, mundane rules. . . . The rule was four people on the boat to race, just four. But my dad, of course, dug around until he found a rule around the rule. . . . Kids under 12, he found out, especially scrawny little redheads like me, could tag along.
>
> That may not mean a lot to many people but it meant a world of difference to me, because where I was not usually seen as a value-added, I was extremely appreciated on the sailboat because I was an extra set of hands and particularly when it came to untangling a line on the deck. Where an adult may not be able to do that without unbalancing the boat, a young person could scurry up there and untangle the lines, thereby not slowing the boat speed. . . . And so when you're feeling as if you have a role to play in life in such a critical team effort, in spite of the fact that you are under twelve, you feel like you matter.[39]

In a speech about his father, Patrick said,

> When we raced in foul weather there was lots of salty water and lots of salty language. Those experiences not only broadened my vocabulary,

sure, but they also built up my self-confidence. I saw a lot of his political philosophy in those sailboat races. One thing I noticed was that on the boat, as in our country, there was a role for everybody. A place for everybody to contribute. Second, in the race as in life, it didn't matter how strong the forces against you were so long as you kept driving forward. There was nothing to lose, maybe you'd even come out a winner. My dad was never bowed, he never gave up and there was no quit in dad.[40]

Chris added,

[Racing] gives younger children an opportunity to play a leadership role. You know, if you're ten years old and know what you're doing on a boat, you're infinitely more competent than the smartest adult who's had no experience. It's a phenomenal confidence builder. It allows them to play a role of peer and maybe leader to some degree, tell somebody to pull in the jib, "no not that line, don't touch that. Whatever you do don't touch that." . . . That's the thing about the Seniors, that boom weighs a lot, if somebody uncleats the halyard and thinks they released the jib and drops the boom, you know, you'll send everybody to the hospital.[41]

~ All that time and learning together made Ted Kennedy and his crew a colorful, competitive presence at the races. David Churbuck, a former journalist and current new media executive, remembered an Edgartown Regatta race against the Kennedys in the 1970s:

A leeward start on a very windy day. I am sailing our Wianno Senior, the yellow *Snafu III*, and manage a good start with a smart spinnaker set right at the gun. It's a very crowded starting line, with a fleet of forty sloops careening just feet apart from each other as they race towards a mark downwind to the north. To leeward of us, being incredibly aggressive and announcing his intention to exercise his right-of-way, is Teddy Kennedy, Jr. in the Kennedy's boat the *Victura*. Maintaining control is nearly impossible as the boats start to death roll in the building swells. As I get ready to douse our spinnaker and avoid the crazed Kennedy boat their spinnaker explodes with a satisfying pop!, and for one magical second the tatters fly forward like a hundred pennants, held out in perfect outline by the tapes along the parachute sail's leeches and foot. We sail on as they fall behind.[42]

With the wind blowing and spinnaker full, losing control of a Senior was a distinct possibility that Kennedys knew firsthand.

Bob's son Joe was at the tiller in one race that was almost called off on account of gale-force wind. A major race of the year—some forty Seniors were competing—with "big Teddy, little Teddy and Patrick," as Joe's crew. Heading downwind, they launched their spinnaker, a powerful sail nicknamed the "chute." "I thought something was a little strange when the only boat in the entire fleet that set a spinnaker was ours, and I thought maybe they know something that we don't," recalled Joe.

The first mark five miles distant, they were soon leading by a wide margin. "I am so happy," said Joe. "I am the happiest guy in the history of sailboat racing. What I haven't bothered to tell big Teddy, little Teddy or Patrick is that I can't steer the boat at all, because it is going wherever the wind is taking it."

About five hundred yards away was a fifteen-foot-tall bell buoy, dead ahead. "And then it's 200 yards, and then it's 100 yards, and Teddy looks around at me and says, 'Hey, don't you think we should turn a little bit?'"

They slammed into the buoy. Damage was minimal, however, so they paid the race-rule penalty, circled the buoy three times, and were now far behind.

The wind kept "blowing like stink," and Ted was on the rail getting cold and very wet. Ted's low spirits notwithstanding, he turned back to Joe and said, "Hey Joe, if last night, before going to bed, I told you we were going to round the first mark in seventh or eighth place, how would you have felt?"

"I guess I would have felt pretty good," said Joe.

"Let's go win this race," said Ted.

Three hours later, ever so slowly, picking off one boat after another, they won.[43]

~ If winning that day seemed unlikely, winning against one sailor in particular seemed a dream too grand to dare contemplate. Karl Anderson was a sailor with a record of such international sailing achievement that the weekend warriors of South Cape Cod—to an outsider—might have looked like 5K runners taking on a Boston Marathoner. Karl seemed of another species entirely. He was five-time world champion in J/24 class sailboats, a boat raced by thousands instead of the scores of Wianno Senior sailors. Today there are 5,300 J/24 sailboats in 150 fleets in forty countries. Karl won three Etchells North American titles. He won or placed national competition wins in other boats too: Melges 24, 12 Meter, Star, Rhodes 18, and the Soling, for which he was an Olympic qualifier. All those boats have large international fleets of competitors.

Karl sailed *Madeline* too, hull #148 in the Wianno Senior class. By 2003 he would win the Scudder Cup four times. But, as Max Kennedy points out, Karl "races [Seniors] every year and he consistently comes in the top four or five, but so do the other five people." He may be world-class, but among Senior racers he is merely very good. Karl knew better than to take these guys for granted, any more than the pros in J/24s. One year, in the Bass River Race, one leg of the Scudder Cup competition, the Kennedys found themselves up against Karl, mano a mano. Ted steered with Teddy Jr. among his crew and a friend named Dave Nunes. They were bow-and-bow with Karl's boat for much of the race, right behind or right beside.

"Dad couldn't believe Karl couldn't get by him," said Ted Jr. "Dad was down on his knees by the centerboard," trying to keep the boat in perfect balance. "It was very intense." They were so close you could hear the waves on Karl's bow.

Ted concentrated on every aspect of his boat, making sure that in that day's moderate breeze the sail shape was perfect and the weight distribution of crew optimal. He was careful not to oversteer, the bow making those tiny circles Ethel taught Max. What about the effect of the current, he might be thinking. Does that ripple on the water mean a quickening breeze?

"Every time Dave opened his mouth Dad would yell, 'would you shut the fuck up!'"[44]

Ted beat Karl Anderson. It was not like getting health care reform through Congress, but for Ted it must have been pretty close.

Max, like the other Kennedys of his generation, knew his Uncle Ted was one of the best sailors on the South Shore. "I'll tell you something else," he said after describing the great Karl Anderson. "My Uncle Teddy? He'll win almost every time. The last time I raced we raced two [in a series] and came in fourth or fifth. And we pulled up to [Ted's] boat and said, 'c'mon, c'mon, c'mon,' and he jumped in and we won. He's really good and my brother Joe is even a little bit better than that."[45]

It took Joe years of sailing with and against his Uncle Ted to become comparable in ability. When they first bought *Resolute*, Joe said, "I was supposed to go out and race against Teddy [in *Victura*]. Every single weekend on Saturday and Sunday I would see the butt end of that boat going over the horizon. Teddy always came in first, second or third."

After so many defeats, Joe remembered actually catching up with his uncle. "We were on the race course in Hyannis Port, and one of the crew said, 'Hey, I actually think we're overtaking your uncle.' I thought 'Oh, my God, I can't believe it.' So we got up next to him and of course the reason why we were catching him was he was up to his bellybutton in water, because the seams of the *Victura* had opened up and the boat was sinking. So we passed Teddy, my one victory."[46]

~ Throughout the 1960s and into the 1980s, Ted, Joe II, and Teddy Jr. raced together on *Victura*, winning major races at least ten times. In 1966 they won the Wianno Yacht Club long-distance race and the Hyannis Port Yacht Club Regatta with Ted at *Victura*'s helm. Joe II won the first race of the Edgartown Regatta in 1976, and then Teddy Jr. started winning races. He won the Edgartown Regatta in 1982, 1983, and 1987.

But the original *Victura*'s time on the water was limited. The boat was approaching fifty years old, and its wood hull planks and seams were harder and harder to repair. After Joe passed Ted as he sank, they got old *Victura* back to the harbor.

"The most people I ever saw on a Senior was 17 and that was in the last real sail that the old *Victura* took," remembered Ted's nephew Chris. "Teddy was our captain and all of the passengers except his sisters were kids."[47]

~ That was probably 1979. Ted's political career was severely set back by Chappaquiddick, but he still maintained a strong national base of support and continued to be mentioned as a candidate to restore the era of Camelot to the White House. Jimmy Carter was elected in 1976, but his term did not go well, and many in the party believed he could not be reelected. At the Democratic Party's midterm election in 1978, Ted was already sounding like a challenger, telling delegates with his booming voice: "Sometimes a party must sail against the wind. We cannot heed the call of those who say it is time to furl the sail. The party that tore itself apart over Vietnam in the 1960s cannot afford to tear itself apart today over budget cuts in basic social programs." Polls soon showed that Democrats by large margins preferred Ted to be the party's nominee in 1980. Labor leaders and other factions of the Democratic Party encouraged him. But, polls of the moment notwithstanding, challenging an incumbent president for his party's renomination was perilous business.

Speculation about Ted's plans was swirling in October 1979 when President Carter traveled to Boston to dedicate the new John F. Kennedy Presidential Library and Museum. In his speech, with Ted, Jackie, and all the Kennedys nearby, Carter found a way to cleverly ease the tension.

"In a press conference in March 1962," said Carter, "when the ravages of being president were beginning to show on his [JFK's] face, he was asked this two-part question: 'Mr. President, your brother Ted said recently on television that after seeing the cares of office on you, he wasn't sure he would ever be interested in being president.'" At that the crowd laughed.

Carter continued, "And the questioner continued, 'I wonder if you could tell us whether, first, if you had it to do over again, you would work for the presidency and, second, whether you can recommend this job to others?' The president replied, 'Well, the answer to the first question is yes, and the second is no. I do not recommend it to others—at least for a while.'"[48]

The following month, three days before he planned to announce his challenge to Carter, Ted granted a TV interview to Roger Mudd of CBS. Mudd asked him, "Senator, why do you want to be president?" Ted's answer was widely regarded as so inarticulate and vague that his campaign was set back before it even began. Afterward, son Patrick recalls his father, shaken, again doing as he had done in past moments of crisis. He returned to Hyannis Port and went sailing, alone, where his brothers had sailed, where he could collect his thoughts.[49]

Despite the setback, Ted's presidential race achieved victories in major states and remained viable all the way to the Democratic Convention. National party conventions were not then the coronations they are now; delegates could be won and the outcome reversed. Ted made desperate last-minute attempts to deprive the president of renomination, but they failed. Within hours of losing, Ted stepped to the podium to acknowledge defeat. Though a concession, it was the greatest speech he ever gave: "And may it be said of us, both in dark passages and in bright days, in the words of Tennyson that my brothers quoted and loved and that have special meaning for me now:

I am a part of all that I have met
Tho' much is taken, much abides
That which we are, we are—
One equal temper of heroic hearts,
Strong in will
To strive, to seek, to find and not to yield.

"For me, a few hours ago, this campaign came to an end.

"For all those whose cares have been our concern, the work goes on, the cause endures, the hope still lives, and the dream shall never die."[50]

~ Carter won the battle but lost the political war to Ronald Reagan. Ted's convention speech was his greatest moment, but it felt like the passing of the Kennedy era. Ted would continue on as a U.S. Senator, a role that from the perspective of the moment seemed an awful letdown. He did not know then as we know now that he would become one of the greatest, longest-serving, and most respected senators in American history.

It was around the time of Ted's failed campaign that old *Victura* had its last sail and was turned over to the JFK Library Foundation as a treasured relic of the Kennedy era. Ted and Joe bought a new Wianno Senior and christened it *Victura* in tribute to the one on its way to eternal dry dock at the John F. Kennedy Library and Museum in Boston, a museum piece ever after. Though never sailed again, *Victura's* influence on the Kennedys endures.

~ Thus began Ted's lost decade. Ted was a warm and loving father, but not in those years so good a husband. People spoke of his drinking and womanizing, and he would allude to them in later public admissions of his shortcomings. A letter said to be by Jackie, auctioned in 2007, counseled Joan to stop putting up with Ted's philandering. He "probably got [that] from his father," Jackie wrote.

"Forbidden fruit is what is exciting," she went on and criticized the constant presence of extended family and friends. "This community living has to stop. The family that really counts is his own. . . . He can go to the graduations of all of Ethel's children & teach John [Jack and Jackie's son] to sail the *Victura*—but, if he botches up his own family . . . that will be a pretty sad record."[51]

Well before 1980 Ted and Joan's marriage was failing, and they had already separated when Ted was running for president in 1980. Joan had problems of her own with alcohol. The couple announced plans to divorce in 1981 and did so the following year.

~ Ted took up residence in Joe and Rose's big house in 1982, and in the basement sipping room created by his father, a favorite hangout of Ted's that resembled a ship's interior, it is said he created a toast he often repeated.

"There are good ships, and there are wood ships, the ships that sail the sea. But the best ships are friendships, and may they always be."

In fact the toast probably has older Irish roots, but it fit him.

One fellow Wianno Senior sailor who knew Ted only slightly in the mid-1980s remembered him at "a wonderful little bar run by Hack Daniels," a few miles' sail west of Hyannis Port. "It was a nice quiet place to have a drink or two, and usually closed when Hack ran out of ice." His friends spotted on Hack's porch, "a small igloo cooler with the words 'Rose Kennedy Cottage' written on the lid. Inside were the makings for additional cocktails. The cooler was pilfered. . . . An hour later the senior senator stood on the steps demanding his cooler be returned for his boat ride back to Hyannis Port. He chided us not by name but by our boat's sail number, '140.'"[52]

Ted's affinity for cocktails was how many remembered him at that time. Ted enjoyed life then, he wrote in his memoir, but did not look forward to things. He loved being a senator and loved his children, friends, books, music, and good food. "I have enjoyed the company of women," he added. "I have enjoyed a stiff drink or two or three, and I've relished the smooth taste of good wine. At times, I've enjoyed these pleasures too much."[53]

A 1990 *Washington Post* profile said,

He remains a figure of controversy and complexity—diligent, shrewd, loud, funny, indiscreet, generous, bibulous, moody, tenacious. An extroverted raconteur with a million friends, he can be his own worst enemy. . . . "If you want to find Ted Kennedy," says Sen. Christopher Dodd (D-Conn.), echoing a similar line about Franklin D. Roosevelt, "listen for the laughter."

Tales of his drinking and raffish behavior have become part of his public persona. . . . Without question, Kennedy likes to drink. During a two-hour stretch on a Lufthansa flight from Boston to West Germany in November [1989], he downed two drinks of Scotch, two of vodka and, with dinner, three glasses of red wine. After three hours of sleep, the senator appeared sharp and refreshed upon arriving in Frankfurt at dawn, and subsequently put in a full day of work. He also is disciplined enough to stop drinking during his annual winter diet; last year, for example, he lost 50 pounds in 49 days, imbibing little more than a weight-loss concoction he refers to as "chocolate goop."[54]

Ted was well aware of his reputation and though some of what was said and written was false, even outrageous, "there was enough that I was doing to cause concern to those who cared about me." For a few years he lived "in the present tense, not despondently . . . but certainly with a sense of the void."[55]

~ That string of years might have been even worse for him had he not continued to have his family around him at the Cape. His family revered him as their leader, but there's no question he drew strength from them too. A highlight of that time was his niece Caroline's wedding in 1986. The ceremony was in Centerville on the Cape and the reception at the big house in Hyannis Port.

Arthur Schlesinger recorded the day in his journal:

> It was a happy day. I have never seen Caroline look more beautiful and the groom went through his paces with commendable aplomb. . . . [Ed Schlossberg] obviously pleases Caroline.
>
> [During the reception] the weather, which had been foggy in the morning and was still overcast in the early afternoon, suddenly became clear, with marvelous Cape afternoon light. The reception was like an alumni reunion [of JFK White House veterans]. The only senator or ex-senator [beside Ted] was John Culver. Where were Claiborne Pell and George McGovern? Still it was a most agreeable time. In due course, dinner was served in a tent with pennants flying in the wind. We ate with Ethel, young Joe and his wife, the Buchwalds and the Goodwins. In the evening there were toasts (Ted's voice breaking when he spoke of JFK), dancing, fireworks. These last were organized by George Plimpton, and some of the displays were dedicated by name to members of the wedding party or of the Kennedy family.[56]

Four years later it was Ted's daughter's turn to wed. The wedding party arrived at the Centerville church rehearsal with hair still wet from sailing and a shower, and Ted's press aide pointed out, "there are more law degrees among the 14 bridesmaids than among the 14 ushers." Afterward, immediate family dined at the Wianno Club. Kara's bridegroom was Michael Allen, an architect, member of the U.S. sailing team that won the 1980 Sardinia Cup, and a founding member of the Museum of Sailing in Newport, Rhode Island. The reception at the big house oversaw the familiar harbor with family sailboats *Victura*, *Mya*, and *Glide*, now colorfully displaying nautical flags that spelled out Kara and Michael. Atop the seven-tiered wedding cake was a replica of *Victura* with riggings of spun sugar.[57]

~ Ted's decade in the void came to a turning point in 1991, the year when his life sunk to one of its lowest points before unexpectedly also rising to a moment of greatest promise. The year began under a cloud of grief from another family loss, this time sister Jean's husband, Stephen Edward Smith, who had been a key member of Jack's presidential campaign in 1960 and was to manage his 1964 reelection campaign. He later managed the presidential primary campaigns of Bob in 1968 and Ted in 1980. Throughout those years he also managed the Kennedy family fortune. Losing Smith was like losing yet another of Ted's brothers.

On Easter weekend 1991, with the family gathered at the Kennedy estate in Palm Beach, Florida, Ted, his son Patrick, and nephew William Kennedy Smith, went out for drinks at a nightclub called Au Bar. When Patrick and William returned home, they had two women with them. One of them went out on the beach with William, and she later charged him with raping her there.

Media frenzy ensued. William was eventually acquitted, and Ted was not accused of doing anything worse than being a bad influence. But the legal proceedings were a font of week-after-week ugliness. *Time* magazine said Kennedy looked like a "Palm Beach boozer, lout and tabloid grotesque."[58] *Newsweek* said the Kennedys were "a family that has fallen from mythic grace to tawdry spectacle" and that Ted, "once the carrier of the family flame [had become] the living symbol of the family flaws."[59] The only people made happy were late night comedians like Jay Leno, who asked, "How many other 59-year-old men still go to Florida for spring break?"[60]

Ted had always been able to drink and party without it ever affecting his work as a senator. That was beginning to change, not because drink affected his performance, but because his reputation sapped his credibility. President George H. W. Bush's nomination of John Tower to be secretary of defense was derailed by accusations of the nominee's excessive fondness for women and wine. Ted's silence on that topic was widely noted. After the Palm Beach incident, when President Bush nominated Clarence Thomas to the U.S. Supreme Court and allegations arose that the nominee had sexually harassed a female lawyer, Ted was shamed into an even more deafening silence. This despite the forceful leadership role he had played in defeating the nomination of an earlier Reagan court nominee, Robert Bork. Ted had the Kennedy name and the Senate title, but he was sinking into irrelevance and political vulnerability.

~ The awfulness of the Palm Beach incident might have been wake-up call enough, but by all accounts what really turned Ted around was the woman he encountered at a dinner party in 1991. At the time his nephew's sexual battery charge was headed for well-publicized trial, and Ted was publicly atoning, telling friends he would change his ways. He was already drinking less and losing weight. At the party was Victoria Anne Reggie, a lawyer and divorced mother of two. From that moment he courted Vicki with dinner invitations, gifts, flowers, and constant attention. The following April he took her snorkeling in the U.S. Virgin Islands. There she found a small treasure among the coral—a gift Ted had planted for her to find. It was an engagement ring.[61]

Ted became a true family man once again. Ted Jr. said, "My father had this old saying: 'Home holds no fear for me,' Do the best you can. Do what's right. And you always can come home. And there's a place that understands, loves and welcomes you. It was an extraordinary part, I think, of the resiliency of the family.[62]

In Vicki he found someone with whom he could create that home that holds no fear. She was a wonderful discovery for a sixty-year-old man entering his elder-statesman years. His poll numbers, however, were plummeting and his future was in doubt. Compared to his colleagues on the Judiciary Committee, his approval ratings in a national Gallup Poll were the lowest at 22 percent.[63] The *Boston Globe* stated that more than three out of five Massachusetts voters thought it was time for somebody else to serve them in the Senate.[64] In the fall of 1991 Ted gave a speech in which he made an extraordinary public confession.

With Vicki's encouragement and as she sat in the audience, Ted spoke at the John F. Kennedy School of Government at Harvard and said, "I am painfully aware that the criticism directed at me in recent months involves far more than honest disagreements with my positions, or the usual criticism from the far right. It also involves the disappointment of friends and many others who rely on me to fight the good fight." He looked not at the audience but above them, straight into a row of television cameras, and spoke "tersely" and "unemotionally," according to the *New York Times*.[65]

"To them I say: I recognize my own shortcomings—the faults in the conduct of my private life. I realize that I alone am responsible for them, and I am the one who must confront them. I believe that each of us as individuals must not only struggle to make a better world, but to make ourselves better, too."⁶⁶

The speech was personal and political. Ted was up for reelection in 1994. In prior elections he was unassailable, a liberal in one of the nation's most liberal states, a Massachusetts Kennedy. But Bill Clinton was elected president in 1992 and, as often happens, the party winning the White House takes a beating in congressional races that follow two years later. On top of that was Ted's still-fresh association with scandal.

That summer of 1994, Ted was on *Mya* with his sister-in-law at Martha's Vineyard, waiting for President and Mrs. Clinton to arrive for a sail.

"Teddy, you go down and greet the President," said Jackie.

"Maurice is already there," said Ted, referring to Jackie's companion in her later years.

"Teddy, you do it," Jackie replied. "Maurice isn't running for re-election."⁶⁷

~ Ted that year needed every advantage. Where in previous years it was hard to find a Republican willing to challenge Ted, this year Republicans locally and nationally saw an extraordinary opportunity to hammer an electoral stake in the heart of the man who personified American political liberalism.

The Republican opponent was a successful business executive and a devout Mormon with five children, married twenty-five years to the woman he'd known since prep school. He made a clear family-values alternative to an incumbent with Ted's roguish reputation. The Republican was also from a prominent family, not as well-known as the Kennedys, but familiar in business and Republican circles. His father had been an automobile industry chief and a governor and in 1968 ran a credible campaign for the Republican presidential nomination. Not yet revealed was the considerable political acumen of the son, ample enough to later win the governorship of Massachusetts and the Republican nomination for president in 2012. Ted's opponent was Mitt Romney.

"He was young and slender and I was not," said Ted.

Romney was smart, well-to-do, a handsome new face of Republicanism;

he drew on vast national financial backing of conservative and business interests salivating for the defeat of a powerful Democratic leader. The Kennedys had a family fortune, but for campaigns they were individually on a short financial leash. To supplement his campaign Ted took out a second mortgage on his Virginia home, a move that surprised all those who thought the Kennedy well deeper.

In the summer of 1994, Romney had been twenty points down in the polls. By September many polls, even including the Kennedy campaign's, had them dead even. The National Democratic Party, seeing a campaign run by Ted's novice nephew Michael, going sour, began to intervene.

A pivotal moment emerged: the first debate. Lesser-known challengers usually benefit from any debate that puts them on a level stage with a famous incumbent. If Ted was not on his game, and if Romney was strong, the identity of both would be irrevocably redefined. All involved thought the debate could decide the outcome.

Ted knew it. On the afternoon of the debate, driving through Boston, he asked his driver to take him to the JFK Library and Museum. He got out and Vicki followed. He stood near the small sailboat on the lawn that his family had donated to the museum. *Victura*, displayed at a tilt as if heeling from the wind, pointed out to Boston Harbor like a great wooden seabird restrained from flight. The temperature was sixty degrees and the October sky turned briefly cloudy while he was there. The west wind blew at fourteen knots over *Victura* and through Ted's mostly white hair.[68] If the wind was fourteen there, it would be strong at the Cape. From the museum lawn he could look south across the water to the land where once stood the naval air station where his oldest brother, Joe Jr., his second father figure, learned fifty years earlier to fly in an open-cockpit yellow Stearman biplane. There was no sign now of the naval air station. Hardly anyone remembered it. He had briefing books and said he studied them, but his attention span must have been short as he let his mind wander and remember his life's turns. Joe. Jack. Bob. Kathleen. His mother, Rose, still alive then at 104. His children, Teddy, Patrick, and Kara.

Of that moment, Ted said, "It was just a thoughtful time. You're sort of reviewing your own thoughts and organizing. You want to collect your thoughts. You're thinking about broader kinds of themes about your life and what it's meant and what your values are and all the rest. You need the time to give some thoughts and some values in order to sift through. And that's what you do from time to time."[69]

Ted arrived ready at Faneuil Hall. The Kennedy campaign had built a case that Romney was flip-flopping on issues; when the topic of abortion came up, Ted said, "I am pro-choice. My opponent is multiple-choice." When Romney accused Ted's family of profiting inappropriately from real estate holdings, Ted reached deep into his diaphragm and said in righteous baritone: "Mr. Romney, the Kennedys are not in public service to make money. We have paid too high a price in our commitment to the public service of this country."

In that and the next debate, Ted more than redeemed himself. On election day, when Democrats had an otherwise bad year, he won 58 percent of the vote. If the previous decade was "lost," he was now found.

~ He easily won again in six years and six years after that. His influence more than rebounded. President Clinton's family returned more than once for a sail on *Mya*. He was a major force behind numerous incremental improvements in health care legislation that, taken together, benefited tens of millions of Americans. He helped his fellow Massachusetts senator John Kerry get the 2004 presidential nomination and, in 2008, his endorsement, along with that of Caroline and other Kennedy family members, was pivotal in Barack Obama's presidential primary campaign against Hillary Clinton. In American history, the number of U.S. senators of comparable achievement can be counted on one hand.

And in those later years he was there for his family too, now a father figure and role model in good times and bad. The schooner *Mya* had replaced *Victura* as his boat of choice; it was beautiful, blue, with a gaff-rigged foremast sail, and plenty big enough to accommodate his growing extended family. At seventy-seven, Ted wrote that looking from his porch at Nantucket Sound never tired him. The ocean "thrilled me and comforted me and protected me for all my life." The sea made a bond with his grandchildren, he said, and that especially pleased him.[70]

In 2000 Ted's nephew Chris fell from a horse and was severely injured—a broken scapula, two cracked ribs, broken bones along his back, nerve damage to his foot, and a concussion. He was thirty-seven, feeling like ninety-seven and using a walker with halting, slow, painful exertion. He moved into his mother's house to recover. Two days out of the hospital Chris received a phone call from Ted.

"Let's go sailing."

Chris was incredulous. "Did anybody tell you . . ."

"I heard about it," Ted said. "C'mon, it's a couple of ribs and those are small bones in your back. You need a bottle of Advil. What's two gonna do?"

It took Chris about twenty minutes just to shuffle his feet and maneuver his walker down the dock toward the launch that would take him to *Mya*. They laid him flat in the cockpit and put a pillow under his head.

Ted thought sailing cured anything. "He thought it was incredibly therapeutic," said Chris, recalling how Ted took his son Patrick out when he was younger and struggling with asthma. Even on rough seas, Patrick felt safer because he was away from allergens in the house, away from dogs and pollen.[71]

~ A summer or two before his death, Ted gathered together cousins, nieces, and other family and friends to sail *Mya* out to watch his grandson race against a fleet of twenty or thirty tiny Optimist sailboats. Optis have a "sprit-rigged" sail that resembles a gaff and are less than eight feet in length, meant for kids the age of Edward M. Kennedy III, "little Teddy," who was eight or nine at the time.

The fifty-foot *Mya* pulled in close to the race, tacking and jibing to stay close enough so "Big Ted" and his son "Medium Ted" could shout instruction to "Little Ted." Soon the older two were loudly disagreeing.

"Pull in the jib," shouted Big Ted.

"No, don't pull it in," countered Medium Ted.

"Jibe!"

"Don't do it! Tack."

Cousin Kerry recalled, "It was so hilariously funny, just to watch, and, of course, a lot of the people on the boat were terrified about us being so close to all those Optis. Of course, my uncle was such a master sailor nobody was in any sort of threat or danger."[72]

Big Ted remembered seeing Little Ted afterward at a sailing-awards presentation: first place for the August series and "Most Improved Sailor," which Ted particularly appreciated as one who always thought Kennedys had to work the hardest to win.

"You couldn't even button up Teddy's coat," said Big Ted, "because his chest was so filled with pride and achievement."[73]

CHAPTER II

Passages

Often beneath the wave, wide from this ledge
The dice of drowned men's bones he saw bequeath
An embassy. Their numbers as he watched,
Beat on the dusty shore and were obscured.

And wrecks passed without sound of bells,
The calyx of death's bounty giving back
A scattered chapter, livid hieroglyph,
The portent wound in corridors of shells.

Then in the circuit calm of one vast coil,
Its lashings charmed and malice reconciled,
Frosted eyes there were that lifted altars;
And silent answers crept across the stars.

Compass, quadrant and sextant contrive
No farther tides . . . High in the azure steeps
Monody shall not wake the mariner.
This fabulous Shadow only the sea keeps.

~ Hart Crane, "At Melville's Tomb"

(Melville's *Moby-Dick* begins in Nantucket, from which *Pequod* set sail.)

Jacqueline Kennedy Onassis died on May 19, 1994, taken by cancer. Always a lover and writer of verse, poems were read at her funeral. Caroline read, "Memory of Cape Cod," by Edna St. Vincent Millay, which concludes with,

We'll find you another beach like the beach at Truro.
Let me listen to the wind in the ash.
It sounds like the surf on the shore.[1]

Jackie's companion, Maurice Templeton, read a poem with a Homeric theme like "Ulysses," one Jackie had requested for her funeral. It was "Ithaka," by C. P. Cavafy and included these lines:

Hope the voyage is a long one.
May there be many a summer morning when,
with what pleasure, what joy,
you come into harbors seen for the first time;
. . . .
Keep Ithaka always in your mind.
Arriving there is what you are destined for.
But do not hurry the journey at all.
Better if it lasts for years,
so you are old by the time you reach the island.
wealthy with all you have gained on the way,
not expecting Ithaka to make you rich.
Ithaka gave you the marvelous journey.[2]

Five years later, as they so often did for occasions happy and sad, for weddings and funerals, holidays and lesser reasons in between, the Kennedy family began gathering at Hyannis Port for the wedding of Robert F. Kennedy's youngest daughter, Rory. Ethel was pregnant with Rory when her husband Bob was killed. Now Rory's wedding to Mark Bailey was set for Saturday, July 17, 1999. On the day before the event a great white tent was standing on the lawn of the Kennedy Compound.

An hour after nightfall that Friday, John F. Kennedy Jr. climbed into the pilot's seat of a single-engine Piper Saratoga II and prepared for a ninety-minute flight from Fairfield, New Jersey, to Martha's Vineyard. His wife, Carolyn Bessette Kennedy, and her sister Lauren, climbed into the plane. He planned to drop Lauren off at the Vineyard, then fly over the Sound to Hyannis Port to spend Friday night. John had earned his pilot's license a little over a year earlier and was not yet fully trained to fly on instruments alone. He still needed to look out the window to orient to the horizon. The night was dark, and haze obscured the line between sea and sky. Absent visual points of reference, a banking plane plays tricks with perception of gravity. At times, up isn't easily told from down. For pilots without instrument rating, "spatial disorientation" was a potentially dangerous consequence.

A flight instructor who had flown the same familiar route with John said later the president's son, thirty-eight, "was methodical about his flight planning and that he was very cautious about his aviation decision-making." But another of John's instructors said he "would not have felt comfortable" with John flying at night in those weather conditions. An instructor offered to fly with him that night, but John said he wanted to do it alone.[3]

The time for John's expected landing at Martha's Vineyard came and went. At two in the morning a family friend called the coast guard office at Woods Hole, whose commander lives in a house at the base of Nobska Point Light, a lighthouse that has watched over the waters of Nantucket and Vineyard sounds since 1876. It stood vigil over all the years Kennedy children sailed those waters. John's plane was reported missing.

With no sign of the plane the next day, police checked John's Manhattan apartment and found it empty. Witnesses confirmed John and his passengers had left Fairfield in his plane. While the search went on, hope diminished, then fell away entirely. The wedding was postponed. A mass was said on Ethel's porch overlooking Nantucket Sound. All that morning, no sign of plane or passengers.

On a beach on Martha's Vineyard, about two miles from the place John's mother, Jackie, lived until her death, items washed shore. A prescription pill bottle with Carolyn's name on it. A briefcase with her sister's business card affixed.

The bodies were recovered in 116 feet of water, seven miles offshore from Gay Head, near his mother's beach, the place where John as a boy was said to have looked for pirate shipwrecks.[4] Ted and his sons boarded the coast guard ship that pulled their remains from the sea.[5] A few days later a coast guard cutter carried the family from Woods Hole back to the same spot the plane had fallen. The ashes of John, Carolyn, and Lauren were gently committed there to the sea, waters near those *Victura* crossed on its ventures from home across Vineyard Sound.

~ Within a day or two of the loss of John's plane, the John F. Kennedy Hyannis Museum put up an easel to display lines from the president's 1962 speech at the America's Cup race: "We are tied to the ocean. When we go back to the sea, whether it is to sail or to watch it, we are going back from whence we came."[6] It was the speech where Jack said, "it is an interesting biological fact that all of us have, in our veins the exact same percentage of salt in our blood that exists in the ocean, and, therefore, we have salt in our blood, in our sweat, in our tears."

The mystery of that biological—one might say spiritual—connection between the human species and the sea has been a Kennedy preoccupation at least since the president's speech. Talking to family members, the theme reemerges in interviews conducted independent of one another.

"I think there have been so many wonderful experiences sailing with mothers, fathers, friends, and cousins," said Mark Shriver, "that it's just like a part of your blood; it's part of your essence."[7]

Without being asked, Jack's nephew Patrick called attention to "this notion that we are tied to something bigger than ourselves, that there is a mystery about the world, that we cannot know for certain, and we're all on a voyage, to find our place in the world. And this notion that we have the same salt in our blood as in the ocean, and that we're intimately tied to the ocean . . . 'from whence we came' . . . is just *powerful*." Patrick maintains that understanding humanity's common evolutionary origins helped open President Kennedy's eyes to civil rights and his declaration that "if, in short, [an American whose skin is dark] cannot enjoy the full and free life which all of us want, then who among us would be content to have the color of his skin changed and stand in his place? Who among us would then be content with the counsels of patience and delay?"[8]

"All of this stuff is a philosophy and it's a notion of us all being in it together. And what the sea, which is arbitrary, and a constant is, it is evolving, and yet it is also predictive, the tides come in and out. What a great metaphor for life."[9]

The ocean, says Kerry Kennedy, gives people "a reverence for life and an understanding of the cycles of life. You live and die and come back again—a sense of renewal. So I think those are all part of our growing up on the ocean. You can't grow up with that experience and not have it influence your worldview."[10]

Max, asked what sailing does for the soul, said, "I have no idea. I really don't know. I think it is different being on salt water than on fresh water." He chuckled and said, "It probably has something to do with having so much liquid inside of us. And I guess we were born in it too, right?" referring to amniotic fluid.[11]

~ Bound as the Kennedys were to the sea, the twenty-first century opened under circumstances that threatened the seascape they knew and loved. The shallows of Horseshoe Shoal that stood between Hyannis Port and the islands, among the places where so often *Victura* and the others struggled to keep from running aground, also happened to be an ideal location for one of the nation's first offshore wind farms. In 2001 developers proposed "Cape Wind," 130 wind turbines, each towering 440 feet from crest of waves to tip of blade. They would spread across twenty-four square miles. Those steady, strong southwest winds to which you could set a clock were ideal for more than sailing. Clean sustainable power generation, a popular notion in a liberal state like Massachusetts, won a warm public reception. Labor unions approved the jobs it would bring.

The Kennedys did not approve. Nor did a number of other affluent residents whose fondness for yachting and ocean views made the thought of a South Cape Cod industrial use appalling. Opponents allying with the Kennedys against the Cape Wind project were of varying political stripes, but they all had affluence and expensive hobbies as a common trait. Walter Cronkite opposed the project. Millionaire Bill Koch poured money into the formation of the Alliance to Protect Nantucket Sound and other efforts to campaign and lobby against Cape Wind. The Kennedys had always been the defenders of the undefended, and now their position seemed too influenced by moneyed personal interest. They were uncomfortably on the opposite side of environmentalists and unions.

Further complicating the conflicted position of the Kennedys was the fact that the leading Kennedy voice against the project was Robert F. Kennedy Jr., by then well into a career as an international and respected voice for environmental causes. He had led legal battles for clean water through

an organization called Riverkeepers, most notably on Hudson River issues. He fought the coal power industry, arguing it should be replaced by
alternate energy sources such as wind turbines. Nonetheless, Robert appeared on a National Public Radio program with the leader of the Cape
Wind development and argued with shrillness against Cape Wind. He
came off as disrespectful, loose with his facts, and hypocritical.

For his part, Ted told people he opposed it but kept his profile low. A
retired utility executive approached Ted at an outdoor concert in Hyannis and asked, "Can you tell me why you're opposed to this wind farm?"
Ted started by saying the developer wasn't paying enough for the use of
Horseshoe Shoal, but he was vague about how much money was necessary. Pressed for another reason, Ted said, "The sight of them bothers
me." Told the turbines would be visible only in the clearest weather, Ted
said, "But don't you realize, that's where I sail."[12]

It was one thing to sail against the wind, but here the Kennedys were
perceived as driven by not-in-my-back-yard self-interest. Massachusetts is
so proudly defined by the Kennedys of Hyannis Port that voters would
give them a pass on this issue. But for the rest of the decade that followed, twisted legal and political fights went on. In 2012 the Kennedy fight
against the wind farm was itself growing unsustainable, and Joseph Kennedy III, running for Congress, grandson of Robert F. Kennedy and son
of Joseph P. Kennedy II, broke with the family and endorsed the Cape
Wind project.

~ In the summer of 2003 Ted sailed *Mya* to second place in the Figawi
race, and Max sailed *Glide* to third place.[13] The name "Figawi" derives
from a story of lost Cape Cod sailors looking around and asking with
their familiar accent, "Wheh the Figk ah we?" It was a good summer's end
and boats were brought out of the water for winter storage. The original
Victura, displayed outdoors in warm weather, was every year shipped back
from the museum in Boston to south Cape Cod and placed into storage
along with the many other actively sailed Wianno Seniors. They all found
dry dock in the big storage sheds at the Crosby Yacht Yard in Osterville,
a kind of annual homecoming. There old *Victura* could be inspected for
weather damage, modest as it would be since it never sailed. It might get

a coat of varnish as needed. It rested out the winters, undercover, an unsailed sailboat, steps from Nantucket Sound, at the boatyard where craftsmen first assembled it seventy-one years before.

On December 10, 2003, a fire started in one of the Crosby sheds. It spread and broke through the roof, making small explosions heard nearby. Soon the glow could be seen for miles. More than 110 firefighters came from surrounding towns—Centerville, Osterville, Marstons Mills. One of the firefighters had his own boat nearby, so he used it to tow boats to safety. Scores of boats were lost, though no lives. Twenty-one of the boats lost were Wianno Seniors.

Old *Victura* was spared. It was in an untouched nearby building, and the fire's spread was contained. But the loss was spectacular otherwise:

Lost was Ethel's *Resolute*, #132, built 1964.

Lost: Eunice's *Headstart*, #139, built 1967.

Lost: Jack Fallon's *Marna*, #120, built 1950.

Also lost: *Shenanigans*, #109, 1947; *Sea Lion*, #118, 1948; *Cochenoe*, #125, 1962; *Cirrus*, #136, 1965; *Circe*, #133, 1965; *Pertelote*, #143, 1968; *Yankee Dime*, #145, 1969, *Intuition*, #147, 1969; *Never Miss*, #156, 1973; *Chanzia*, #157, 1973; *Molly*, #158, 1973; *Quest*, #159, 1973; *Owl*, #164, 1974; *Eowyn*, #169, 1975; *Lady Luck*, #171, 1976; *Betsy Ross*, #178, 1988; *Althaea*, #185, 1990; and *Shadowfax*, #192, 2003.[14]

It was one of the few times Ethel was seen with tears in her eyes.

"Tears came easily that night," a boatyard neighbor said. "They say the pain is what you feel after a barn fire. But horses don't live as long as these boats lived."[15]

Interviewed just afterward, Bob's son Chris said of *Resolute*: "We learned from our parents, we taught our kids, we bonded with our friends and we raced on it. It was a family boat more than anything else."[16]

To save the memory, Chris wrote a letter to his children in 2004. "My grandpa [Joe] bought a Senior for his kids. It was No. 94, which meant that it was the 94th Senior made. My dad learned to sail on it from his older brother Jack. Jack also taught Uncle Teddy how to sail. Teddy taught my brother Joe, and Joe taught me, and I taught you guys. Hopefully, when you are older, you can teach your kids."[17]

~ In May of 2008 Ted was diagnosed with a malignant brain tumor. In the year that followed, as he battled it, his sister Eunice's health worsened too. Strokes, car accidents, and more were finally catching up with Eunice, and she was nearing the end.

In June 2009 Ted and Vicki took a golf cart the short distance from the main house to the Shriver house. Eunice's son Bobby was there, along with his six-month-old daughter, Rosemary. Illness weighed on Eunice, and she needed cheering up.

They gossiped awhile about family, what guests were expected that week and, of course, who won the sailboat races. That was when Ted had an idea. Here was something to take Eunice's mind off her failing health. Eunice loved to rank people, give them passing or failing grades. She particularly loved to judge them as sailors. So Ted started with their older brother Joe and asked her if he was a good sailor or not.

"Yes," said Eunice, and they pondered that a moment.

"Bobby?"

"Not serious," she said. Ted thought she was being harsh.

On down the list Ted went, all nine brothers and sisters. Jack? Jean? Each one earned a pass or fail until Ted came to Kick. She was dismissed as wholly uninterested in the sport. With all nine cases so adjudicated, one question remained—the most important of all. Ted asked Eunice to pick the best sailor of the nine.

"I was."

Ted's laugh came from deep down. The firmer Eunice held to that position, the more Ted laughed.

That was in June of another of their warm, windswept summers on the Cape. Nantucket Sound and their boats were in view out their windows. Eunice died a few weeks later, on August 11, 2009. Ted died two weeks after Eunice.[18]

~ The story of *Victura* is a story of the power of shared experience. Families and friendships are not made strong by genetics or chance but by time spent together in common purpose. The Kennedys enjoyed one of the few sports where members of a family could compete as a team—gender, age, and physical strength notwithstanding. They raced together, or set a compass for distant Nantucket together, and they made it there together, strategizing, suffering the cold or enjoying the sun, talking about other topics, each with something to contribute. A family can get much the same experience if they farm together or build a house together or hike the Appalachian Trail. It's the shared experience, intentionally arranged by the parents, that brings families closer. Kennedys did not just sail together but also dined together with purposeful intent to have intelligent and enjoyable conversation. They made a simple poem about an ancient mariner a part of their shared heritage. Many families make little intentional effort to create shared experience, and they are weaker for it.

At Ted's funeral two sons, one nephew, and one lifelong friend eulogized him by telling stories of the *Victura*. Every big family has funerals to attend, but they have been particularly numerous for the Kennedys in recent years. Services are typically at Cape Cod before noon, leaving the family an afternoon to be together. Niece Kerry said that in recent years, without a conscious effort, another family tradition has emerged. After the funeral, they usually go sailing, typically on the bigger boats so they can all be together.

Ted's daughter, Kara, for whose cancer Ted so aggressively sought a cure, whose wedding cake had a little *Victura* on top, succumbed to a recurrence of cancer two years after Ted's death. At Kara's funeral brother Patrick read from Eugene O'Neill, a passage Ted also quoted in the opening pages of his memoir:

> I lay on the bowsprit, facing astern, with the water foaming into spume under me, the masts with every sail white in the moonlight, towering high above me. I became drunk with the beauty and the singing rhythm of it, and for a moment I lost myself—actually lost my life. I was set free! I dissolved in the sea, became white sails and flying spray, became beauty and rhythm, became moonlight and the ship and the high dim-starred sky! I belonged, without past or future, within place and unity and wild joy, within something greater than my own life, or the life of Man, to Life itself. To God, if they want to put it that way.[19]

Afterword

In August 2012 I knocked on the door of Brambletyde, once known as the Summer White House of Jack and Jacqueline Kennedy. Chris and Sheila Kennedy own it now. The night before my arrival their house had been battered by what Chris guessed were fifty-knot winds. It stands higher than most beach homes near it, up on a bluff, exposed. A window repair truck was outside.

Six months earlier, meeting north of Chicago to discuss my book on a winter day, Chris was enthusiastic about the project and invited me out for a sail at the Cape. Taking him up on the offer, I arrived in August. Sheila opened the door, and we walked toward the kitchen, where she offered me a sandwich to have before the sail. Would she be sailing too? No, she needed to take her daughter to a sailing lesson.

Chris was to take me on a wooden Wianno Senior, just like *Victura*. The available boat was *Ptarmigan*, Max's. Chris's own wood boat, named after the original *Victura*, had sprung a leak and was back at Crosby Yacht Yard for repairs. Arriving at the dock, there was Max Kennedy, hand pumping water from *Ptarmigan*'s bilge, something all owners of old Seniors find themselves doing with grudging frequency. *Ptarmigan*'s name was an homage to the family's beloved lost *Resolute*. The nineteenth-century Arctic exploration barque *Resolute*, with which the old Wianno Senior shared its name, was initially named *Ptarmigan* before being purchased in 1850 by the Royal Navy and refitted for Arctic service.

Chris, Max, and I set out with, I think, four youngsters aboard. Chris immediately offered to let me steer, entrusting the passengers to my unsteady hand. In short order, still in the harbor, another Senior was astern, also heading out, filled with kids and sailors, none older than about eighteen. I did not ask, but the other crew almost certainly included at least a Kennedy and a Shriver or two. "If they catch us, you're going to have to swim back," said Chris. We were only a couple hundred yards from the dock, with no original intent of racing, but there we were, racing. Happens a lot on a Senior.

Their boat grew closer, of course. I love sailing, but I am not a natural helmsman by any stretch, and I was sailing this boat for the first time. And, thanks to me, a younger generation is about to pass us by, too campy a metaphor for a book about new Kennedy generations passing older ones. The chasers grew closer, and Max wasn't going to let that happen, so he asked to take over the steering. Mischievously, he angled to port. I found Kennedys full of boating mischief this day. Max forced them to fall off to avoid hitting a moored boat. There would be no passing this generation this day.

At another moment of this short sail, the group of children on our boat suddenly stood, crouched, and leapt into the water, sent by Chris and Max to swim to a yacht a short distance away and, pirate-like, demand booty from the owners on deck. "Make them give you snacks or candy or something," I think Max said. I was later told to steer back to recollect the little pirates, all now treading water with as much ease and comfort as others find strolling on the beach. As we approached, I came too close to the yacht and Max directed me farther to port, aiming in a straight line toward the swimming children. We mustn't damage *Ptarmigan* or the larger boat to starboard, he said. I expressed concern for the fate of children directly in our path. Any Kennedy child has a better-than-average chance of becoming president some day, and I had a fleeting image of an America deprived of its future leader. Max knew the children would simply part like water lilies. They did and grabbed our rail to climb back aboard. One straggling skinny kid struggled to get his knee over the stern, so I offered one hand, my other on the tiller, while looking back and forth at child behind and yachts ahead so as not to ram anything. The bony white boy got his other knee up and made it aboard.

~ In researching this book I was struck by the family's love of Tennyson's "Ulysses" and the role the poem played in their public and private lives through the years. To this day there are Kennedy children who not only know the poem's history with the family, dating to the day young Jackie

recited it from memory to Jack, but also memorize verses. Chris's children have recited lines for dinnertime performances. Robert F. Kennedy
Jr.'s son Conor, who turned eighteen in 2012, some months earlier chose
"Ulysses" for a class assignment that required recitation of a poem from
memory. The timeless quality of the legend of Ulysses, like the limitless-
ness one experiences at ocean's edge and in the night sky, puts the complicated tabloid lives of the Kennedys in a better perspective. Most of us
do not have our daily lives played out in the media as do the Kennedys,
so they have more reason than most to find a healthier historical perspective. Who couldn't use that? "Ulysses" tells us that great ambitious figures
with boundless aspirations, struggling with human weakness and confronting tricks of fate, are not new to the world, but a persistent trope for
as long as humans have lived.

The memorizing of poems, the passing on of sailing technique, the
money, important as they are, are not the greatest of the family's inheri-
tances.

Mark Shriver is now a leader of Save the Children and in that capacity
traveled to Newtown, Connecticut, to do what he could shortly after the
shooting of twenty children and six school staff just days before Christmas 2012. Mark's brother Timothy P. Shriver is chair and CEO of the Special Olympics and has been on a campaign to ban the word "retard" from
polite conversation. Chris Kennedy, a four-month-old baby when his
uncle Jack was assassinated, became president of his grandfather's Merchandise Mart in Chicago. He chairs the University of Illinois Board of
Trustees, chaired his nephew Joseph P. Kennedy III's successful 2012 run
for Congress, and also that year started Top Box Foods, a not-for-profit
venture to provide nutritious foods for needy families.

Kerry Kennedy established the Robert F. Kennedy Memorial Center
for Human Rights and travels the world advocating social justice. Robert F. Kennedy Jr. has been a long-time activist in environmental law and
for clean rivers, lakes, and coastal waters. Max founded the Urban Ecol-
ogy Institute at Boston College and follows an eclectic range of academic
and public-purpose pursuits, including a documentary about suicide as
a weapon of war. Ted's son Patrick served two terms in Congress, then
cofounded One Mind for Research, a not-for-profit organization that

promotes the study of brain disorders and fights the social stigma associated with mental illness. Caroline Kennedy, an author, attorney, and mother of Rose, Tatiana, and John, lends her name to numerous causes and annually presents the Profiles in Courage Award, given in 2012 to three elected Iowa Supreme Court justices who ruled for same-sex marriage. In fall 2013, President Obama named Caroline the U.S. ambassador to Japan. There are other children of Kennedys and Shrivers doing too many good deeds to be listed here.

The Kennedys owe both much success and much pain to incessant media attention. Their voices are amplified and their foibles magnified, countervailing forces they struggle daily to navigate. They all have inherited wealth, but few people with a lot of money ever think they have enough, and nobody has seriously accused the Kennedys of using their position or influence to improperly further enrich themselves. The Kennedys have a family commitment and tradition to use their name and financial position to better the lives of others, and they have been impressively successful at encouraging younger generations to embrace that choice.

Bruce Feiler, who writes a popular column for the *New York Times* called "This Life," devoted years of research to a 2013 book, *The Secrets of Happy Families*. He surveyed extensive academic research that showed children who grew up with a strong family narrative history, especially those who understood that their families made it through big successes, awful tragedies, personal failures, and redemptions, fared best. "If you want a happier family, create, refine and retell the story of your family's positive moments and your ability to bounce back from the difficult ones. That act alone may increase the odds that your family will thrive for many generations to come."[1]

The Kennedys, now a large extended family, have had more than their share of the positive and the difficult, including their share of personal failings. What family of that size hasn't, if not quite to the extremes of the Kennedys? The strongest families own up to their failings, celebrate their victories, and draw strength by doing both.

~ As a child I spent countless hours on summer vacations with my father and brothers on fishing boats drifting on Wisconsin lakes. When not there, back home we read *Field and Stream* and dreamt of the summer to come, when we would catch the biggest walleye ever. My father once bought himself a big new plastic tackle box with many compartments and trays that fanned up and out to display his ever-expanding collection of Rapalas, Red Devils, Pinkies, and glistening rubber worms. He gave me his old tackle box, slightly rusted, but big, heavy, and sturdy, a serious angler's box with cork linings he cut for each small compartment. It was not the child's tackle box I had been using, a pathetic thing the size of a quarter gallon of milk. Now I am fifty-seven, and that metal tackle box is still among my prized possessions. It was like getting his gold watch, though he had no idea. Living in the moment as we all do, we parents rarely have a good sense that what we do with our children—consciously or unconsciously, large or small—stays with them forever, gets passed on, and lingers in their subconscious thought long, long after we die. The Kennedys have a stronger sense of that.

~ In the summer of 1932 *Victura* made its first sail out of Crosby Yacht Yard's harbor and headed east to Hyannis Port and the Kennedy home. No one knows for sure, but at such a thrilling moment for a couple of boys like Jack and his brother, Joe, surely they wanted to be along for the sail. Eighty years later another newly acquired Wianno Senior, *Dingle*, sailed into Hyannis Port to join the rest of the Kennedy-Shriver fleet, bobbing at its mooring by the breakwater, visible from their collection of homes around the old main house, not far from Max's *Ptarmigan* and Chris's newer *Victura*.

How many hours and days have they spent together in those boats and the others, like *Resolute*, rolling over swells, carving through white-crested waves, leaning over the gunwale to lessen the heel, experiencing every kind of wind—maddeningly slow, becalming, exhilarating—taking turns pulling in the jib sheet or skippering, arguing over whose turn it is to pump the bilge, punching the arm of somebody who did something tactically stupid, talking through career issues and family troubles, executing a tack, talking some more, heading off on a reach, back and forth like that, day by day, decade by decade.

~ Dockside, I met Max's daughter Summer, eighteen, fit, thin, and pretty and, like her siblings and cousins, spending most of her summer days in a bathing suit, almost always on, in, or by the water. She introduced herself confidently and politely, hand outstretched, elbow straight. A couple of years earlier, when she was fifteen or sixteen, with friends her age she sailed *Ptarmigan* from Hyannis Port to Nantucket, a distance of more than thirty miles. You can't see Nantucket from Hyannis Port. She literally sailed over the horizon.

Mark Shriver, who had just acquired the secondhand *Dingle* in 2012, told me he hopes his fourteen-year-old daughter will solo sail their boat next year, though perhaps not so far quite yet.

After my sail on *Ptarmigan*, Chris and I walked down the dock, and we saw his thirteen-year-old daughter among a group of kids in a sailing class, in bathing suits of bright colors fading from a summer-long wear, practicing the proper folding of a sail. As we walked by, Chris waved his hand in their direction and casually observed, "They're all Kennedys . . . or Shrivers." Kerry remembered when Chris, on a sail, pointed over his child's shoulder to a lighthouse and said, "If you draw a line from here to there and follow the line onward after the light, you'll end up in Ireland."[2]

~ In 1925, the same year Joe and Rose rented Malcolm Cottage, the same year Henry Beston bought his patch of dune for his "Outermost House," F. Scott Fitzgerald published *The Great Gatsby*. It would be hard to close this with lines better than those Fitzgerald chose to close his, when he wrote of a "future that year by year recedes before us."

"It eluded us then, but that's no matter—tomorrow we will run faster, stretch out our arms farther. . . . And one fine morning—

"So we beat on, boats against the current, borne back ceaselessly into the past."[3]

ACKNOWLEDGMENTS

Christopher G. Kennedy, son of Robert F. and Ethel Kennedy, in addition to sharing so much information himself, right down to a sail on a Wianno Senior, generously introduced me to cousins, siblings, spouses, and his extraordinary mother. Several members of the Kennedy and Shriver families kindly agreed to be interviewed. The staff of the John F. Kennedy Presidential Library and Museum were wonderfully helpful. My thanks go to Al Lawson and Jennifer Morgan Williams of the charming Osterville Historical Museum and to Timothy W. Fulham, chair of the Wianno Senior Class Association. I met many wonderful people, among them artist Henry Koehler, who shared stories and his only surviving photographs of his 1963 paintings of *Victura*. The process of bringing *Victura's* story to the printed page was aided by my friends Sallie Smith and John Montgomery; my agent, Claire Gerus; my editor Stephen Hull; Beth Aldrich; and Rhea and Earl Kingman. As important as the contributions so far noted have been, combined they do not equal those of my wife, Linda Kingman, supportive at every step, in innumerable ways, and for much longer, of course. And, speaking of the longer term, the original encourager of my written works was my mother, Virginia P. Graham, who to this day inspires and encourages both by example and thoughtful effort.

NOTES

CHAPTER 1. METAPHOR FOR LIFE

1 William Manchester, *The Death of a President* (New York: Harper and Row, 1967), 81–82.
2 Caroline Kennedy and Michael Beschloss, *Jacqueline Kennedy: Historic Conversations on Life with John F. Kennedy* (New York: Hyperion, 2011), 100–102.
3 Christopher G. Kennedy, interview with the author, Wilmette, IL, February 13, 2012.
4 Edward M. Kennedy, *True Compass* (New York: Twelve, 2009), 6.
5 Some sources say 1926 was their first year there, but the JFK Library holds correspondence with a household moving company scheduling their arrival for the summer of 1925. Joe Sr.'s biographer David Masaw says it was 1924.
6 C. G. Kennedy, interview, February 13, 2012.
7 Doris Kearns Goodwin, *The Fitzgeralds and the Kennedys: An American Saga* (New York: St. Martin's Press, 1991), 325.
8 Arthur M. Schlesinger Jr., *Robert Kennedy and His Times* (Boston: Houghton Mifflin Harcourt, 1978), 6.
9 Kearns Goodwin, *Fitzgeralds and the Kennedys*, 367.
10 Kennedy and Beschloss, *Jacqueline Kennedy*, 76.
11 Charles Higham, *Rose: The Life and Times of Rose Fitzgerald Kennedy* (New York: Pocket Books, 1995), 102–3.
12 Kearns Goodwin, *Fitzgeralds and the Kennedys*, 366.
13 Michael O'Brien, *John F. Kennedy: A Biography* (New York: St. Martin's Press, 2005), 36.

CHAPTER 2. BRED TO WIN

1 Caroline Kennedy, *The Best-Loved Poems of Jacqueline Kennedy Onassis* (New York: Hyperion, 2001), 31.
2 Edna St. Vincent Millay, *The Selected Poetry of Edna St. Vincent Millay* (New York: Modern Library, 2002), 49.
3 Henry Beston, *The Outermost House* (New York: Henry Holt, 1988), 6.
4 Ibid., 191.
5 Leo Damore, *The Cape Cod Years of John Fitzgerald Kennedy* (Englewood Cliffs, NJ: Prentice-Hall, 1967), 25.

6 Gail Cameron, *Rose: A Biography of Rose Fitzgerald Kennedy* (New York: Putnam's Sons, 1971), 127.

7 Damore, *Cape Cod Years*, 26.

8 O'Brien, *John F. Kennedy*.

9 Edward M. Kennedy, *The Fruitful Bough: A Tribute to Joseph P. Kennedy* (Privately published, printed by Halliday Lithographic, 1965), 255.

10 A 1943 fleet roster of Wianno Juniors and a *Daily Boston Globe* article spelled it "*Tenovus*," with an "o." The roster, also showing "*One More*," is displayed at the Osterville Historical Museum, Osterville, Mass. See also "Prevailing Wind, Pequod Hyannis Port Winners," *Daily Boston Globe*, September 9, 1936, 22.

11 Higham, *Rose*, 104.

12 Kearns Goodwin, *Fitzgeralds and the Kennedys*.

13 Damore, *Cape Cod Years*, 26.

14 Tazewell Shepard Jr., *John F. Kennedy: Man of the Sea* (New York: Morrow, 1965), 27–28.

15 Henry David Thoreau, *Cape Cod* (Boston: Houghton, Mifflin, 1893), 76-77.

16 Beston, *Outermost House*, 47.

17 Joseph P. Kennedy Jr. to Joseph P. Kennedy Sr., January 26, 1930, Rose Fitzgerald Kennedy Papers Collection, JFK Library and Museum, Boston.

18 Correspondence between Joseph P. Kennedy Jr. and Edward Moore, May 1930, Joseph P. Kennedy Papers Collection, JFK Library and Museum.

19 Kennedy Jr. to Kennedy Sr., April 7, 1931, Fitzgerald Kennedy Papers.

20 John F. Kennedy to Rose and Joseph P. Kennedy Sr., [1932?], Fitgzerald Kennedy Papers.

21 Wilton B. Crosby to Joseph P. Kennedy, January 12, 1932, Joseph P. Kennedy Papers.

22 Joseph P. Kennedy Jr. to C. J. Scollard, n.d., Joseph P. Kennedy Papers.

23 John F. Kennedy to Rose Kennedy, Spring 1932, John F. Kennedy Personal Papers, JFK Library and Museum, doi JFKPP-001–010, accessed August 25, 2013, http://www.jfklibrary.org.

24 Wilton Crosby to Joseph P. Kennedy Sr., January 12, 1932; Joseph P. Kennedy Jr. to C. J. Scollard, [March 1932?]; and C. J. Scollard to Wilton Crosby, March 18, 1932, Joseph P. Kennedy Papers.

25 "The President-to-Be in Action," *Sports Illustrated* 13, no. 26 (December 26, 1960): 22–23.

26 Ariane Schwartz, PhD, e-mail message to author, March 21, 2013.

27 Wianno Senior Class Association, *Wianno Senior One Design Rules*, accessed August 11, 2013, http://www.wiannosenior.org.

28 Malcolm Howes, "The Wianno Senior," *Wooden Boat* 91 (November–December 1989): 61.

29 *Lady of the Sound, the Wianno Senior*, produced and written by Andrew Fone (Centerville, MA: Pearl River Productions, 2005), documentary film.

30 Howes, "Wianno Senior," 61.

31 Ibid., 60.

32 Ibid., 60–61.

33 *Lady of the Sound.*

34 Len Edgerly, "Sailing with My Friend Max Kennedy," YouTube video, 8:46, Mile High Pod Chronicles Productions, August 4, 2006, accessed August 27, 2013, http://www.youtube.com.

35 David Arnold, "Blue-Blooded Racers Costly, Cherished, and Original to the Cape," *Boston Globe*, May 23, 2004, 24.

36 Ibid.

37 Mark K. Shriver, telephone interview with the author, January 5, 2013.

38 Richard Ulian, *Sailing: An Informal Primer* (New York: Van Nostrand Reinhold, 1982).

39 Ibid., 57–58.

40 "New Securities Chief Flies from Washington for Weekend on Cape," *Boston Globe*, July 15, 1934, A42.

41 Damore, *Cape Cod Years*, 40.

42 Ibid., 41.

43 Roger Whitcomb and Wendy Williams, *Cape Wind: Money, Celebrity, Class, Politics, and the Battle for Our Energy Future* (New York: Public Affairs, 2007), 126.

44 Ibid., 126.

45 Damore, *Cape Cod Years*, 25.

46 Ibid., 35–36.

47 George Connelly to Joseph P. Kennedy Sr., June 16, 1932, Joseph P. Kennedy Papers.

48 J. Julius Fanta, *Sailing with President Kennedy* (New York: Sea Lore, 1968), 25.

49 Damore, *Cape Cod Years*, 36.

50 Robert Dallek, *An Unfinished Life: John F. Kennedy* (Boston: Little, Brown, 2003), 32.

51 Damore, *Cape Cod Years*, 36–37.

52 Luella Hennessey-Donovan, recorded interview by Ed Martin, November 26, 1964, John F. Kennedy Oral History Collection, JFK Library, Boston.

53 Kearns Goodwin, *Fitzgeralds and the Kennedys*, 457.

54 Vincent Bzdek, *The Kennedy Legacy: Jack, Bobby and Ted and a Family Dream Fulfilled* (New York: Palgrave Macmillan, 2009), 49.

55 Nigel Hamilton, *JFK: Reckless Youth* (New York: Random House, 1992), 115.

56 O'Brien, *John F. Kennedy*, 47.

57 Rose Fitzgerald Kennedy, *Times to Remember* (Garden City, NY: Doubleday, 1974), 143.

58 Robert Kennedy's tribute to his father read at Joseph Kennedy's funeral by Edward

M. Kennedy, November 20, 1969. Reported in *Congressional Record* 115 (November 25, 1969): 35877.

59 Whitcomb and Williams, *Cape Wind*, 153.

60 Jack Newfield, *RFK: A Memoir* (New York: Nation Books, 2009) 42.

61 O'Brien, *John F. Kennedy*, 48.

62 Seymour Hersch, *The Dark Side of Camelot* (Boston: Little, Brown, 1997), 17.

63 Joanna Barboza, recorded interview by Sheldon M. Stern, March 24, 1982, John F. Kennedy Library Oral History Program, 13.

64 Hamilton, *JFK*, 94.

65 Ralph G. Martin, *A Hero for Our Time: An Intimate Story of the Kennedy Years* (New York: Scribner, 1983), 26. The interview with JFK was in 1959.

66 O'Brien, *John F. Kennedy*, 48.

67 Damore, *Cape Cod Years*, 23.

68 Lynne McTaggart, *Kathleen Kennedy, Her Life and Times* (Garden City, NY: Dial; Doubleday, 1983), 14.

69 Hank Searls, *The Lost Prince: Young Joe, the Forgotten Kennedy; The Story of the Oldest Brother* (New York: World, 1969), 60.

70 Hamilton, *JFK*, 162–63.

71 Cameron, *Rose*, 128.

CHAPTER 3. AT ONCE RIVALROUS AND LOYAL

1 Joseph P. Kennedy Sr. letter to Joseph P. Kennedy Jr., May 4, 1934; Joseph P. Kennedy Jr. to Robert Kennedy, May 3, 1934; Kathleen Kennedy letter to Rose Kennedy, May 27, 1934, Joseph P. Kennedy Papers.

2 Laurence Leamer, *The Kennedy Women* (New York: Villard Books, 1994), 209–10.

3 "Prevailing Wind, Pequod Hyannis Port Winners," *Daily Boston Globe*, September 9, 1936.

4 "Nearly 200 Boats Turn Out in Half-Gale off Edgartown," *Daily Boston Globe*, July 25, 1937.

5 Searls, *Lost Prince*, 59.

6 C. G. Kennedy, interview, February 13, 2012.

7 Jean Kiley Wells, "Memories of the Thirties," in *The Senior—75 Years of the Wianno Senior Class* (Osterville, MA: Wianno Senior Class Association, 1989), 19.

8 Wells, "Memories of the Thirties," 19.

9 John F. Kennedy, ed., *As We Remember Joe* (Cambridge, MA: privately published by University Press, 1945).

10 Searls, *Lost Prince*, 60.

11 Kennedy Sr. to Kennedy Jr., May 4, 1934, Joseph P. Kennedy Papers.

12 Thomas Bilodeau, recorded interview by James Murray, May 12, 1964, John F. Kennedy Library Oral History Program, 8–9.

13 Searls, *Lost Prince*, 96.

14 J. F. Kennedy, *As We Remember Joe*, 59. His boyhood spelling and grammatical errors are corrected here.

15 Kearns Goodwin, *Fitzgeralds and the Kennedys*, 355.

16 Bilodeau, interview, 10.

17 Bzdek, *Kennedy Legacy*, 20.

18 Bilodeau, interview, 7–8.

19 C. G. Kennedy, interview, February 13, 2012.

20 Ibid.

21 Ulian, *Sailing*, 42.

22 Fanta, *Sailing with President Kennedy*, 22–26.

CHAPTER 4. CHEMISTRY

1 McTaggart, *Kathleen Kennedy*, 13–23.

2 Leamer, *Kennedy Women*, 225. Leamer's footnote cites an interview with Tom Egerton.

3 "Prevailing Wind," 22.

4 Carla Baranauckas, "Eunice Kennedy Shriver, Influential Founder of Special Olympics, Dies at 88," *New York Times*, August 11, 2009.

5 Andrew Jacobs, "Patricia Kennedy Lawford Dies at 82," *New York Times*, September 18, 2006. See also Kearns Goodwin, *Fitzgeralds and the Kennedys*.

6 Troy McMullen, "The Last Kennedy: Jean Kennedy Smith," *ABC News*, August 26, 2009.

7 Martha T. Moore, "JFK's Sister Jean Kennedy Smith reflects," *USA Today*, September 26, 2010.

8 Bilodeau, interview.

9 David Bolles and Guy Gurney, "The Kennedy Brothers and the Stars," International Star Class Yacht Racing Association, accessed August 22, 2013, http://www.starclass.org.

10 Kennedy Jr. to Kennedy Sr., telegram, August 15, 1934, Joseph P. Kennedy Papers.

11 Paul Murphy to Joseph P. Kennedy Sr., May 1, 1936, Joseph P. Kennedy Papers.

12 Edward Moore to Joseph P. Kennedy Jr., August 27, 1936, Joseph P. Kennedy Papers.

13 "Harvard Skippers Win M'Millan Cup," *New York Times*, June 25, 1938, 9.

14 Leonard Fowle, "The McMillan Cup in Seniors," in *Senior*, 26.

15 Herbert S. Parmet, *Jack: The Struggles of John F. Kennedy* (New York: Deal, 1982), 47.

16 "Hyannisport Defeats Wianno Y. C. for Trophy," *Boston Globe*, July 23, 1938.

17 Edward J. Renehan Jr., *The Kennedys at War* (New York: Doubleday, 2002), 95.

18 Francis Ann Cannon to John F. Kennedy, telegram, February 25, 1939, John F. Kennedy Personal Papers.

19 J. F. Kennedy, *As We Remember Joe*, 53.
20 Michael R. Beschloss, *Kennedy and Roosevelt: The Uneasy Alliance* (New York: Norton, 1980), 190.
21 John Bartlett, *Familiar Quotations* (Boston: Little, Brown, 1968), 921.
22 Damore, *Cape Cod Years*, 57–58.
23 Ibid., 58.
24 "Lightning Splits Mast of Young Kennedy's Boat at Osterville," *Daily Boston Globe*, July 12, 1936.

CHAPTER 5. WAR AND DESTINY

1 Robert J. Donovan, *PT 109: John F. Kennedy in World War II* (New York: McGraw Hill, 1961), 34.
2 O'Brien, *John F. Kennedy*, 113–14.
3 Damore, *Cape Cod Years*, 61.
4 Searls, *Lost Prince*, 179, 197.
5 Recorded interview of JFK, *John F. Kennedy Presidential Library and Museum Introductory Film*, 1992, John F. Kennedy Library Foundation.
6 Renehan, *Kennedys at War*, 191–92.
7 Ron McCoy, son of Inga Arvad, e-mail correspondence with the author, June 29, 2013. McCoy said Hitler was not in the box the day Inga sat there.
8 Searls, *Lost Prince*, 181.
9 Donovan, *PT 109*, 36.
10 Robert F. Kennedy to Joseph Kennedy Sr., n.d., Joseph P. Kennedy Papers.
11 Damore, *Cape Cod Years*, 62–65.
12 Ibid., 63.
13 Robert F. Kennedy to Rose and Joseph Kennedy Sr., n.d., Joseph P. Kennedy Papers.
14 "Guadalcanal-Tulagi Invasion, 7–9 August, 1941," "Guadalcanal Campaign, August 1942–February 1943," and "Conquest of Tulagi, 7–8 August, 1942," U.S. Navy, accessed August 22, 2013, http://www.history.navy.mil/.
15 John F. Kennedy to sister Kathleen Kennedy, June 1943, Joseph P. Kennedy Papers.
16 Ibid.
17 John Hersey, "PT Squadron in the Pacific," *Life*, May 10, 1943, 74–87.
18 Kearns Goodwin, *Fitzgeralds and the Kennedys*, 649.
19 Vivian M. Baulch and Patricia Zacharias, "The 1943 Detroit Race Riots," *Detroit News*, February 10, 1999.
20 Hersey, "PT Squadron."
21 O'Brien, *John F. Kennedy*, 157.
22 Inga Arvad, "Lt. Kennedy Saves His Men as Japs Cut PT Boat in Half," *Pittsburgh Post-Gazette*, January 13, 1944), 4.
23 John Hersey, "Survival," *New Yorker* 20, no. 18 (June 17, 1944): 31–43.

24 Donovan, *PT 109*, 163.

25 Hersey, "Survival."

26 Ibid.

27 Ibid.

28 M. Lynn Landweer and Peter Unseth, "An Introduction to Language Use in Melanesia," *International Journal of the Sociology of Language* 214 (2012): 1–3.

29 This account of PT-109 is based primarily on Donovan, *PT 109*, with some details added from O'Brien, *John F. Kennedy*. The native Gasa's own account of their role was recorded many years later and told by Ted Chamberlain in "JFK's Island Rescuers Honored at Emotional Reunion," *National Geographic*, November 20, 2002. Gasa claimed it was his idea to carve a message in a coconut.

30 Interview with Edward Kennedy, *Lady of the Sound*.

31 Parmet, *Jack*, 108.

32 O'Brien, *John F. Kennedy*, 161.

33 Edward Kennedy, *True Compass*, 75.

34 O'Brien, *John F. Kennedy*, 161.

35 Kearns Goodwin, *Kennedys and the Fitzgeralds*, 662.

36 Damore, *Cape Cod Years*, 69.

37 Searls, *Lost Prince*, 202–3.

38 Laurence Leamer, *The Kennedy Men: 1901–1963* (New York: HarperCollins, 2001), 212.

39 Kearns Goodwin, *Kennedys and the Fitzgeralds*, 659.

40 John F. Kennedy to Inga Arvad, courtesy of Ron McCoy.

41 Renehan, *Kennedys at War*, 178–79.

42 Arvad, "Lt. Kennedy," 4.

43 McTaggart, *Kathleen Kennedy*, 143.

44 J. F. Kennedy, *As We Remember Joe*, 54.

45 Renehan, *Kennedys at War*, 191.

46 Amanda Smith, ed., *Hostage to Fortune: The Letters of Joseph P. Kennedy* (New York: Viking, 2001), 587, 581.

47 J. F. Kennedy, *As We Remember Joe*, 54.

48 Kearns Goodwin, *Fitzgeralds and the Kennedys*, 687.

49 Ibid., 683.

50 A. Smith, *Hostage to Fortune*, 598.

51 Cari Beauchamp, "Two Sons, One Destiny," *Vanity Fair*, December 2004, accessed August 20, 2013, http://www.vanityfair.com.

52 Kearns Goodwin, *Fitzgeralds and the Kennedys*, 685.

53 A. Smith, *Hostage to Fortune*, 598.

54 Searls, *Lost Prince*, 270.

55 Kearns Goodwin, *Fitzgeralds and the Kennedys*, 687.

56 Christopher Buckley, "Family Guy," review of *The Patriarch*, by David Nasaw, *New York Times*, November 18, 2012, Sunday Book Review, BR1.

57 John F. Kennedy, "Letter Written by Ensign James Simpson, U.S.N.," in J. F. Kennedy, *As We Remember Joe*.

58 A. Smith, *Hostage to Fortune*, 599.

59 Bzdek, *Kennedy Legacy*, 52.

60 Edward Kennedy, *True Compass*, 86; Joe Gargan, WXGK News, John F. Kennedy Hyannis Museum, November 5, 2010, accessed August 24, 2013, http://jfkhyannismuseum.org.

61 J. F. Kennedy, *As We Remember Joe*, 16.

62 Kearns Goodwin, *Fitzgeralds and the Kennedys*, 687.

63 Renehan, *Kennedys at War*, 308.

64 "U.S.S Warrington (DD-383)," U.S.S. Warrington Alumni Association, accessed May 5, 2013, http://www.usswarrington.org/.

65 Multiple sources describe this storm, including H. C. Sumner, "The North Atlantic Hurricane of September 8–16, 1944," *Monthly Weather Review* 72, no. 9 (September 1944): 187–89. See also Ken Adams, "The Great Atlantic Hurricane of September 1944: My Remembrances," *Destroyer Escort Sailors Association*, May 2008, accessed August 20, 2013, http://www.desausa.org.

66 "Vineyard Sound Lightship," Executive Office of Energy and Environmental Affairs, State of Massachussets, accessed August 20, 2013, http://www.mass.gov/eea/.

67 O'Brien, *John F. Kennedy*, 170. On August 17, 1944, JFK underwent rectal surgery at the Chelsea naval hospital.

68 Damore, *Cape Cod Years*, 71–75, tells the story of saving *Victura* from the storm and the aftermath with his new friend from *Life* and the two sisters.

69 A. Smith, *Hostage to Fortune*, 601.

70 Kearns Goodwin, *Fitzeralds and the Kennedys*, 697.

71 Ibid.

CHAPTER 6. JACK

1 Recorded interview of JFK, *Introductory Film*.

2 Dallek, *Unfinished Life*.

3 O'Brien, *John F. Kennedy*, 188.

4 Ibid., 196.

5 Damore, *Cape Cod Years*, 93.

6 Barboza, interview, 14–15.

7 Accounts of the strain Kick's relationship had on the family are told by Kearns Goodwin, *Fitzgeralds and the Kennedys*, and others.

8 O'Brien, *John F. Kennedy*, 228.

9 Edward Kennedy, *True Compass*, 91.

10 Ibid., 91.

11 Ibid., 91–92.

12 Fanta, *Sailing with President Kennedy*, 21.

13 Sarah Bradford, *America's Queen: The Life of Jacqueline Kennedy Onassis* (New York: Viking, 2000), 54.

14 O'Brien, *John F. Kennedy*, 265.

15 Bradford, *America's Queen*, 990.

16 Dinah Bridge, recorded interview by Joseph E. O'Connor, October 30, 1966, John F. Kennedy Library Oral History Program, 4.

17 Bradford, *America's Queen*, 88.

18 O'Brien, *John F. Kennedy*, 266.

19 "Life Goes Courting with a U. S. Senator: John Kennedy and His Fiancée Enjoy an Outing on Cape Cod," *Life* 35, no. 3 (July 20, 1953): 96–99.

20 Victor Lasky, *JFK: The Man and the Myth* (New York: MacMillon, 1963), 160.

21 C. Kennedy, *Best-Loved Poems*, 71.

22 Jacqueline Kennedy, "Meanwhile in Massachusetts," JFK Family Papers, JFK Library and Museum.

23 Bradford, *America's Queen*.

24 Edward Klein, *All Too Human: The Love Story of Jack and Jackie Kennedy* (New York: Simon and Schuster, 1997), 213.

25 Ibid., 214.

26 C. Kennedy, *Best-Loved Poems*, 71–72.

27 *New York Times* articles on the two weddings coincidentally cited the same number of spectators for both weddings—three thousand.

28 O'Brien, *John F. Kennedy*, 279.

29 Ibid., 283.

30 Rose Kennedy, *Times to Remember*, 146.

31 O'Brien, *John F. Kennedy*, 316.

32 Ibid., 322–23.

33 Jerry Oppenheimer, *The Other Mrs. Kennedy: An Intimate and Revealing Look at the Hidden Life of Ethel Skakel Kennedy* (New York: St. Martin's, 1994), 196.

34 O'Brien, John F. Kennedy, 328.

35 Ibid.

36 Dallek, *Unfinished Life*.

37 O'Brien, *John F. Kennedy*, 331.

38 Christopher Andersen, *Jack and Jackie: Portrait of an American Marriage* (New York: Avon Books, 1997), 135.

39 Arthur M. Schlesinger Jr., *Journals, 1952–2000*, edited by Andrew Schlesinger Jr. and Stephen Schlesinger (New York: Penguin, 2007), 56–58.

40 Damore, *Cape Cod Years*, 185.

41 Norman Mailer, "Superman Comes to the Supermarket," *Esquire*, November 1960.

42 Damore, *Cape Cod Years*, 188.

43 "Jack Kennedy Practices the Fitness That He Preaches," *Sports Illustrated* 13, no. 26 (December 26, 1960): 18-23.

44 John F. Kennedy, "Remarks of Senator John F. Kennedy at Milwaukee, Wisconsin, October 23, 1960," JFK Library and Museum, accessed August 30, 2013, http://www.jfklibrary.org.

45 Verse by George D. Lottman, added in 1926 to Alfred H. Miles's original 1906 lyrics, "Anchors Aweigh," Naval Academy Band, United States Naval Academy, accessed August 17, 2013, http://www.usna.edu. The song's lyrics vary according to verse, and it is not known which verse was sung to JFK that day.

46 O'Brien, *John F. Kennedy*, 445.

47 John F. Kennedy, "Remarks of Senator John F. Kennedy, Springfield, Mass., City Hall," November 7, 1960, quoted in Gerhard Peters and John T. Woolley, *American Presidency Project*, accessed August 17, 2013, http://www.presidency.ucsb.edu.

48 Damore, *Cape Cod Years*, 214.

49 Ibid., 226.

50 Andersen, *Jack and Jackie*, 226.

51 Ibid., 226.

52 Thoreau, *Cape Cod*, 232–33.

CHAPTER 7. THE PRESIDENCY

1 T. Shepard, *John F. Kennedy*, 29.

2 Ibid., 23–24.

3 Ibid., 25.

4 John F. Kennedy, "Remarks to the Faculty and Students of the French Institute of High Studies for National Defense," March 25, 1963, *American Presidency Project*, August 17, 2013, http://www.presidency.ucsb.edu.

5 John F. Kennedy, "Remarks in Philadelphia at a Dinner Sponsored by the Democratic County Executive Committee," October 30, 1963, *American Presidency Project*, accessed August 17, 2013, http://www.presidency.ucsb.edu.

6 Tazewell Shepard, USS *Constitution* correspondence, Papers of John F. Kennedy, Presidential Papers, President's Office Files, JFK Library and Museum, accessed August 24, 2013, http://www.jfklibrary.org.

7 Robert Frost, "Education by Poetry" (speech, Amherst College, MA, ca. 1930), revised for publication in *Amherst Graduates' Quarterly*, February 1931. This version appears on the website of the Department of English at the University of Texas at Austin, accessed August 17, 2013, http://www.en.utexas.edu.

8 James Geary, *I Is an Other: The Secret Life of Metaphor and How It Shapes the Way We See the World* (New York: Harper Collins, 2011), 3.

9 Patrick J. Kennedy, interview with the author, Providence, RI, March 19, 2012.

10 O'Brien, *John F. Kennedy*, 575.

11 Hugh Sidey, *John F. Kennedy, President* (New York: Atheneum, 1964), 95–96.

12 Ibid., 101–2.

13 Michael R. Beschloss, "Kennedy and the Decision to Go to the Moon," in *Spaceflight and the Myth of Presidential Leadership*, ed. Roger D. Launius and Howard E. McCurdy (Urbana: University of Illinois Press, 1997), 56.

14 Wernher von Braun to the Vice President of the United States, April 29, 1961, NASA Historical Reference Collection, NASA, Washington, DC.

15 John F. Kennedy, "Special Message by the President on Urgent National Needs," May 25, 1961, Papers of John F. Kennedy, Presidential Papers.

16 Beschloss, "Kennedy and the Decision," 63.

17 David Callahan and Fred I. Greenstein, "Eisenhower and U.S. Space Policy," in Launius and McCurdy, *Spaceflight*, 42.

18 Presidential meeting in the Cabinet Room of the White House, "Supplemental Appropriations for the National Aeronautics and Space Administration (NASA)," November 21, 1962, presidential recordings collection tape 63, President's Office files, John F. Kennedy Library.

19 Matt Novak, "How Space-Age Nostalgia Hobbles Our Future," *Slate*, May 15, 2012.

20 John F. Kennedy, address at Rice University, September 12, 1962, accessed August 17, 2013, http://www.jfklibrary.org.

21 John H. Glenn, recorded interview by Walter D. Sohier, June 12, 1964, John F. Kennedy Library Oral History Program, 2.

22 Ibid., 23.

23 Alan B. Shepard Jr., recorded interview by Walter D. Sohier, June 12, 1964, John F. Kennedy Library Oral History Program, 12.

24 John F. Kennedy, "Remarks Following the Orbital Flight of Col. John H. Glenn, Jr.," February 20, 1962, *American Presidency Project*, accessed August 17, 2013, http://www.presidency.ucsb.edu.

25 Glenn, interview, 21.

26 Dr. Wernher von Braun, recorded interview by Walter D. Sohier and Eugene M. Emme, March 31, 1964, at Huntsville, AL, John F. Kennedy Library Oral History Project, 17.

27 Ibid., 14.

28 Ross Anderson, "Neil Armstrong's Solemn but Not Sad Memorial at the National Cathedral," *Atlantic*, September 14, 2012, accessed August 27, 2013, http://www.theatlantic.com.

29 Sally Bedell Smith, *Grace and Power: The Private World of the Kennedy White House* (New York: Random House, 2004), 280.

30 E. W. Kenworthy, "President Sails in 30-Knot Wind," *New York Times*, July 29, 1962, 32.

31 "President and Caroline Have Picnic on Sandbar," *Boston Globe*, August 5, 1962, 12.

32 Rose Styron, ed., *Selected Letters of William Styron* (New York: Random House, 2012), 338.

33 "President and Family Run Aground in Sloop," United Press International, *New York Times*, July 30, 1962.

34 Frank Falacci, "Kennedy Race Sloop Runs Aground in Mud," *Boston Globe*, July 30, 1962, 1.

35 Helen Thomas, *Front Row at the White House* (New York: Scribner, 1999), 83–84.

36 John F. Kennedy, "Remarks in Newport at the Australian Ambassador's Dinner for the America's Cup Crews," September 14, 1962, *American Presidency Project*, accessed August 27, 2013, http://www.presidency.ucsb.edu.

37 Chief of Naval Operations, "The Naval Quarantine of Cuba, 1962: Quarantine, 22–26 October," report on the Naval Quarantine of Cuba, Post 46 Command file, box 10, Operational Archives Branch, Washington, DC, accessed August 24, 2013, http://www.history.navy.mil.

38 John Ahern, "Ted Kennedy Shows Skill in Edgartown Y. C. Races," *Boston Globe*, July 20, 1963, 13.

39 Frank Falacci, "Kennedys, 2 Children Cruise to Nantucket," *Boston Globe*, September 3, 1963, 5.

40 Henry Koehler, telephone interview with the author, March 6, 2013.

41 Ted Widmer, *Listening In: The Secret White House Recordings of JFK* (New York: Hyperion, 2012), 246.

42 Koehler, interview.

43 Edward Kennedy, *True Compass*, 208–10.

44 Anthony Mason, "JFK Painting Finds Its Way Back to Artist 50 Years after Brush with Camelot," news broadcast, *CBS This Morning*, March 1, 2013, accessed August 24, 2013, http://www.cbsnews.com.

45 E. B. White, "The Talk of the Town: Notes and Comment," *New Yorker*, November 30, 1963, 51. The last sentence is best known because Ted Kennedy quoted it in a speech.

46 Associated Press, "Kennedy Family Divided over Mass. Compound," *USA Today*, July 15, 2011, accessed August 17, 2013, http://usatoday30.usatoday.com.

47 Edward Kennedy, *True Compass*, 213.

CHAPTER 8. BOBBY AND ETHEL

1 C. David Heymann, *RFK: A Candid Biography of Robert F. Kennedy* (New York: Dutton, 1998), 351. The account of items added to the casket also appears in Oppenheimer, *Other Mrs. Kennedy*, 354.

2 Steven M. Gillon, *The Kennedy Assassination: 24 Hours after, Lyndon B. Johnson's Pivotal First Day as President* (New York: Basic Books, 2010), 214.

3 Robert F. Kennedy, *Tribute to John F. Kennedy at the Democratic National Convention, Atlantic City, New Jersey, August 27, 1964*, accessed August 18, 2013, http://www.jfklibrary.org.

4 Ted Sorensen, *Kennedy: The Classic Biography* (1965; repr., New York: HarperCollins, 2009), 34.

5 Schlesinger, *Robert Kennedy*, 21–23.

6 Ibid., 33.

7 Evan Thomas, *Robert Kennedy: His Life* (New York: Simon and Schuster, 2000), 32–34.

8 Robert F. Kennedy to Rose Kennedy, n.d.; Robert F. Kennedy to Joseph P. Kennedy, n.d., Joseph P. Kennedy Papers.

9 Robert F. Kennedy to Rose Kennedy, n.d., Joseph P. Kennedy Papers. Hershey served as director of the Selective Service through the presidencies of Kennedy and Johnson, until 1970, when Nixon removed him in the wake of controversy surrounding the "Hershey Directive," which stated that anyone demonstrating against a military recruiter could be subject to immediate reclassification of his draft status. The Supreme Court voided the directive.

10 Michael Knox Beran, *Last Patrician: Bobby Kennedy and the End of the American Aristocracy* (New York: St. Martin's Press, 1998).

11 C. G. Kennedy, interview, February 13, 2012.

12 Schlesinger, *Robert Kennedy*, 88.

13 Ibid., 60–65.

14 Patricia Kennedy Lawford, ed., *That Shining Hour* (privately published, printed by Halliday Lithograph, 1969), 15.

15 C. G. Kennedy, interview, February 13, 2012; Christopher G. Kennedy, "Resolute," letter to his children, January 26, 2004, 2.

16 Rory Kennedy, *Ethel*, directed by Rory Kennedy (Malibu, CA: Moxie Firecracker Films, 2012), documentary film.

17 Schlesinger, *Journals, 1952–2000*, 122.

18 Heymann, *RFK*, 337–38.

19 R. Kennedy, *Ethel*.

20 O'Brien, *John F. Kennedy*, 735.

21 R. Kennedy, *Ethel*.

22 E. Thomas, *Robert Kennedy: His Life*, 282–83.

23 Edith Hamilton, *The Greek Way* (New York: Norton, 2010), 182.

24 Robert F. Kennedy, *Statement on Assassination of Martin Luther King, Jr., Indianapolis, Indiana, April 4, 1968*, accessed August 18, 2013, http://www.jfklibrary.org.

25 R. Kennedy, *Ethel*.

26 C. G. Kennedy, interview, February 13, 2012.

27 Schlesinger, *Robert Kennedy*, 677.

28 Heymann, *Bobby and Jackie: A Love Story* (New York: Atria Books, 2009), 180–81. Heymann's footnote cites Jacqueline Kennedy Onassis to Rose Kennedy, December 1, 1968, JFK Library.

29 E. Thomas, *Robert Kennedy: His Life*, 183.

30 C. David Heymann, *American Legacy: The Story of John and Caroline Kennedy* (New York: Atria Books, 2007), 4.

31 This account is drawn from the author's May 30, 2012, telephone interview with Kerry Kennedy, who was aboard but very young, and from Schlesinger, *Robert Kennedy*, and Oppenheimer, *Other Mrs. Kennedy*, 381. All three versions differ in details, but together they confirm the basic facts.

32 R. Kennedy, *Ethel*.

33 Dolly Connelly, "How Did I Get Myself into This?" *Sports Illustrated* 22, no. 14 (April 5, 1965): 58–67.

34 Jim Whittaker, *A Life on the Edge: Memoirs of Everest and Beyond* (Seattle: Mountaineers, 1999), 129–31.

35 Ibid., 136. See also Michael Shnayerson, "1963 American Summit: Jim Whittaker—Back on Earth," *National Geographic Adventure*, May 2003, accessed August 19, 2013, http://adventure.nationalgeographic.com.

36 Edward Kennedy, "Senator Edward M. Kennedy," in Lawford, *That Shining Hour*, 305.

37 Lawrence Durrell, *Reflections on a Marine Venus: A Companion to the Landscape of Rhodes* (Rockville, MD: Olympia, 2009), 221.

38 Schlesinger, *Journals, 1952–2000*, 295.

39 C. G. Kennedy, interview, February 13, 2012.

40 K. Kennedy, interview.

41 C. G. Kennedy, "Resolute."

42 Ibid.

43 Ethel Kennedy; Ted Kennedy Jr. and wife, Kiki; Max Kennedy; Christopher and Sheila Kennedy; and family friend David Nunes, interviews with the author, who sailed with the family on *Glide*, August 6, 2012.

44 Ethel Kennedy, interview with the author, Hyannis Port, MA, August 6, 2012; C. G. Kennedy, interview, August 6, 2012.

45 C. G. Kennedy, "Resolute."

46 Ethel Kennedy, interview.

47 C. G. Kennedy, "Resolute."

48 Tim Fulham, Wianno Senior Class Association board chair, interview with the author, Osterville, MA, August 5, 2012.

49 Ethel Kennedy, interview.

50 C. G. Kennedy, "Resolute."

51 K. Kennedy, interview; C. G. Kennedy, "Resolute."

52 Karl Zimmerman, "Final Chapter: The Islander and Other Bygone Ferries," *Martha's Vineyard Magazine*, August 2010, accessed August 24, 2013, http://www .mvmagazine.com.

53 C. G. Kennedy, "Resolute."

54 Ethel Kennedy, interview.

55 R. Kennedy, *Ethel.*

56 Ethel Kennedy, interview; C. G. Kennedy, interview, August 6, 2012.

57 K. Kennedy, interview.

58 Max Kennedy, interview with the author aboard *Ptarmigan*, Hyannis Port, MA, August 6, 2012.

59 Ethel Kennedy, interview.

CHAPTER 9. EUNICE

1 M. Shriver, interview, January 4, 2012.

2 Searls, *Lost Prince*, 59.

3 Leamer, *Kennedy Women*, 209.

4 Edward Kennedy, *Fruitful Bough.*

5 Scott Stossel, *Sarge: The Life and Times of Sargent Shriver* (Washington, DC: Smithsonian Books, 2004), 96.

6 Leamer, *Kennedy Women*, 225.

7 Edward Kennedy, *True Compass*, 25–26.

8 Eunice Kennedy Shriver, "Hope for Retarded Children," *Saturday Evening Post*, September 22, 1962, 71.

9 Leamer, *Kennedy Women*, 374.

10 John F. Kennedy to Eunice Kennedy, 1939, JFK Family Papers.

11 Leamer, *Kennedy Women*, 208.

12 Martha Kearney, "Eunice Kennedy Tackles Job to Cut Delinquency, " *Times Herald*, January 20, 1947; and "Eunice Kennedy Praised for Fight on Delinquency," *Traveler*, November 11, 1947, news clips, Fitzgerald Kennedy Papers.

13 "Eunice Kennedy Praised."

14 Stossel, *Sarge*, 104.

15 Ibid., 113–15.

16 Scott Stossel, "Eunice the Formidable," *Atlantic*, August 2009.

17 Maria Shriver, "Maria Shriver's Eulogy for Her Mother," *Boston.com*, August 14, 2009, accessed May 5, 2013, http://www.boston.com.

18 Arnold Schwarzenegger, *Total Recall: My Unbelievably True Life Story* (New York: Simon and Schuster, 2012), 495.

19 Stossel, *Sarge*, 262.

20 Leamer, *Kennedy Women*, 530.

21 Stossel, *Sarge*, 263.

22 Ibid., 659.

23 Kennedy Shriver, "Hope for Retarded Children," 71.

24 Schwarzenegger, *Total Recall*, 376.

25 Leamer, *Kennedy Women*, 580.

26 M. Shriver, interview, January 4, 2012.

27 Schwarzenegger, *Total Recall*, 224.

28 M. Shriver, interview, January 4, 2012.

29 "Ted Kennedy Jr. Eunice was a great competitor," New England Cable News, August 13, 2009, accessed Nov. 26, 2013, http://www.necn.com.

30 Joe Mathews, "Arnold's Debt to Eunice," *Daily Beast*, August 11, 2009, accessed May 5, 2013, http://www.thedailybeast.com.

31 Leamer, *Kennedy Women*, 761.

32 Stossel, "Eunice the Formidable."

33 Stossel, *Sarge*, 667–78.

34 Mathews, "Arnold's Debt to Eunice."

35 C. G. Kennedy, interview, February 13, 2012.

36 M. Shriver, interview, January 4, 2012.

37 Mark K. Shriver, *A Good Man: Rediscovering My Father, Sargent Shriver* (New York: Holt, 2012), 193.

CHAPTER 10. TED

1 Robert F. Kennedy to Rose and Joseph P. Kennedy Sr., n.d., Joseph P. Kennedy Papers.

2 Harvard Kennedy School, "JFK50 Playing Football with JFK—John Culver," recorded interview of John Culver, YouTube video, 2:27, posted on February 10, 2011, accessed May 5, 2013, http://www.youtube.com.

3 John Culver, tribute to EMK in, *Edward M. Kennedy, Late a Senator from Massachusetts, Memorial Addresses and Other Tributes* (Washington, DC: U.S. Government Printing Office, 2010), 287–91. Culver's memorial speech can be viewed at http://www .youtube.com.

4 Ahern, "Ted Kennedy Shows Skill," 13.

5 Ibid.

6 Frank Falacci, "Ted Loses Boat Race," *Boston Globe*, August 4, 1963, 6.

7 Falacci, "Kennedys, 2 Children Cruise," 5.

8 Edward M. Kennedy Jr., interview with the author, Hyannis Port, MA, August 6, 2012.

9 C. G. Kennedy, interview, February 13, 2012.

10 Ethel Kennedy, interview.

11 Jack Fallon, "Tuning Up with Jack Fallon," *Wooden Boat* 91 (November–December 1989): 68.

12 Ibid., 67–69.

13 C. G. Kennedy, interview, February 13, 2012. Attempts to obtain a copy of the photo were unsuccessful.

14 David Churbuck, "Ted Kennedy in Glimpses," *Churbuck.com*, August 29, 2009, accessed May 5, 2013, http://www.churbuck.com.

15 Patrick Kennedy, interview with the author, Providence, RI, March, 19, 2012.

16 C. G. Kennedy, interview, February 13, 2012.

17 Marion J. White, *Eldridge Tide and Pilot Book, 2002* (Medfield, MA: White, 2001), 27.

18 Edward Kennedy, *True Compass*, 273. See also Elizabeth Deane, "The Kennedys," *American Experience*, Public Broadcasting Service, 2003, accessed August 27, 2013, http://www.pbs.org.

19 Deane, "Kennedys."

20 P. Kennedy, interview.

21 Edward Kennedy, *True Compass*, 274.

22 P. Kennedy, interview.

23 Peter Kunhardt and Sheila Nevins, *Teddy in His Own Words*, edited by Phillip Schopper (Pleasantville, NY: Kunhardt-McGee Productions, 2009), HBO documentary.

24 Edward Kennedy, *True Compass*, 283.

25 Ibid., 287.

26 Knox Beran, *Last Patrician*, has EMK coming in ninth. EMK's recollection comes from Edward Kennedy, *True Compass*, 290.

27 Edward Kennedy, *True Compass*, 288.

28 Beston, *Outermost House*, 165.

29 Edward M. Kennedy Jr., eulogy to his father, in *Edward M. Kennedy, Late a Senator from Massachusetts, Memorial Addresses and Other Tributes* (Washington, DC: U.S. Government Printing Office, 2010), 287–91.

30 Edward Kennedy Jr., interview.

31 Christopher Andersen, *Sweet Caroline: Last Child of Camelot* (New York: Avon Books, 2003), 166.

32 Edward Kennedy, eulogy to his father, in *Edward M. Kennedy*.

33 Ibid.

34 Edward Kennedy Jr., interview.

35 P. Kennedy, interview.

36 K. Kennedy, interview.

37 Alexandra Styron, "Life with Father," article adapted from Styron's book, *Reading My Father, Vanity Fair*, April 2011, accessed May 5, 2013, http://www.vanityfair.com.

38 K. Kennedy, interview.

39 Patrick Kennedy, eulogy to his father, in *Edward M. Kennedy*, 329; P. Kennedy, interview.

40 P. Kennedy, eulogy to his father, in *Edward M. Kennedy*.

41 C. G. Kennedy, interview, February 13, 2013.

42 Churbuck, "Ted Kennedy in Glimpses."

43 Joseph P. Kennedy II, eulogy to EMK, in *Edward M. Kennedy*, 255–56.

44 Edward Kennedy Jr., interview.

45 Edgerly, "My Friend Max."

46 J. Kennedy, eulogy to EMK, in *Edward M. Kennedy*.

47 C. G. Kennedy, "Resolute."

48 Jimmy Carter, *Remarks Delivered by President Jimmy Carter at the October 20, 1979 Dedication Ceremony of the John F. Kennedy Presidential Library*, accessed August 18, 2013, http://www.jfklibrary.org.

49 P. Kennedy, interview.

50 Edward M. Kennedy. "Transcript of Kennedy's Speech on Economic Issues at Democratic Convention," *New York Times*, August 13, 1980.

51 Gayle Fee and Laura Raposa, "Jackie's Private Letter to Joan Up for Bid," *Boston Herald*, February 23, 2007, accessed August 24, 2013, http://www.freerepublic.com.

52 Churbuck, "Ted Kennedy in Glimpses."

53 Edward Kennedy, *True Compass*, 421.

54 Rick Atkinson, "Why Ted Kennedy Can't Stand Still," *Washington Post*, April 29, 1990, W11.

55 Edward Kennedy, *True Compass*, 421.

56 Schlesinger, *Journals, 1952–2000*, 618.

57 Jay Mulvaney, *Kennedy Weddings: A Family Album* (New York: St. Martin's Griffen, 2002). Another source is the Jack Thomas, "Kennedy Wedding Bells Ring Out, Senator's Daughter Marries Architect," *Boston Globe*, September 9, 1990, 25.

58 Bzdek, *Kennedy Legacy*, 201.

59 "Sobering Times," *Newsweek*, December 8, 1991, accessed August 24, 2013, http://www.thedailybeast.com.

60 Bzdek, *Kennedy Legacy*, 201.

61 Edward Kennedy, *True Compass*, 427.

62 Laurence Leamer, *Sons of Camelot: The Fate of an American Dynasty* (New York: HarperCollins, 2004), 569.

63 Alessandra Stanley, "Facing Questions of Private Life, Kennedy Apologizes to the Voters," *New York Times*, October 26, 1991, 8.

64 Leamer, *Sons of Camelot*, 354.

65 Stanley, "Facing Questions."

66 Ibid., 8.

67 Edward Kennedy, eulogy to Jacqueline Kennedy Onassis, in *First Lady Jacqueline Kennedy Onassis: Memorial Tributes in the One Hundred Third Congress of the United States* (Washington, DC: U.S. Government Printing Office, 1995), 58.

68 U.S. Department of Commerce, weather data, accessed spring 2013, http://www1 .ncdc.noaa.gov.

69 Leamer, *Sons of Camelot*, 430. Edward Kennedy in *True Compass* confirms he visited the library and sat outside preparing for the debate.

70 Edward Kennedy, *True Compass*, 506.

71 C. G. Kennedy, interview, February 13, 2012.

72 K. Kennedy, interview.

73 Edward Kennedy, *True Compass*, 507.

CHAPTER 11. PASSAGES

1 Caroline Kennedy, reading from "Memory of Cape Cod," in *First Lady*, 61.

2 Maurice Templeton, reading from "Ithaka," in *First Lady*, 62.

3 Matthew L. Wald, "Safety Board Blames Pilot Error in Crash of Kennedy Plane," *New York Times*, July 7, 2000.

4 Mike Allen, "The Kennedy Burial: The Overview," *New York Times*, July 23, 1999.

5 Mike Allen, "Bodies from Kennedy Crash Are Found," *New York Times*, July 22, 1999.

6 Ibid.

7 M. Shriver, interview, January 4, 2013.

8 John F. Kennedy, "Radio and Television Report to the American People on Civil Rights, June 11, 1963," accessed August 24, 2013, http://www.jfklibrary.org.

9 P. Kennedy, interview.

10 K. Kennedy, interview.

11 Edgerly, "My Friend Max."

12 Whitcomb and Williams, *Cape Wind*, 128.

13 Barbara Veneri, "Warren Navigated His Way to Win," *South Coast Today*, June 1, 2003, accessed May 5, 2013, http://www.southcoasttoday.com.

14 "Fleet Roster—Spring 2013," Wianno Senior Class, accessed May 5, 2013, http:// www.wiannosenior.org.

15 Arnold, "Blue-Blooded Racers," 24.

16 Emily C. Dooly, "Sturdy Wianno Boats, Now Lost, Helped Foster Kennedys' Love of Sea," *Cape Cod Times*, December 12, 2003, accessed August 24, 2013, www .capecodonline.com.

17 C. G. Kennedy, "Resolute."

18 Bobby Shriver, "A Last Summer in Hyannis Port," *Newsweek*, August 26, 2009, accessed August 24, 2013, www.thedailybeast.com.

19 Eugene O'Neill, *Long Day's Journal into Night* (New Haven, CT: Yale University Press, 2002), 156.

AFTERWORD

1 Bruce Feiler, "The Stories That Bind Us," *New York Times*, March 15, 2013.

2 K. Kennedy, interview.

3 F. Scott Fitzgerald, *The Great Gatsby* (New York: Charles Scribner's Sons, 1953), 182.

INDEX

Note: Terms found in the photo gallery are designated with an italicized *G.*

The author gratefully acknowledges permission to reproduce the following:

David Arnold, "Blue-Blooded Racers, Costly, Cherished, and Original to the Cape," *Boston Globe*, May 23, 2004, 24. Used by permission of David Arnold.

Hart Crane, "At Melville's Tomb," in *The Complete Poems and Selected Letters and Prose of Hart Crane*, ed. Brom Weber, 24 (New York: Library of America/Penguin-Putnam, 2006). Copyright 1933, 1958, and 1966 by Liveright Publishing Corporation. Copyright 1952 by Brom Weber. Used by permission of Liveright Publishing Corporation.

Christopher G. Kennedy, "Resolute," a letter to his children, January 26, 2004. Used by permission of Christopher G. Kennedy.

John F. Kennedy to Inga Arvad. Courtesy of Ron McCoy.

Arthur M. Schlesinger Jr., *Journals 1952–2000*, ed. Andrew Schlesinger and Stephen Schlesinger (New York: Penguin, 2007). Copyright © 2007 by the Estate of Arthur M. Schlesinger, Jr. Used by permission of The Penguin Press, a division of Penguin Group (USA) LLC.

Hank Searls, *The Lost Prince: Young Joe, the Forgotten Kennedy; The Story of the Oldest Brother* (New York: World, 1969). Copyright 1969 by Hank Searls. Used by permission of Hank Searls.

"Superman Comes to the Supermarket," from *The Presidential Papers* by Norman Mailer. Copyright © 1963 by Norman Mailer, used by permission of the Wylie Agency LLC.